MW01473461

TREES & SHRUBS
of the Maritimes

Todd Boland

Boulder Publications also publishes these field guides:

Birds of Newfoundland
Edible Plants of Atlantic Canada
Edible Plants of Newfoundland and Labrador
Geology of Newfoundland
Trees and Shrubs of Newfoundland and Labrador
Whales and Dolphins of Newfoundland and Labrador
Wildflowers of Newfoundland and Labrador

And these gardening guides:

Atlantic Gardening
Newfoundland Gardening

TREES & SHRUBS
of the Maritimes

Todd Boland

BOULDER PUBLICATIONS

Library and Archives Canada Cataloguing in Publication

Boland, Todd
    Trees and shrubs of the Maritimes : field guide / Todd Boland.

Includes index.
ISBN 978-0-9865376-5-3

    1. Trees--Maritime Provinces--Handbooks, manuals, etc.
2. Shrubs--Maritime Provinces--Handbooks, manuals, etc.
3. Trees--Maritime Provinces--Identification. 4. Shrubs--
Maritime Provinces--Identification. I. Title.

QK203.M35B65 2012   582.16'09715   C2012-901257-2

Published by Boulder Publications
Portugal Cove-St. Philip's, Newfoundland and Labrador
© 2012
www.boulderpublications.ca

Editor: Sandy Newton
Copy editors: Iona Bulgin, Charis Cotter
Design and layout: Vanessa Stockley, granitestudios.ca
Cover images: Todd Boland

> Front cover main image: pin cherry (*Prunus pensylvanica*)
> Front cover detail images (left to right): red pine (*Pinus resinosa*), sheep laurel (*Kalmia angustifolia*), red-osier dogwood (*Cornus stolonifera*)
> Back cover detail images (top to bottom): white spruce (*Picea glauca*), red maple (*Acer rubrum*), Canada blackberry (*Rubus canadensis*)

Printed in China

All rights reserved. No part of this work covered by the copyrights hereon may be reproduced or used in any form or by any means without written permission of the publisher. Any requests for photocopying, recording, taping, or information storage and retrieval systems of any part of this book shall be directed in writing to the Canadian Reprography Collective, One Yonge Street, Suite 1900, Toronto, Ontario, Canada, M5E 1E5.

We acknowledge the financial support of the Government of Newfoundland and Labrador through the Department of Tourism, Culture and Recreation.

We acknowledge financial support for our publishing program by the Government of Canada and the Department of Canadian Heritage through the Canada Book Fund.

CONTENTS

Preface	vii
Acknowledgements	ix
Introduction	1
First: The Big Picture	1
Where One Forest Meets Another	2
A Distinctive Plant Group / Atlantic Coastal Plain Species	3
Telling the Trees from the Shrubs	3
How to Use This Guide	5
Identifying Plants with Needles or Scales	6
Identifying Plants with Broad Leaves	6
Using Nature's Clues	7
Even with a System, Identifying Plants Can Be Tricky	8
A Few Words about Plant Names and Terms	9
Not All Plants Like the Same Locations	9
Habitat Notes / Forests	9
Habitat Notes / Barrens	11
Habitat Notes / Dunes	11
Habitat Notes/ Wetlands	12
Habitat Notes / Disturbed Areas	13
Woody Plants / Supporting Wildlife	14
Sample Page	16
Icon Legend	17
Plant profiles	19
Plants with needles	20
Plants with scaled leaves	38
Plants with broad leaves	
Simple / Opposite	42
Simple / Alternate	72
Whorled	167
Compound / Opposite	170
Compound / Alternate	179

Woody Species with At-risk Status   205
Glossary   208
Maritimes' Woody Plants / By Family   212
Index / Plants by Latin Name   221
Index / Plants by Common Name   225
Photo Credits   232
About the Author   235

PREFACE

Trees & Shrubs of the Maritimes will introduce you to more than 240 species of trees and shrubs that grow in the Canadian Maritime provinces—Nova Scotia, New Brunswick, and Prince Edward Island. They are what botanists term "woody plants."

I have profiled both the species that are native to the Maritimes and many introduced species that have become naturalized (and sometimes invasive), which they've done either by "jumping the fence" from cultivated areas into wild ones or simply by persisting long after the original homesteads on which they were planted have disappeared.

Why create this book now? Because a gap in the literature seemed to exist and because interest in Maritimes flora is on the rise, especially among visitors from outside the region. Guides to wildflowers of North America are available—but few are devoted solely to the species found in the Maritimes.

Three resources *do* exist: *Flora of Nova Scotia* by A. E. Roland and E. C. Smith, Marian Zinck's revised editions of that book, and *Flora of New Brunswick* by Harold R. Hinds. These volumes cover all the flora—native and introduced—of two of the Maritime provinces and have significant overlaps with the flora found on Prince Edward Island. However, both are technical and include botanical drawings for illustration—which, for the novice naturalist, may make them somewhat daunting resources. So it seemed that a dedicated field guide to the woody plants of the Maritimes—illustrated with photographs and aimed at beginners—was warranted.

Trees & Shrubs of the Maritimes is designed to help readers who know little to nothing about botany identify the woody plants they will encounter in the region, as well as some of the noteworthy rare or uncommon species. Unlike many other plant guides, this book is not organized by flower colour or by scientific plant families. Rather, it is based on the one feature that all people can recognize on a woody plant: its leaves. This approach relies on identification clues and a process of elimination and is described in detail in the Introduction.

Concerns about the environment are often in the forefront these days, and one way to understand nature's inter-connected web better is by learning to recognize and appreciate its plants. By helping you identify the woody plant species in the Maritimes, I hope this guide will give you a solid foundation for a thoughtful and observant connection to the natural world around you.

ACKNOWLEDGEMENTS

My thanks to Jim Goltz and David Carmichael for their careful review of the text and for providing up-to-date regional details such as species' locations, habitats, and population status. I would also like to thank everyone who graciously allowed me to use their photographs to fill the gaps in my own image archive. (They are listed by name in the photo credits, page 232.)

I note with gratitude the contributions of Vanessa Stockley (Granite Studios) for both the book's design and her attention to detail in the layout.

Finally, special thanks go to Sandy Newton, Iona Bulgin, and Charis Cotter for their care with my prose and grammar, which helped this non-English major write with greater definition and focus.

INTRODUCTION

Canada's Maritime provinces are home to nearly 275 species of native and naturalized woody plants. This guide will help you identify most of them using their most easily noticed feature: their leaves.

Reading the following pages is key to your ability to use this book successfully: they explain this guide's system of icons and notations and how to use them in a process of elimination to identify a tree or shrub in the field. However, before you get into the "how" of the book, it helps to understand some of the larger forces at play in the Maritimes that influence where different types of woody plants grow.

First: The Big Picture

Relative to the size of North America, the Canadian Maritimes do not cover a large area. The entire region is just over 134,000 square kilometres, only a little more than the island of Newfoundland located just to the northeast. Nevertheless, these three provinces—New Brunswick, Nova Scotia, and Prince Edward Island—experience wide climatic variation.

Prince Edward Island is completely surrounded by the Gulf of St. Lawrence—the furthest you can get from it is 17 kilometres. Nova Scotia is almost surrounded by salt water, and there you can go only 67 kilometres inland away from it before you start approaching it again. Both of these provinces thus have oceanic climates: relatively mild winters and cool summers.

New Brunswick is another story, however. Although flanked by salt water on two sides, its climate is more influenced by its connections to mainland North America. It has a more continental climate in western and northern areas, and more oceanic conditions near its coasts. Inland temperatures can be much colder in winter and warmer in summer than they are by the sea.

Not surprisingly, considerable variation occurs in the types and distribution of woody species across the Maritimes. The greatest diversity of woody plants is found in southwestern New Brunswick, especially in the Saint John River valley.

Southwestern Nova Scotia has a unique assemblage of plants—the Coastal Plain flora—which is discussed on page 3.

In addition to the effects of geographical location, elevation also influences plant life. In the Maritimes, its effects are most clearly seen in parts of the Cape Breton Highlands of Nova Scotia, where the hills can reach more than 500 metres. In this coastal area, trees are stunted and some arctic-alpine flora are at home. In contrast, the Miramichi Highlands, Chaleur Uplands, and Notre Dame Mountains of northwestern New Brunswick (where elevations can be 800 metres or more) are mostly forested—thanks to the insulation of the North American landmass to the west and south, and the distance from cold North Atlantic winds.

The nature of the soil also influences vegetation. Limestone and gypsum outcrops, for example, are scattered throughout the Maritimes; the most prominent are near Windsor, Upper Stewiacke, and in the Cape Breton Highlands in Nova Scotia, in extreme western and northern regions (upper Saint John and Restigouche river valleys) of New Brunswick, as well as in the Albert Mines area in the southeast. The soil in these areas is naturally alkaline and generally rocky—as a result, it supports several arctic-alpine-affinity species.

Where One Forest Meets Another

The forests of the world are divided into various zones that are defined by their major plant groups. Most of the Maritimes region falls within the Acadian Forest (which, with the Great Lakes–St. Lawrence Forest, forms the larger Northern Hardwood Forest). This forest type marks the transition between the North American Boreal Forest region to the north and the Central Hardwood Forest region to the south. As a result, the Acadian Forest has considerable plant diversity. The main species that defines the Acadian Forest, however, is red spruce (*Picea rubens*), a tree that, though present in the Great Lakes–St. Lawrence Forest, is not as prominent there.

Northwestern New Brunswick and Cape Breton Island have considerable areas of Boreal Forest, which is dominated by balsam fir (*Abies balsamea*), black spruce (*Picea mariana*), white spruce (*P. glauca*), paper birch (*Betula papyrifera*), and heart-leaved birch (*B. cordifolia*). Trembling aspen (*Populus tremuloides*), red pine (*Pinus resinosa*), and jack pine (*P. banksiana*) are also present, in fire-prone areas. Red spruce, on the other hand, is conspicuously rare or absent.

Southwestern New Brunswick, especially along the Saint John River, has a stronger affinity to the Central Hardwood Forest. The signs of this are the presence of silver maple (*Acer saccharinum*), burr oak (*Quercus macrocarpa*), black willow (*Salix nigra*), butternut (*Juglans cinerea*), and basswood (*Tilia americana*)—tree species that are not native to Nova Scotia or Prince Edward Island.

Elsewhere in the Maritimes, the natural forest includes pockets of coniferous species or deciduous species, or—more commonly—a mixture of both.

A Distinctive Plant Group / Atlantic Coastal Plain Species

Nova Scotia is home to an assemblage of plants that is almost unique in the Canadian context. It is known as the Atlantic Coastal Plain (ACP) flora. Although ACP plants do occur as far east as Newfoundland and west through parts of New Brunswick (as well as along the Great Lakes in Ontario, Michigan, and Wisconsin), Nova Scotia has the best developed ACP flora of any Canadian province. The main North American ACP flora regions are coastal areas from Nova Scotia south to eastern Texas.

The Atlantic Coastal Plain was formed at the end of the last glacial period, approximately 10,000 to 14,000 years ago. In that era, the sea level was 60 to 100 metres lower than it is today and southern Nova Scotia was connected to the eastern seaboard of North America. The range of several ACP species extended north as far as what is now Nova Scotia—and some even to Newfoundland. When the glaciers melted and sea levels rose, the southern Nova Scotia plant populations were cut off from the rest of the eastern seaboard by the newly formed Bay of Fundy. These "outliers" are now at the northern end of each species' distribution range.

Over time, more aggressive species from the interior of Nova Scotia have pushed the Atlantic Coastal Plain species into isolated pockets. Most are found on gravelly or sandy shores of freshwater lakes and streams and in boggy areas; a few are located in salt marshes. Look for ACP plants in the southwestern Nova Scotia counties of Lunenburg, Annapolis, Yarmouth, Queens, and Shelburne. There is also a small pocket in the southeastern Cape Breton Island counties of Richmond and Cape Breton.

Ninety species in Nova Scotia belong to the Atlantic Coastal Plain flora. Most are herbaceous, but there are several woody plants. These include northern bayberry (*Morella pensylvanica*), smooth alder (*Alnus serrulata*), common buttonbush (*Cephalanthus occidentalis*), common greenbrier (*Smilax rotundifolia*), poison ivy (*Toxicodendron radicans*), swamp rose (*Rosa palustris*), and coastal sweet pepperbush (*Clethra alnifolia*).

Telling the Trees from the Shrubs

What is the difference between a tree and a shrub? It may seem like a simple question but the definitions of each term can vary widely.

For the purposes of this book, a "tree" is a plant that is often more than 5 metres tall and usually has a trunk diameter of at least 10 centimetres when mature. It can have one trunk or several but its branches are supported clear of the ground. In exposed locations, a "tree" species may be more shrub-like.

A "shrub" is typically shorter than 5 metres and has several stems that are 10 centimetres or smaller in diameter. Branches occur near or at ground level.

A "sub-shrub" is a short woody plant (generally under 20 centimetres) that superficially appears to be herbaceous—but the base of the plant actually contains wood cells. An example is bunchberry (*Cornus canadensis*), which appears to be herbaceous but at its base is woody.

HOW TO USE THIS GUIDE

Trees & Shrubs of the Maritimes organizes plants by leaf shape—starting with the main differences between leaf types and working down to the finer details. Why? Because this approach provides a reliable and easy first step to plant identification for people who have not studied plant science.

Leaves are the most obviously visible feature on any given plant. And although flowers, scientifically, can be the most definitive characteristic in plant identification, many woody plants in the Maritimes have a limited blooming period, so blossoms are not always present (this is also true for fruit). Thus leaves are the obvious feature that remains on a plant for the longest period of time, and so are the most useful starting point for novice botanists.

To use this guide, then, you begin by looking at a leaf on the plant you wish to identify. Next, ask yourself these three questions:

Are the leaves needle-like?

Are they like tiny scales?

Or are they flat and broad?

These are the three largest groupings of plants in this book; one of these three icons appears on each species page. So, too, does one of the two icons at right, which indicate if a tree is evergreen (keeps green leaves all year) or deciduous (loses its leaves in fall or winter and grows new foliage in the spring).

Evergreen

Deciduous

Identifying Plants with Needles or Scales

Because relatively few woody plants in the Maritimes have needle- or scale-like leaves, you will find them to be some of the easiest to identify. In these categories, your next step is to determine if your mystery plant produces cones (the next broadest sub-grouping). Once you determine this, you should be able to narrow down your possible identification by comparing the tree you are looking at with the notes and images in the relevant section in the book.

Identifying Plants with Broad Leaves

If your unknown plant is broad-leaved, then you need to note a few other leaf characteristics to narrow down the possibilities:

- does a single leaf grow on each stem ("simple") or do multiple small leaflets combine to create a larger leaf ("compound")?

- do the leaves extend from either side of the stem in an alternating sequence ("alternate"), are they paired ("opposite"), or do three or more leaves grow from the same point on the stem ("whorled")?

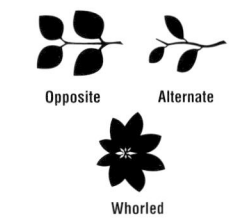

- what is the overall shape of the leaf? For simplicity, leaf shapes in this guide are categorized as
   - elongate or lance-shaped
   - elliptical
   - oval to egg-shaped
   - having three connected arms (tri-lobed)
   - hand-shaped ("palmate")

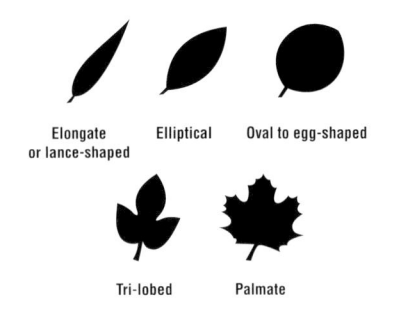

- if the leaf is compound, does it have three leaflets (making it "trifoliate"), five leaflets ("palmately compound"), or many leaflets ("pinnately compound")?

- is the leaf edge smooth ("untoothed" or "entire"), toothed ("serrated"), or lobed?

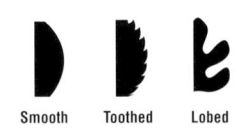

All the plants included in this guide are grouped according to shared leaf characteristics. The groupings of specific attributes are captured in the quick-reference icons at the top of each page, the details of each species are summarized in the text, and key characteristics are illustrated in the photographs. With broad-leaved plants, if you follow your observations about leaf shape and arrangement to the corresponding section of the book, then compare what you are looking at with the descriptions and photos on the pages, you should once again be able to narrow down the possibilities and identify your specimen.

Using Nature's Clues

In the warmer seasons of the year, flowers or fruit may be present to help you make your identification. "Flowers" can take the form of

- a cone
- a catkin (which is an elongate cluster of many tiny flowers that lack petals)
- a single flower
- a single "bell-shaped" flower
- a rounded cluster of individual flowers
- an elongate spray of many flowers
- unusual blooms that lack petals

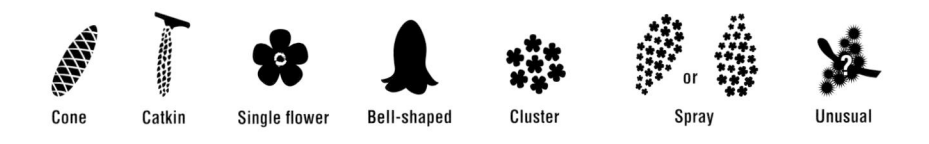

| Cone | Catkin | Single flower | Bell-shaped | Cluster | Spray | Unusual |

When observing fleshy fruit, it is important to note if it is
- a single smooth berry
- a berry with a "crown" (the remnants of the calyx)
- a single berry with many tiny berries packed together (like a raspberry)
- a looser cluster of berries

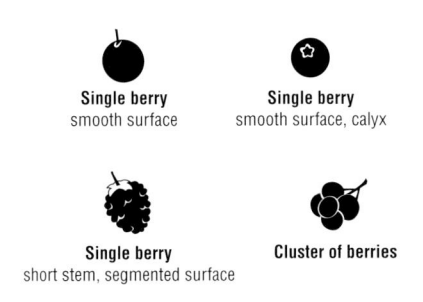

Single berry
smooth surface

Single berry
smooth surface, calyx

Single berry
short stem, segmented surface

Cluster of berries

7

Icons on each page also illustrate at a glance which of these features each plant has. Where possible, photo images of flowers and berries are also included.

It is important to remember that plants do not strictly follow the rules of these categories. For example, they may exhibit more than one flower type (producing individual *and* clustered blooms), or they may produce single *and* multiple berries. In such circumstances, all the relevant icons for flower/fruit forms are included.

Finally, icons also appear if a plant's fruit is edible or not (or is poisonous). The plant's status as native or introduced is also included. (The Plant List by Family, page 212, specifies the provinces in which each species is native or introduced.)

Can You Eat the Fruit?

Edible   Inedible or harmful

Native or Introduced?

Native Species   Introduced Species

Even with a System, Identifying Plants Can Be Tricky

More than 240 of the woody plants commonly encountered in the wild in the Maritimes are described in this guide. Most have a dedicated page, and I hope that by using all the information you will be able to identify them in the field.

Of course, I do realize any attempt to simplify nature is not foolproof—nature is far too complex for an across-the-board system! It is important, for example, to keep in mind that plants can show considerable variation in their leaf shape. Look around for similar specimens and compare the leaves on the same tree and on its neighbours. The more you practice and observe, the easier plant identification will become.

In a few cases, however, physical details may not be sufficiently different to allow the system to work. This is why I have grouped three of the most difficult genera to identify: the serviceberries, the hawthorns, and the blackberries/dewberries (the latter [*Rubus*] species have only minor differences in the leaves).

Eleven serviceberry (*Amelanchier*) species grow in the Maritimes—but many of them hybridize so freely that their features cannot be easily distinguished. Consequently, the serviceberries are described in just three entries.

The willows (*Salix*) present a similar challenge, as the differences between each species can be subtle. So you'll find only the most distinctive species in these pages.

Even the professionals have difficulty telling some of these species apart using only observational techniques. Confirming the identification of similar species can require a microscope, which can show minute details not visible to the naked eye, and also visits throughout the year to examine flowers, fruit, and leaves as they appear and change. So take heart—if you manage to identify the genus of some of these difficult species, you are doing well.

A Few Words about Plant Names and Terms

All known living organisms have a scientific name. The naming process is a science itself—taxonomy. Taxonomic names are created in Latin, considered by scientists to be a "universal" language. Over time, as new information is learned about an organism (especially about its genetic makeup), its scientific name may change.

Plants are commonly affected by such name changes. For this reason, each plant in this book is listed by its most-accepted common name, but the most current botanical (Latin) name and other common synonyms are also included. Both the common and taxonomic names applied generally follow VASCAN (the Database of Canadian Vascular Plants, http://data.canadensys.net/vascan/search/). Family names follow the system listed on the Angiosperm Phylogeny website (www.mobot.org/mobot/research/apweb).

If you are keenly interested in following botanical name changes, you might want to look at the ongoing Flora of North America project which, when complete, will be a 30-volume online encyclopedia of the entire North American flora (see http://fna.org).

Even though this guide is designed for the novice plant enthusiast, some botanical terms are used. This is because they have precise meanings. Think of the book as an introductory Botany 101 course—and refer to the glossary for explanations of terms that may be new to you.

For those who are more botanically inclined, there is a complete list of the Maritimes' woody plants according to their taxonomic family relationships (see page 212). You can also search for plants by either their (accepted) common name, or their Latin name, using the indexes.

Not All Plants Like the Same Locations

Along the edges of each species listing in this guide are habitat tabs. They indicate the major and minor habitat types favoured by the plant described. These habitat indicators provide general guidelines only—you should refer to the habitat description in the text for specific habitat details and locations, since they can vary by province. In some cases, reference is made to specific counties, shown on the map on the next page.

Habitat Notes / Forests

Three major forest habitat tabs are used: coniferous forest, mixed forest, and hardwood forest. Generally, the Maritimes region is part of the Acadian Forest, in which both coniferous softwoods and deciduous hardwoods grow. In addition to large swathes of mixed forest, there are areas in which one or the other type of tree predominates.

THE COUNTIES

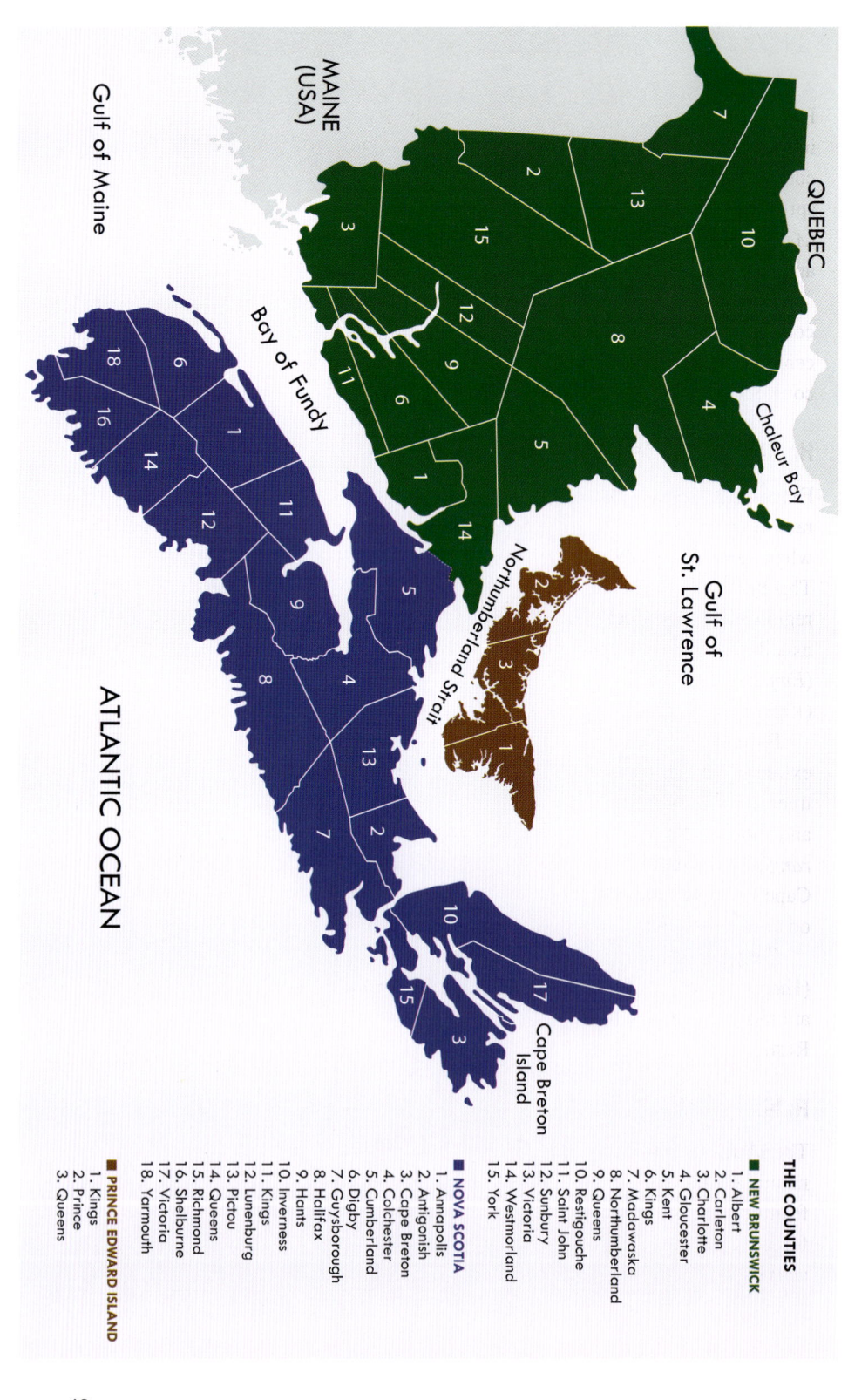

NEW BRUNSWICK
1. Albert
2. Carleton
3. Charlotte
4. Gloucester
5. Kent
6. Kings
7. Madawaska
8. Northumberland
9. Queens
10. Restigouche
11. Saint John
12. Sunbury
13. Victoria
14. Westmorland
15. York

NOVA SCOTIA
1. Annapolis
2. Antigonish
3. Cape Breton
4. Colchester
5. Cumberland
6. Digby
7. Guysborough
8. Halifax
9. Hants
10. Inverness
11. Kings
12. Lunenburg
13. Pictou
14. Queens
15. Richmond
16. Shelburne
17. Victoria
18. Yarmouth

PRINCE EDWARD ISLAND
1. Kings
2. Prince
3. Queens

Some woody plants prefer a specific forest type; others are not so particular. For example, yellow birch (*Betula alleghaniensis*) may occur sporadically in coniferous or hardwood forests (indicated as minor habitats) but is more commonly found in mixed forest situations (indicated as its major habitat). Black spruce (*Picea mariana*) is rarely found outside of coniferous forests. Silver maple (*Acer saccharinum*) is hardly ever found among conifers, rarely in mixed forests, and almost always in pure hardwood stands.

For the purposes of this guide, if at least 80 per cent of a forest is made up of coniferous trees, then the forest type is considered coniferous. If a forest is 80 per cent hardwood, then it is considered a hardwood forest. Any other combination is considered a mixed forest.

Habitat Notes / Barrens

Extensive barrens—common in Newfoundland and Labrador—are relatively rare in the Maritimes (though they do exist). Usually they are coastal, and result when areas with shallow rocky soil are exposed to windy oceanic conditions. This type of large coastal barrens is found primarily in Nova Scotia, in the Canso region and on the Chebucto peninsula—the area around Peggy's Cove is an excellent example. Dominant woody plants on coastal barrens include crowberries (*Empetrum* species), huckleberries (*Gaylussacia* species), and blueberries (*Vaccinium* species).

Barrens are often formed in higher elevations, which expose plant cover to extreme climatic conditions. Higher elevation barrens are dominated by stunted trees, especially conifers or birch/heath-like plants (many of which are evergreen and shorter than one metre), and an abundance of caribou moss (*Cladonia rangiferina*). In the Maritimes, this type of barrens is mostly found in the Cape Breton Highlands and features a range of species similar to that found on coastal barrens.

Frequent forest fires yield barrens dominated by early lowbush blueberry (*Vaccinium angustifolium*) and sheep laurel (*Kalmia angustifolia*). These barrens are most common in the east and northeastern counties of Gloucester and Restigouche in New Brunswick.

Habitat Notes / Dunes

The Maritime provinces are blessed with an abundance of sandy beaches. Under natural conditions—that is, undisturbed by human activity—these areas would feature a series of dunes that marked the transition from sand beach to coastal forest vegetation. Today, many sand dunes areas are severely degraded by human activity.

Not all dunes are created equal. Fore-dunes—closest to the sea—are held loosely in place by specialty grasses. Wind and tides will cause them to move and shift over time; they are rarely static.

As you move inland, secondary and tertiary dunes appear. They are the products of uninterrupted plant succession. Secondary dunes are almost completely covered by vegetation, which is, again, mostly herbaceous with a few woody species. Tertiary dunes, furthest inland, feature more woody species, many of which are wind-stunted versions of the coastal forest vegetation.

Several woody plant species are associated with secondary and tertiary dunes. They include woolly heather (*Hudsonia tomentosa*), creeping juniper (*Juniperus horizontalis*), and northern bayberry (*Morella pensylvanica*).

Occasionally sandy regions may appear some distance from the ocean. They developed as a result of glacial activity—as deposits of glacial outwash material (in Nova Scotia) or larger rivers (in New Brunswick). The upper Annapolis Valley has the best example of inland sand barrens; it is home to specialty woody plants such as pinebarren golden heather (*Hudsonia ericoides*) and broom crowberry (*Corema conradii*). The sandy riverbanks of New Brunswick's larger rivers, in turn, often feature sand cherry (*Prunus pumila*).

Habitat Notes / Wetlands

Another habitat tab used in this guide is wetlands, which occupy a relatively small area of the total landmass in the Maritimes. New Brunswick has the most wetland areas—about 8 per cent of its landmass. In Nova Scotia that drops to about 3 per cent, and on Prince Edward Island to less than 1 per cent. (In contrast, the nearby island of Newfoundland is 18 per cent wetlands.)

What is meant by "wetlands"? The term applies to several types of habitats where water plays a key role. One major wetland group includes the margins of streams, rivers, and lakes, where the ground may be covered by water for at least a few weeks each year. In some of these places, water is present all year except during the driest summer months. Either way, the soil is always quite moist.

A second major wetland type is peatlands. These areas remain wet year-round, which means that, because of a lack of oxygen in the waterlogged substrate, plant detritus is slow to decompose. It forms a relatively thick layer of organic matter known as peat.

Bogs are the most prevalent category of wetland in the Maritimes. Four types occur in the region: raised, sloped, flat, and blanket. Raised bogs often form in valleys and cover a relatively large area. Typically, their central section is raised above their edges, appearing dome-like. In Nova Scotia, raised bogs are restricted mostly to southwestern areas. In New Brunswick, they occur in the southern counties of Charlotte and Saint John and the northeastern counties of

Restigouche and Gloucester. On Prince Edward Island, they occur mostly in Prince County, especially between East Bideford and Black Bank.

Sloped bogs occur in regions with high rainfall, poor drainage, and sloped terrain. In Nova Scotia they are most prevalent on Cape Breton Island and in Guysborough County.

Flat bogs are relatively small, form in wet depressions, and are scattered throughout the Maritimes. High groundwater tables are usually the reason they form.

Blanket bogs, on the other hand, cover vast areas on both level and sloped terrain, and form mostly in exceptionally wet, cool regions. Generally, they feature many small ponds and exposed bedrock. Blanket bogs are most common on Cape Breton Island and in eastern coastal regions of Nova Scotia. Bogs are the most nutrient-poor of the various wetland types. Their nutrients come from rain and snow rather than from the mineral soils of surrounding forested areas. Sphagnum moss and dwarf ericaceous shrubs are the dominant plants. Insectivorous herbaceous plants also abound, as do many species of orchids. Trees are generally absent, except for stunted tamarack (*Larix laricina*) and black spruce (*Picea mariana*).

Fens are another type of wetland. Generally much smaller than bogs, they often occur in poorly drained areas next to larger streams and lakes or as patches inside forests. Because they receive nutrients from surrounding upland areas, they are more nutrient-rich than bogs. As a result, they can support more plant life. Fens often resemble meadows because grasses and sedges dominate. They are usually tree-less, but they do support a diversity of shrubs including red-osier dogwood (*Cornus stolonifera*), shrubby cinquefoil (*Dasiphora fruticosa*), and broad-leaved meadowsweet (*Spiraea latifolia*).

Swamps and marshes are terms that are often used interchangeably. Both are wetlands that are flooded on a regular basis. For the purposes of this guide, however, a "marsh" is an area dominated by herbaceous plants with few or no woody plants, while a "swamp" has a high proportion of woody plants.

Swamps are the most nutrient-rich wetlands. They are small and localized within the Maritimes, usually found near larger river estuaries, especially where rivers flow into freshwater lakes. Swamps look like fens but, unlike them, they are home to many woody species. Red maple (*Acer rubrum*) and eastern white cedar (*Thuja occidentalis*) are typical woody trees encountered in Maritimes swamps.

Habitat Notes / Disturbed Areas

In this guide, disturbed areas include roadsides and railway beds; urban areas such as scrublands, vacant lots, and city/town trails; old pastures; and burned areas. All of these types of habitat have had their natural vegetation removed and underlying soil disturbed. Several native woody species are primary colonizers of disturbed habitats. They include trembling aspen (*Populus tremuloides*), pin cherry (*Prunus pensylvanica*), white spruce (*Picea glauca*), speckled alder (*Alnus incana* subsp. *rugosa*), and American green alder (*A. viridis* subsp. *crispa*).

Disturbed habitat is "new" habitat and so is the type of area most often occupied by introduced species. Mostly of European origin, introduced (or "alien") species arrived during the last five centuries. Some were brought as ornamentals, but many arrived accidentally—as seeds in ship ballast or packing materials. Nearly 20 per cent of all the plant species found in the Maritimes are not native to the region; they include woody ornamental species that have escaped from our gardens. Wych elm (*Ulmus glabra*), European ash (*Fraxinus excelsior*), and Scotch pine (*Pinus sylvestris*) are good examples.

Some introduced plants have increased in population so much that they are now inhabiting natural areas and displacing native species. They are considered "invasive alien plants"—a phenomenon that is a concern worldwide. Major invasive alien woody plants in the Maritimes include glossy buckthorn (*Frangula alnus*) and European buckthorn (*Rhamnus cathartica*).

Woody Plants / Supporting Wildlife

All woody plant species help support wildlife by providing food sources, places to shelter, and/or breeding sites. Some groups of shrubs and trees are widely known for their attraction and service to birds and animals.

Birds in particular are keenly attracted to specific woody plants, and their movements—especially in winter—are often highly dependent upon these plants' seed or fruit production. When birds move in dramatic numbers from one region to another in winter, they display "irruptive" behaviour. Despite what folklore suggests, their arrival in your area does not necessarily indicate a long harsh winter. Irruptions are more likely driven by a lack of food on the species' normal wintering grounds, which forces the birds to become more nomadic and move to an unusual (for them) overwintering area.

Birds commonly associated with winter irruptions are the winter finches: pine grosbeak, red crossbill, white-winged crossbill, purple finch, pine siskin, common redpoll, American goldfinch, and evening grosbeak. They each have particular food source preferences, which influence their movements. For example, over the course of their lives conifers have good and bad cone years. If your area has a particularly good cone crop, you may find pine grosbeaks, pine siskins, purple finches, and the crossbills in much higher overwintering numbers than usual—or they may appear in your area where they are not normally seen. Evening grosbeak movements are often determined by production levels of beechnuts (*Fagus grandiflora*) as well as ash (*Fraxinus* species) and maple (*Acer* species) keys, while American goldfinches and common redpolls are more influenced by the production of alder (*Alnus* species) seeds.

Other irruptive birds are more dependent on berry production. Quantities of mountain-ash (*Sorbus* species) fruit, in particular, can vary dramatically from year to year. In years of heavy fruit production, you may find American robins remaining through the winter months. Cedar waxwings—and especially Bohemian waxwings—will also often move into an area of productive mountain-ash fruit in winter, gorge themselves, then promptly move on. Pine grosbeaks, purple finches, and northern flickers may often overwinter in higher than normal numbers if mountain-ash berries are prolific.

Birds are not the only wildlife with a strong dependence on woody plants. Black bears, for example, also rely heavily on them as a food source. In mid- to late summer, they eat vast quantities of blueberries (*Vaccinium* species), raspberries (*Rubus idaeus*), red elderberries (*Sambucus racemosa*), and dogwood (*Cornus* species) fruit. In September, they seek out mountain-ash, mountain holly (*Ilex mucronata*), hazelnuts (*Corylus cornuta*), and blackberries (*Rubus* species) for their fruit. Later in the fall, beechnuts and, in some areas, acorns (*Quercus* species) are key food resources, along with wild apple (*Malus pumila*) and the fruit of the viburnums particularly arrowwood (*Viburnum recognitum*) and northern wild raisin (*Viburnum nudum* subsp. *cassinoides*). The breeding success of bears is highly dependent on the abundance of these fruits and nuts.

In addition, red squirrels and eastern chipmunks favour the nuts of hazelnut and beech, as well as the seeds from balsam fir (*Abies balsamea*) and spruce (*Picea* species). Raccoons and coyotes supplement their fall diets with the bounty from fruit-bearing woody plants that grow in the Maritimes.

SAMPLE PAGE

Evergreen or deciduous

Main leaf type

At-a-glance leaf characteristics

Bar colour for plants with shared characteristics**

At-a-glance information about cones, flowers, berries, edibility, etc.

Family name
Common name

Heath family / Ericaceae

Large cranberry

Scientific species name

Vaccinium macrocarpon

American cranberry, cranberry

Native Species

Other common names

VITAL STATISTICS

Maximum height: 10 centimetres
Flowering season: July

Height the plant can achieve in the Maritimes

Months in which flowers usually appear

Habitat type the plant is often found in (solid colour)

Wetlands

Habitat type the plant is sometimes found in (outline)

Barrens

Habitats are not shown if plant does not appear in them

Images show leaves, flowers, fruit, and other details that aid in identification

HABITAT: Wetlands—especially coastal wetlands—are the preferred habitat for large cranberry, which is fairly common throughout the Maritimes.

CHARACTERISTICS: Large cranberry is a trailing, broad-leaved evergreen with brown, flaking bark. The alternate, 5- to 10-millimetre, elliptical leaves are crowded on the stems. Shiny green on the upper surface, they have whitened undersides and untoothed, slightly revolute edges. New leaves often have a reddish tint; in winter, they may be tinted purple.

Nodding pink flowers are composed of four backward-curving petals and eight fused stamens that point downward, appearing beak-like. Produced in July, flowers are usually in twos or threes and sub-terminal; leafy stems extend beyond the blossoms.

Flowers develop into relatively large, deep red to dark purple berries that ripen in October and November. Large cranberry's tart berries are prized for jams and preserves, sauces, and desserts.

The similar small cranberry (*V. oxycoccus*) can be distinguished from the large cranberry by its flowers and berries, which are located at the ends of the stems.

Top: Leaves have pale undersides and untoothed, slightly revolute edges. Note the red tint on edges, typical in spring. **Middle:** Flowers have four backward-curving petals. Leafy stems extend beyond the flowers. **Bottom:** In winter, leaves are tinted purple. Berries are dark red when ripe.

112

**BAR COLOUR KEY

- Needles
- Scaled
- Broad Leaves: Simple, Opposite
- Broad Leaves: Simple, Alternate
- Broad Leaves: Whorled
- Broad Leaves: Compound, Opposite
- Broad Leaves: Compound, Alternate

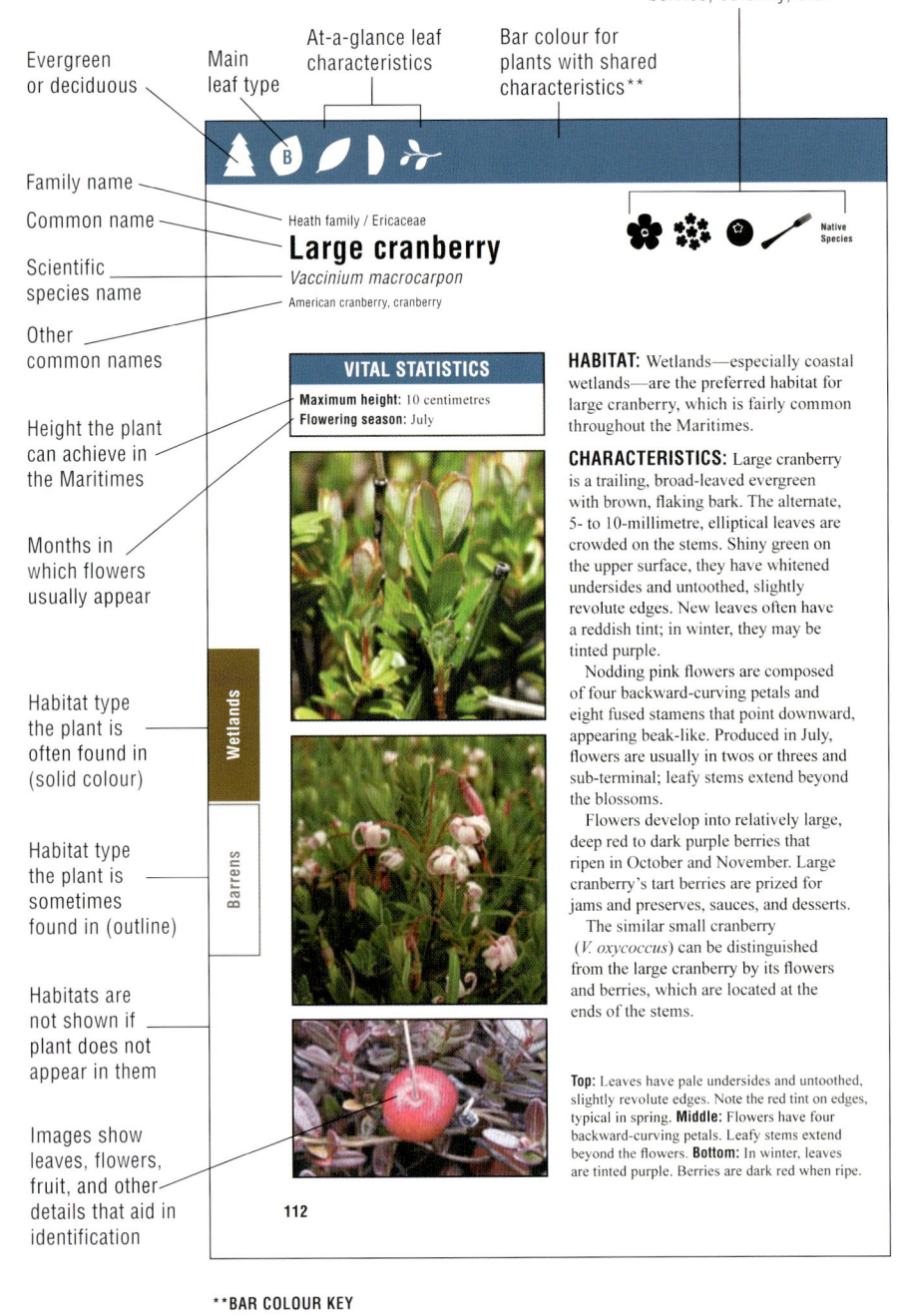

16

ICON LEGEND

Tree Type
- Evergreen
- Deciduous

Leaf Type
- Needle-like leaves
- Scale-like leaves
- Broad leaves

Leaf Edge
- Smooth
- Toothed
- Lobed

Leaf Arrangement on Branch (Simple)
- Opposite
- Alternate
- Whorled

Leaf Arrangement on Branch (Compound)
- Trifoliate
- Palmately compound
- Pinnately compound

Broad Leaf Shapes
- Elongate or lance-shaped
- Elliptical
- Oval to egg-shaped
- Tri-lobed
- Palmate

Flower Types
- Catkin
- Single flower
- Bell-shaped
- Cluster
- Spray
- Unusual

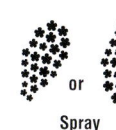

Berry Types
- Single berry, smooth surface
- Single berry, smooth surface, calyx
- Single berry, short stem, segmented surface
- Cluster of berries

Additional Information
- Cone
- Edible
- Inedible or harmful
- Native Species
- Introduced Species

17

PLANT PROFILES

Yew family / Taxaceae
Canada yew
Taxus canadensis
Ground-hemlock, dwarf yew

Native Species

VITAL STATISTICS
Maximum height: 1.5 metres
Flowering season: May

HABITAT: Canada yew grows throughout the Maritimes in moist to moderately dry woodlands, in ravines, as well as in wooded swamps.

CHARACTERISTICS: A spreading shrub that can reach a height of 1.5 metres, Canada yew has 1- to 2-centimetre-long, dark green needles. Flat and flexible, the needles have pointed tips but are not particularly prickly. They have a prominent midrib and are arranged spirally or, more commonly, horizontally.

This species is dioecious. Unlike other conifers, the female cones in yew family species produce berry-like fruit, not woody cones.

The flowers of both sexes are rather insignificant. Males produce a small cone in May, which lasts only a few weeks. By September the female flowers become red pulpy "cups" (arils); each aril has a large central seed.

The aril is edible **but the seed and the rest of the plant is poisonous.**

Top: Yew needles in typical two-sided arrangement. **Middle:** Each pulpy but edible red aril surrounds a poisonous central seed. **Bottom:** Small, short-lived cones appear in May.

Native Species

Pine family / Pinaceae
Balsam fir
Abies balsamea
Canada balsam

HABITAT: Balsam fir grows in woodlands throughout the Maritimes and can be prolific after clear-cutting.

CHARACTERISTICS: Balsam fir's flattened and blunt-tipped needles either extend horizontally from the stem or arch upward. Needles are somewhat flexible and are often white on the underside and shiny green on the top surface. Winter buds are rounded and often waxy or resinous. Both the bark and dead twigs are smooth, although the trunk may have resinous blisters.

Balsam fir is monoecious. Male cones are small, about 1 centimetre long, and purple-red. They are often clustered at branch tips. The 5- to 8-centimetre-long female cones, which point upward, are pale green initially, become purplish grey, then turn brown before they shatter and release seeds in the fall. Female cones often exude a sticky resin.

Balsam fir is the provincial tree of New Brunswick. Its flat needles, smooth twigs, and erect cones make it easy to distinguish from a tree it otherwise resembles: spruce, which has rounded needles, scaly twigs, and pendant cones.

VITAL STATISTICS
Maximum height: 25 metres
Flowering season: May to June

Top: Needles are often positioned horizontally on smooth stems. **Middle:** These late-summer, nearly mature female cones show sticky resin. Note the stiffly upright growth and the needles' pale undersides. **Bottom:** The smooth bark has resinous blisters.

Pine family / Pinaceae
European larch
Larix decidua
Tamarack

Introduced Species

VITAL STATISTICS
Maximum height: 30 metres
Flowering season: May

HABITAT: This introduced larch species is occasionally seen along roadsides and has been infrequently planted in reforestation projects throughout the Maritimes.

CHARACTERISTICS: European larch has a narrow, upright shape. Young twigs are golden brown and smooth; older bark becomes light grey-brown with furrows.

Needles are 2 to 3 centimetres long, bright green, soft, and flexible; in autumn, they turn golden yellow before falling off. Needles grow individually around the stem of current-season growth or, on older stems, in rounded clusters atop short spurs.

Plants are monoecious. Pale brown male cones, about 1 centimetre long, release pollen throughout May. Female cones are purple-red when young and become golden brown to grey-brown when mature, reaching 2 to 3.5 centimetres in length. They shed their seeds in their first autumn; old cones may remain attached to the trees for several years.

Top: The needles on all larch trees grow in distinct clusters on older stems. Also shown are immature female cones. **Middle:** All larch species' needles turn yellow before being shed in the fall. **Bottom:** Female cones in transition from purplish to brown.

Native Species

Pine family / Pinaceae
Tamarack
Larix laricina
Eastern larch, hackmatack, larch

HABITAT: Tamarack grows on poorly drained sites throughout the Maritimes.

CHARACTERISTICS: Young tamarack trees can be pyramidal in outline, but older trees are often quite gnarled and irregular in shape. In exposed locations, the treetop often leans to the east.

The needles, 1 to 2.5 centimetres long, are bluish green, soft, and flexible. In autumn, they turn golden yellow before falling off. They may be produced individually around the stem of current-season growth or, on older stems, appear in rounded clusters atop short spurs. Twigs and bark are grey-brown.

Plants are monoecious. Tiny male cones, shorter than 1 centimetre and pale yellow, shed their pollen during May. Female cones are 1.5 to 2 centimetres long and bright purplish red at first; when mature, they are a light reddish brown.

Cones shed their seeds during their first autumn but may remain attached to the tree for two to three years.

VITAL STATISTICS
Maximum height: 20 metres
Flowering season: May

Top: Tamarack's soft, clustered needles often show a blue tint. **Middle:** Female tamarack cones are purple-red in early summer. **Bottom:** These old female cones have shed their seeds.

Coniferous Forest

Pine family / Pinaceae
Norway spruce
Picea abies
Dwarf yew, ground-hemlock

Introduced Species

VITAL STATISTICS
Maximum height: 35 metres
Flowering season: May

HABITAT: Native throughout Europe, Norway spruce has been used experimentally in tree plantations in Nova Scotia and New Brunswick.

CHARACTERISTICS: The needles of this tall conifer are somewhat square in cross-section, sharply pointed, and a shiny dark green on all sides. They are 1 to 2 centimetres long and usually grow horizontally from the stems.

Dead twigs are covered in peg-like leaf bases. Young twigs are orange-brown and hairless, while older stems and the trunk are brownish grey and scaly. Winter buds are somewhat pointed and scaly.

Norway spruce is monoecious. Male cones are about 1 centimetre long, but the pendant female cones can eventually reach 9 to 17 centimetres, the longest of any spruce species worldwide. Cones shed their seeds in the first year but may remain attached for an additional season.

Top: Spruce needles growing from smooth, golden brown stems. **Bottom:** These mature female cones have shed their seeds but have not yet fallen from the tree.

Disturbed

Native Species

Pine family / Pinaceae
White spruce
Picea glauca
Canadian spruce, cat spruce, old field spruce

HABITAT: White spruce occurs in a variety of well-drained sites throughout the Maritimes, especially in coastal and upland areas.

CHARACTERISTICS: White spruce stems are hairless; bark is rough and scaly. Winter buds are somewhat pointed and scaly. As on all spruce, old dead twigs have peg-like leaf bases. White spruce emits a urine-like smell when bruised (which relates to the name "cat spruce").

Needles are four-sided, stiff, and sharply pointed. Often pale green or blue-tinted, they are arranged around the stem but often arch upward.

White spruce is monoecious. Male cones are about 1 centimetre long and purplish red; the elongate female cones, 3 to 5 centimetres long, are purple-red and upright at first, becoming pendant and greenish red, then brown, as they mature.

Although cones shed their seeds in their first autumn, they may remain on the tree for an additional year. Unlike the cones of fir or pine trees, spruce cones do not shatter before they fall.

VITAL STATISTICS
Maximum height: 30 metres
Flowering season: Mid-May to mid-June

Top: White spruce needles surround the stems and often arch upward. **Middle:** A group of pendant female cones after the release of seeds; these cones will soon drop but will remain intact. **Bottom:** Old dead twigs have peg-like leaf bases.

Pine family / Pinaceae
Black spruce
Picea mariana
Bog spruce, swamp spruce

Native Species

VITAL STATISTICS
Maximum height: 15 metres
Flowering season: Late May to June

HABITAT: Black spruce grows on various types of wetlands, in poorly drained forest sites, and in upland areas throughout the Maritimes.

CHARACTERISTICS: Black spruce has a narrow, pyramidal shape. Bark is rough and scaly. Dead twigs are covered in peg-like leaf bases; new twigs are densely hairy. Winter buds are somewhat pointed and scaly.

Needles, which are four-sided, stiff, but not particularly sharp, are arranged around the stems and are usually more densely packed than those of white or red spruce. They are dark green, often with a blue tint.

Plants are monoecious. Male cones are about 1 centimetre long and purplish red. The ovate and pendant female cones are the shortest of any spruce species: just 2 to 3 centimetres long. Dark purple in their first summer, they turn dark reddish brown late in the season. Unlike the cones of white spruce, which drop after they shed their seeds, the cones of black spruce may remain attached to the tree for many years.

Black spruce is the provincial tree of Newfoundland and Labrador. It is used to make spruce beer in some areas of the Maritimes.

Top: The relatively short, densely packed needles of black spruce are arranged around the entire stem. **Middle:** Developing pendant female cones as they appear in mid-summer's purple stage. **Bottom:** Female cones that have shed their seeds often remain attached for an additional season.

Native Species

Pine family / Pinaceae
Red spruce
Picea rubens
Eastern spruce, yellow spruce

HABITAT: Red spruce—the provincial tree of Nova Scotia—grows on well-drained sites throughout the Maritimes and is especially predominant near the Bay of Fundy. Its presence distinguishes the Acadian Forest region.

CHARACTERISTICS: Red spruce bark is rough and scaly. Winter buds, somewhat pointed, are also scaly but twigs are hairy, a characteristic that differentiates this species from the similar white spruce. Branches are often well spaced and curve upward at the tip.

Red spruce needles are four-sided, stiff, and sharply pointed. They are dark green or yellow-green and occasionally blue-tinted. Arranged around the stem, they often arch upward.

Plants are monoecious. Male cones are about 1 centimetre long and purplish red; the elongate female cones, 3 to 4 centimetres long, are purple-red. The elongate cones help distinguish this species from black spruce, which has ovate cones; initially upright, they become pendant and green-red then red-brown as they mature. Although they shed their seeds in their first autumn, these cones may remain on the tree for an additional year.

VITAL STATISTICS
Maximum height: 35 metres
Flowering season: Mid-May to mid-June

Top: The needles are arranged around the stem and often angle upward. Also seen here are the small purple-red male cones. **Middle:** Mature female cones are about to shed their seeds. **Bottom:** Branches are often well spaced and curve upward at the tips.

Pine family / Pinaceae
Jack pine
Pinus banksiana
Grey pine, scrub pine

Native Species

VITAL STATISTICS
Maximum height: 20 metres
Flowering season: Late May to June

HABITAT: Jack pine grows on dry sandy or gravelly sites and rocky outcrops throughout the Maritimes.

CHARACTERISTICS: Conical in shape when young, jack pine often becomes more irregular in outline with age. A fire-adapted species, jack pine cones remain attached to the tree and unopened until exposed to temperatures above 50°C, sometimes for many years.

Twigs are grey to brown. Bark is brown-grey and scaly; the scales become more plate-like with age. Jack pine's short needles, 2 to 5 centimetres long, are olive to yellow-green and relatively stiff but have a noticeable twist. They grow in pairs and have a distinct basal sheath.

Jack pine is monoecious. Typical of pines, male cones are 1 to 2 centimetres long and clustered at the base of the current season's new growth; female cones are located at its tips. Mature female cones are 3 to 5 centimetres long, and rounded at the base with a tapered tip. They are green in the first year, becoming brown to grey in the second. They often curve in on branch stems rather than hang down. Old female cones may remain attached for several years.

Pinus banksiana was named to honour Sir Joseph Banks (1743–1820), the British naturalist and botanist on James Cook's first great Pacific voyage (1768–1771).

Top: Always paired, jack pine needles are relatively short. Note the papery basal sheath at the base of each pair. **Bottom:** First-year female cones are green and point inward, hugging the stems.

Native Species

Pine family / Pinaceae
Red Pine
Pinus resinosa
Norway pine

HABITAT: Red pine is scattered throughout the Maritimes on sandy and rocky soils.

CHARACTERISTICS: Red pine is the only Maritimes species that retains a conical shape even in old age. Young tree bark is brown and scaly; the scales become more plate-like as the tree matures.

Red pine needles, 8 to 15 centimetres long, are deep green and relatively stiff. They grow in pairs with a distinct basal sheath.

Like other pines, red pine is monoecious. The male cones are 1 to 2 centimetres long and purple, becoming yellow as they shed pollen. Typical of all pines, male cones are clustered at the base of the current year's growth.

When mature, female cones are somewhat rounded, 4 to 6 centimetres long, and green in the first year, becoming brown in the second. Cones may remain on the tree for several years after seeds have been shed.

VITAL STATISTICS
Maximum height: 25 metres
Flowering season: June

Top: Long and stiff, red pine needles can give branches a brush-like appearance. **Middle:** Old grey female cones can remain attached for several years after seed release. **Bottom:** Male cones are clustered where the current year's growth begins.

Pine family / Pinaceae
Eastern white pine
Pinus strobus
Northern white pine, white pine

Native Species

VITAL STATISTICS
Maximum height: 30 metres
Flowering season: June

HABITAT: Eastern white pine grows mostly on well-drained, naturally sandy or gravelly sites throughout the Maritimes. It is common to most such areas except on Cape Breton Island.

CHARACTERISTICS: Unlike most conifers, which have a pyramid-like silhouette, mature white pines are often flat-topped and irregular in shape. Twigs are smooth and green. Young trees have smooth green bark, which becomes furrowed and brown, and grows large scales, as the trees age.

White pine needles are 5 to 12 centimetres long, bluish green, and flexible. They grow in clusters of five and have no basal sheath.

White pine is monoecious. Male cones are clustered, 1 to 2 centimetres long, and purplish red; they become yellow as they shed pollen. Female cones are green during their first year, turning brown in their second. These elongated cones (7 to 15 centimetres) drop from the tree during the autumn and winter after seeds have been shed. They are the longest cones of any local pine.

Top: Needles are produced in clusters of five with no papery basal sheath. **Middle:** White pine's female cones are the longest of any local pine. **Bottom:** Purplish red male cones become yellow as they shed pollen.

Introduced Species

Pine family / Pinaceae
Scotch Pine
Pinus sylvestris
Caledonian pine, Scots pine

HABITAT: Scotch pine is native throughout Europe and across northern Asia to eastern Siberia. In the Maritimes, it has been used experimentally for reforestation projects but has also started to naturalize from ornamental plantings.

CHARACTERISTICS: Conical in shape when young, Scotch pine trees often become more irregularly contoured as they age. Twigs are grey-brown to brown; grey-brown bark becomes distinctive orange-brown as trees age.

The needles, 3 to 7 centimetres long, are bluish green, relatively stiff, somewhat flattened, and have a characteristic twist. They grow in pairs and have a distinct basal sheath.

Male cones, clustered at the base of the current season's growth, are 1 to 2 centimetres long and purple-red, becoming yellow as they shed pollen. Female cones change over time. In the first year, they are 4 to 7 centimetres long, dark green, and rounded at the base, with a tapered tip. In the second year, they become wholly round and brown to greyish brown.

VITAL STATISTICS
Maximum height: 25 metres
Flowering season: June

Top: Scotch pine needles are relatively short, often blue-tinted, and have a distinct twist. **Middle:** Female cones in their green phase. Note the paired needles. **Bottom:** Male cones cluster where current-season growth begins.

Coniferous Forest | Mixed Forest | Disturbed

31

Pine family / Pinaceae
Eastern hemlock
Tsuga canadensis
Canadian hemlock

Native Species

VITAL STATISTICS
Maximum height: 25 metres
Flowering season: Mid-May to mid-June

HABITAT: Eastern hemlock grows on moist northern slopes and in ravines. It is found throughout the Maritimes but is most common in southwestern Nova Scotia and south-central New Brunswick. It is uncommon on Prince Edward Island.

CHARACTERISTICS: Young trees are pyramidal in shape, although the leader and tips of horizontal branches usually droop. Trees become more rounded as they age. Twigs are densely pubescent and golden to grey-brown. The bark becomes dark red-brown, flaky, and furrowed with age.

The short (8 to 13 millimetres) flattened needles have round to pointed (though not sharp) tips. They are shiny green above with two whitened lines on the underside and usually arranged in a double-row horizontal pattern. Needles are attached to the stems by a narrow stalk.

Plants are monoecious. Tiny yellow male cones are produced along the sides of the branchlets; blue-green female cones are located at the branch ends. When mature, pendant female cones are 1.5 to 2 centimetres long and light brown. They shed their seeds in the autumn.

Eastern hemlock are among the oldest trees in the Maritimes—some specimens are more than 400 years old.

Top: Twigs are densely pubescent; needles extend horizontally from them. **Bottom:** This mature female cone has released its seeds.

Native Species

Cyprus family / Cupressaceae
Common juniper
Juniperus communis
Dwarf juniper, ground juniper, low juniper

HABITAT: Common juniper grows throughout the Maritimes in open, exposed habitats such as old burned sites, barrens, coastal headlands, and old pastures.

CHARACTERISTICS: Common juniper is the most widely distributed woody plant on Earth. A sprawling low evergreen shrub, it can grow completely prostrate in exposed habitats. In sheltered areas, plant shape is more fountain-like and needles are more widely spaced. Bark is brownish grey and scaly.

The 1- to 2-centimetre-long needles—concave, stiff, and sharply pointed—grow in whorls of three and densely on the stems. Their upper surface is shiny and varies in colour from olive to blue-green; the underside is white to bluish white. In winter, the needles often turn a bronze hue.

Common juniper is dioecious, but its flowers are insignificant. Unlike typical conifers, the female fruit (cone) is an aromatic berry that changes from greenish blue to blue, and gains a white bloom during its long maturation period of two to three years. The berry-like cones are the source of the flavour in gin; some people use them to season wild game.

VITAL STATISTICS
Maximum height: 1.5 metres
Flowering season: May

Top: This close-up shows the convex shape of juniper needles and their whitened underside.
Bottom: This prostrate branch has prolific berry-like female cones.

Rockrose family / Cistaceae

Pinebarren golden heather
Hudsonia ericoides

False heather, golden heather, hudsonia

Native Species

VITAL STATISTICS
Maximum height: 20 centimetres
Flowering season: Late May to early July

HABITAT: An Atlantic Coastal Plain species, pinebarren golden heather grows on dry exposed sandy to rocky barrens and on pine barrens. Generally uncommon in the Maritimes, it is found on the Atlantic coast and in the Annapolis Valley in Nova Scotia, as well as on Prince Edward Island. It is absent from New Brunswick.

CHARACTERISTICS: Pinebarren golden heather has small, somewhat downy, needle-like leaves that spread outward. Older leaves turn brown-black but remain attached to the stems. Plants grow 10 to 20 centimetres tall and form clumps that are 20 to 60 centimetres in diameter.

The 1-centimetre-diameter yellow flowers have five petals, giving the tiny blossoms a star-like shape. The flowers are held on 4- to 10-millimetre-long stems.

Top: This plant's narrow, pointed, evergreen leaves look like moss, making the plant difficult to identify when it is not in bloom.
Bottom: The five-petalled flowers resemble little stars.

Native Species

Heath family / Ericaceae
Broom crowberry
Corema conradii
Poverty grass

HABITAT: Broom crowberry, an Atlantic Coastal Plain species, grows on sandy to rocky coastal barrens and pine barrens of mainland Nova Scotia. It is rare on Prince Edward Island, rare and probably introduced in New Brunswick, and absent from Cape Breton Island.

CHARACTERISTICS: This sub-shrub produces evergreen mats up to 2 metres in diameter. Superficially, broom crowberry looks like a more upright version of black crowberry (*Empetrum nigrum*) but its leaves usually have a more upward angle and twigs are yellow-green rather than reddish brown.

The needle-like, 3- to 6-millimetre-long leaves, a shiny bright green in summer, turn rusty brown in winter. They are strongly revolute, meeting on the underside to produce a white groove.

Plants are dioecious. Both male and female flowers are produced in small clusters at the tips of the branches. The flowers have no petals, just purple-red stamens or pistils. The female flowers later develop into tiny (5-millimetre-long), hard, green to brown fruit.

VITAL STATISTICS
Maximum height: 50 centimetres
Flowering season: Late April to early May

Top: The needle-like leaves often point upward. **Middle:** The flowers have no petals and are clustered at stem tips. **Bottom:** Needles turn rusty brown in winter.

Barrens

Dunes

Heath family / Ericaceae
Pink crowberry
Empetrum eamesii
Purple crowberry, rock crowberry

Native Species

VITAL STATISTICS
Maximum height: 5 centimetres
Flowering season: Late April to May

HABITAT: Pink crowberry grows in the most exposed locations—coastal headlands, high hills, and alpine locations—primarily on Cape Breton Island and in the Chebucto and Canso regions of Nova Scotia. It is rare on Prince Edward Island and absent from New Brunswick.

CHARACTERISTICS: This species is a sub-shrub that forms a prostrate evergreen mat. Pink crowberry is more compact than black crowberry (*E. nigrum*), which it otherwise resembles.

Branchlets are densely covered in white hairs. Needle-like leaves are 2.5 to 4 millimetres long, dull-tipped, shiny green, and densely crowded on the stems. Leaves have smooth, strongly revolute margins that nearly meet on the underside, forming a white groove. Dense white hairs make the stems appear pale. Old leaves turn rusty red and remain attached to the plant.

Plants are dioecious. The minute flowers (inconspicuous and purple-red) are produced in the axils of upper leaves. Female flowers become light pink berries that mature to translucent red by late July. The fruit is edible but has little flavour.

Purple crowberry (*E. atropurpureum*), which is similar but whose fruit is dark red-purple, is also restricted to Nova Scotia. It grows on sand dunes and exposed coastal headlands.

Top: Pink crowberry has a low, mat-like form and reddish pink fruit. **Bottom:** Purple crowberry's drupes, shown here, are similar to those of pink crowberry but are more distinctly purple-red.

Native Species

Heath family / Ericaceae
Black crowberry
Empetrum nigrum
Heathberry, northern crowberry

Coniferous Forest

HABITAT: Black crowberry grows throughout the Maritimes but is most common along the coasts, on high exposed hills, and in the drier acidic bogs.

CHARACTERISTICS: Black crowberry is a sub-shrub that produces prostrate evergreen mats.

Branchlets are hairless and shiny. The short, needle-like leaves (3 to 7 millimetres long) are dull-tipped, shiny dark green, and relatively crowded on the stems. Leaf margins are smooth and strongly revolute, resulting in a thin white groove on the leaf's underside. Old leaves turn rusty brown but remain attached.

The purple-red axillary flowers are minute and inconspicuous. Plants may be dioecious or hermaphroditic (recently, plant taxonomists have reclassified the hermaphroditic plants as a separate species: *E. hermaphroditica*). Female flowers develop into juicy, dull black, berry-like drupes that ripen by late July. The black fruit is edible.

VITAL STATISTICS
Maximum height: 5 centimetres
Flowering season: April to May

Wetlands

Barrens

Dunes

Top: Needle-like leaves are short but quite thick. **Middle:** Black crowberry has a low, mat-like form. **Bottom:** Flowers are minute and hard to see (males shown).

Cypress family / Cupressaceae
Creeping juniper
Juniperus horizontalis
Creeping savin, horizontal juniper

Native Species

VITAL STATISTICS
Maximum height: 10 centimetres
Flowering season: May to early June

HABITAT: Although it grows most prolifically along exposed coastal headlands, creeping juniper can occur in any open, exposed location. It is distributed throughout the Maritimes but is most common along the shores of the Bay of Fundy and the Northumberland Strait, as well as along the eastern Quebec–New Brunswick border.

CHARACTERISTICS: Creeping juniper is a prostrate evergreen shrub that can form large mats several metres wide. Its foliage is a dense arrangement of overlapping scale-like leaves; individual leaves are sharply pointed. The foliage colour varies from blue-green to blue-grey and often has a purple tint in winter.

Plants are dioecious. Minute male cones shed pollen throughout May and into June. Female cones mature into aromatic, berry-like cones over two seasons. First-year "cones" are pale blue-green. Once mature, they become blue-black with a waxy bloom.

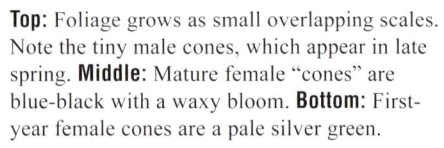

Top: Foliage grows as small overlapping scales. Note the tiny male cones, which appear in late spring. **Middle:** Mature female "cones" are blue-black with a waxy bloom. **Bottom:** First-year female cones are a pale silver green.

Native Species

Cypress family / Cupressaceae
Eastern white cedar
Thuja occidentalis
Cedar, eastern arborvitae, swamp cedar, white cedar

HABITAT: Eastern white cedar grows in damp to relatively dry, limestone-based soils in swamps, along rivers and lakeshores, and in uplands and old pastures. Although found throughout the Maritimes, it is considered rare in Nova Scotia (but found in Annapolis Valley, and Cumberland and Digby Counties) and on Prince Edward Island (found in western areas).

CHARACTERISTICS: This species forms a conical evergreen tree with arching branches. The young stems of eastern white cedar are grey-brown; the bark and trunk become red-brown as they age. The mature trunks are furrowed and the bark peels in long strips.

The small, overlapping, scale-like foliage is arranged in flat fan-like branchlets. The olive green summer foliage is tinted with brown in winter.

Plants are monoecious with clusters of male and female cones produced on separate branchlets. The tiny yellow male cones are produced in the axils of the branchlets; the green female cones are produced near the tips. When mature, the egg-shaped female cones are 8 to 13 millimetres long. They turn from green to brown by late summer. In autumn, the cones open to release seeds, but they can remain attached for another year.

Top: The small, overlapping, scale-like leaves form flat fan-like branchlets. Note the green, egg-shaped, immature female cones.
Bottom: These mature female cones have shed their seeds.

VITAL STATISTICS
Maximum height: 20 metres
Flowering season: May

Rockrose family / Cistaceae
Woolly heather
Hudsonia tomentosa
Sand heather, woolly beach heather, woolly hudsonia

Native Species

VITAL STATISTICS
Maximum height: 20 centimetres
Flowering season: June and July

HABITAT: Woolly heather grows on coastal sand dunes and freshwater sandbars and occasionally in open, sandy fields and woods and on high, gravelly hills. Generally uncommon in the Maritimes, it is most likely to be found along the Northumberland Strait.

CHARACTERISTICS: This evergreen sub-shrub forms a mound. From a distance, its foliage appears grey-green with pale tips. Branchlets are white with a dense covering of hairs; older stems are grey to red-brown.

The tiny, triangular-shaped leaves appear scale-like and densely overlap along the branches. They are grey-green and covered in a thick coating of hair, a feature that distinguishes them from the similar pinebarren golden heather (*H. ericoides*).

The yellow five-petalled flowers are nearly stemless and are produced at the tips of the branches. The fruit is a smooth ovoid capsule surrounded by a persistent calyx.

This species has a deep taproot that can provide stability in the shifting sand-dune habitat it prefers.

Top: Scale-like leaves are thickly covered in hair.
Middle: Yellow flowers are nearly stemless.
Bottom: From a distance, foliage appears grey-green with paler tips.

Introduced Species

Heath family / Ericaceae
Scottish heather
Calluna vulgaris
Heather, Scotch heather

HABITAT: Scottish heather is native to Europe and Asia Minor, where it grows on acidic open barrens. In the Maritimes, localized introduced populations are restricted to Nova Scotia and New Brunswick.

CHARACTERISTICS: Scottish heather is an upright to sprawling evergreen shrub that reaches only 20 to 60 centimetres in height. Paired leaves—minute and scale-like—are dark green in summer but can have a bronze tint in winter.

Scottish heather produces narrow spikes of tiny, rose-purple, bell-shaped flowers at branch tips. Flowers have four petals and four petal-like sepals.

In Europe during the Middle Ages, heather was a key ingredient in brewing beer. Today, natural honey made from heather nectar is an important product in moorland regions of Europe. The Latin name *Calluna* comes from the Greek *kalluno*, which means "to sweep"—a reference to the historic custom of tying together branches of heather to make a rough broom.

There are more than a thousand cultivars of Scottish heather; a beautiful collection can be viewed at the Agricultural College in Truro, Nova Scotia.

VITAL STATISTICS
Maximum height: 60 centimetres
Flowering season: August to October

Top: Scottish heather foliage consists of tiny, overlapping, scale-like leaves. **Middle:** An impressive display of flowers on Scottish heather. **Bottom:** Flowers have four petals and four petal-like sepals.

Heath family / Ericaceae
Pale bog laurel
Kalmia polifolia
Bog laurel, swamp laurel

Native Species

VITAL STATISTICS
Maximum height: 30 centimetres
Flowering season: June

HABITAT: Pale bog laurel is scattered throughout the Maritimes, growing primarily on bogs but occasionally on open, damp barrens.

CHARACTERISTICS: Often confused with bog rosemary (*Andromeda polifolia* var. *latifolia*), this laurel can best be identified by examining its leaves. Shiny and green, they grow opposite each other, while the dull grey-green leaves of bog rosemary alternate up the stem.

Pale bog laurel's smooth leaf stems have two conspicuous vertical ridges. Leaves are linear to lance-shaped, 1.5 to 3 centimetres long. Shiny dark green on the top surface, they are whitened on the underside. Leaf margins are untoothed and strongly revolute. Leaves remain deep green in winter.

This shrub produces terminal clusters of pink saucer-shaped flowers, each with five lobes. Stamens are set into cups on the corolla and spring outward when touched. The fruit—rounded, reddish capsules—grows atop erect, slender but stiff stems. The similar sheep laurel (*K. angustifolia*) has whorled, broader leaves and flowers a month later.

Top: Pale bog laurel growing among black crowberry (bottom) and low sweet blueberry (upper right). **Middle:** Stamens are set into small pockets on the saucer-shaped flowers (visible on centre and right-hand flowers). **Bottom:** Globular seed capsules are produced atop slender but stiff stems.

Native Species

Diapensia family / Diapensiaceae
Lapland diapensia
Diapensia lapponica
Diapensia

HABITAT: Lapland diapensia is an arctic-alpine plant that extends as far north as land exists. In the Maritimes it is restricted to north-facing slopes on the highest hills of the Cape Breton Highlands, where it is considered a rare species.

CHARACTERISTICS: This evergreen sub-shrub forms a rounded to flat hummock 5 to 8 centimetres high. Leaves are opposite, smooth, narrow, downwardly curved, and somewhat spoon-shaped with untoothed edges. Olive to dark green in summer, they turn purple-red in winter.

Flowers are relatively large and showy. Solitary, white, and five-petalled, they grow just above the foliage. They are bell-shaped but not pendulous, growing outward or upward. The fruit is a capsule enclosed by a greenish red or purplish red calyx.

VITAL STATISTICS
Maximum height: 8 centimetres
Flowering season: June and July

Top: Lapland diapensia's deep green leaves are narrow, smooth, and somewhat spoon-shaped.
Bottom: Single white flowers extend just above the leaves, which here show some of their purple-red winter colour.

Barrens

Bush-honeysuckle family / Diervillaceae

Northern bush-honeysuckle
Diervilla lonicera
Bush honeysuckle

Native Species

VITAL STATISTICS
Maximum height: 1 metre
Flowering season: Late June through July

HABITAT: Common throughout the Maritimes, northern bush-honeysuckle grows along roadsides, in old pastures and fields, on rocky slopes, and as an understorey shrub in dry, open forests.

CHARACTERISTICS: Northern bush-honeysuckle is a deciduous, suckering, sprawling shrub. Leaf stems are brownish green and generally smooth, although occasionally scaly. Leaves are opposite and may be elliptical to oval; usually they have a rounded base and an elongate pointed tip. Somewhat wrinkled, they have finely toothed edges. When exposed to at least partial sun, fall foliage is an impressive mix of orange, red, and yellow.

Throughout July, clusters of two or three flowers are produced at twig tips or in upper leaf axils. Flowers are tubular to funnel-shaped, straw yellow, and have five petals. The lower petal is larger and a deeper yellow than the others, which helps attract the main pollinator: the bumblebee. Flowers often turn orange to red as they age. A narrow curved seed capsule, topped with a small star-like calyx, is produced in autumn.

Top: Leaves are elliptical to oval, with a rounded base, elongate pointed tip, and finely toothed edges. **Middle:** Flowers are tubular to funnel-shaped with five petals. Note the slightly larger, modified lower petal. **Bottom:** The narrow curved seed capsules have a small star-like calyx.

Muskroot family / Adoxaceae
Northern wild raisin
Viburnum nudum var. *cassinoides*
(formerly *V. cassinoides*)

Wild raisin, witherod

HABITAT: Northern wild raisin is a common shrub that occurs in a variety of moist habitats throughout the Maritimes, such as thickets, forests, swamps, and lakeshores.

CHARACTERISTICS: This species is a medium to tall deciduous shrub. Its newest twigs are light greyish brown and somewhat felted with scattered pale lenticels. Older stems are purple-brown and smooth. The winter buds of northern wild raisin are narrow, scurfy, and covered in minute golden or rust-coloured scales.

The opposite leaves vary from lance-shaped through elliptical to oval. A dull coppery green at first growth, they later become shiny dark green on their upper surface. Some have slightly toothed edges. Anywhere from 6 to 12 centimetres long, leaves turn shades of red in autumn.

Flat-topped clusters of tiny, five-petalled, yellowish cream flowers have a musty scent. They become loose clusters of berry-like drupes that ripen from greenish white through pink then to blue-black—sometimes fruit in all three colours may be in the same cluster. Each drupe contains one flattened seed. Berries are edible and are commonly used dried.

The rare nannyberry (*V. lentago*) resembles northern wild raisin. Restricted to southwestern New Brunswick, it can be distinguished by its distinctly serrated leaves and shorter-stalked flower clusters.

VITAL STATISTICS
Maximum height: 4 metres
Flowering season: Late June through July

Top: Flat-topped clusters of tiny, creamy flowers among lance-shaped to oval leaves.
Bottom: Loose clusters of fruit in pink and blue-black with late autumn's burgundy red foliage.

Aster family / Asteraceae

Big-leaved marsh-elder
Iva frutescens subsp. *oraria*
Marsh-elder

Native Species

VITAL STATISTICS
Maximum height: 2 metres
Flowering season: August to September

HABITAT: Big-leaved marsh-elder occurs among salt marshes and adjacent roadside embankments. It is a rare species in Nova Scotia, seen in central and southern areas, as well as in Cape Breton County. Considered an Atlantic Coastal Plain species, it is not found in New Brunswick or on Prince Edward Island.

CHARACTERISTICS: This species is a multi-stemmed shrub. The bark of big-leaved marsh-elder is smooth and grey-brown. Young stems are green, later becoming grey-brown. The leaf scars completely encircle the stem, forming a ring.

The leaves are lance-shaped to elliptical with fine teeth along their edges. They are fleshy with a rough texture and have three prominent veins. They range from 4 to 10 centimetres in length. Most leaves are opposite, but the smaller upper leaves are often alternate. This species has no appreciable fall colour, and leaves are quite late to drop.

In late summer, plants produce nodding clusters of dull brownish pink flowers (resembling the flowers of ragweed) from the upper leaf axils. The base of each small flower is surrounded by five green, petal-like bracts. Small, naked, purple-brown seeds are shed in autumn.

Top: Fleshy leaves are lance-shaped to elliptical with fine teeth along their edges. **Bottom:** Near the flowers, leaves are often alternately arranged.

Native Species

Oleaster family / Elaeagnaceae
Soapberry
Shepherdia canadensis
Canada buffaloberry, soopolallie

HABITAT: Soapberry is primarily restricted to limestone or gypsum-based rocky slopes and ledges, seacoasts, and open woods. In New Brunswick, it is most likely to be found in the northwest and near Hillsborough, Albert County; in Nova Scotia, it is most common on the north side of Cape Breton Island and on the Avon peninsula, Hants County. It is not native to Prince Edward Island.

CHARACTERISTICS: Although it may grow to its full height as an upright deciduous shrub in sheltered sites, soapberry is often prostrate in exposed locations.

Twigs are reddish brown, scurfy, and covered in minute scales. Winter buds are somewhat pointed and also scurfy. Leaves are opposite, smooth-edged, and elliptical to oval. The upper surface is smooth and dark green with small white dots; the underside is silvery and scurfy.

Plants are dioecious. Both sexes produce small, yellowish, four-petalled flowers just as the leaves unfurl. Male flowers grow in small clusters in the leaf axils; female flowers are solitary.

Female plants produce small, solitary, translucent red, berry-like drupes in August. The fruit's surface is peppered with white spots, and the calyx persists as a crown-like extension at the fruit tip. The fruit is edible but tastes bitter.

Top: Fruiting soapberry has reddish brown, scurfy stems and silvery white scales on leaves. **Bottom:** The small male flowers are yellow-green.

VITAL STATISTICS
Maximum height: 2 metres
Flowering season: April to June

Coniferous Forest
Mixed Forest
Barrens
Dunes

47

Madder family / Rubiaceae
Common buttonbush
Cephalanthus occidentalis
Buttonbush, honey-bells

Native Species

VITAL STATISTICS
Maximum height: 3 metres
Flowering season: July and August

HABITAT: Common buttonbush is a rare Atlantic Coastal Plain species restricted to southwestern Nova Scotia and south-southwestern New Brunswick. It grows in swamps, on lakeshores, and along streams and rivers. It is not native to Prince Edward Island.

CHARACTERISTICS: This species forms a medium-sized, multi-stemmed shrub. The young stems of common buttonbush are smooth and green, aging to red-brown with pale lenticels. Older bark is brown-grey, fissured, and flaky.

Smooth-edged leaves are 8 to 14 centimetres in length and vary in shape from elliptical to ovate. They may be opposite or in whorls of three. The upper leaf surface is smooth and shiny green, while the underside is paler.

The white flowers are terminal or produced in the upper leaf axils. Individual flowers are minute and tubular but are arranged in a dense, 2.5-centimetre-wide, spherical head. Later, this becomes the "fruit": a dense rusty red head of tiny nutlets that often remains attached all winter.

The leaves are toxic to both humans and livestock.

Top: On this stem, leaves are in whorls of three. **Middle:** Narrow tubular flowers are produced in a spherical head. **Bottom:** A rusty red head of nutlets may remain throughout winter.

Wetlands

Honeysuckle family / Caprifoliaceae

Canada fly honeysuckle
Lonicera canadensis

American fly honeysuckle

Native Species

VITAL STATISTICS
Maximum height: 1.5 metres
Flowering season: Late April to May

HABITAT: Canada fly honeysuckle prefers cool, damp, mixed or deciduous woodlands. It is widely distributed throughout the Maritimes.

CHARACTERISTICS: This plant is a short, sprawling shrub. New twigs are smooth and red-brown; older twigs commonly shed their bark in long, narrow strips. The winter buds of Canada fly honeysuckle are paired, red-brown, and pointed.

Paired, ovate to elliptical leaves are bright green on the upper surface and paler on the underside. Leaf edges are smooth and covered in fine hairs. Fall foliage is yellow.

Leaf axils produce paired, nodding, pale yellow flowers, 2 to 2.5 centimetres long, at the end of a distinct flower stem. Each blossom has five petals and is bell- to funnel-shaped. The fruit consists of two red, teardrop-shaped berries, which are connected at their base.

Swamp fly honeysuckle (*Lonicera oblongifolia*), a rare species, is found in limestone-based swamps in New Brunswick. It is distinguished from Canada fly honeysuckle by its leaves' downy white underside.

Top: Paired ovate leaves are bright green on upper surfaces. Note the twinned teardrop-shaped fruit. **Middle:** Paired flowers are pale yellow and bell-shaped. **Bottom:** Look under the leaf to distinguish the similar swamp fly honeysuckle; note unripe fruit and downy white leaf undersides (on left).

Honeysuckle family / Caprifoliaceae

European honeysuckle
Lonicera periclymenum
Woodbine

Introduced Species

VITAL STATISTICS
Maximum length: 6 metres
Flowering season: July and August

HABITAT: Native throughout most of Europe, European honeysuckle is a garden ornamental in the Maritimes and has become established in the wild only in the province of Nova Scotia, primarily from Halifax south to Yarmouth.

CHARACTERISTICS: European honeysuckle is a tall twining vine that climbs up neighbouring shrubs and trees or spreads along the ground where upright supports are not available. Current-season stems are smooth and often purple-tinted. Older stems are tan brown and can shed their bark in thin strips.

Winter buds are paired, red-brown, and pointed. The paired, oblong to ovate leaves are waxy blue-green on the upper surface and distinctly pale underneath. The leaf edges are smooth and the leaves hairless. They have no distinctive fall colour.

Clusters of 5-centimetre-long, elongate, tubular flowers are produced at the stem tips. Unopened, buds are pink-tinted; open, they are white to pale yellow, aging to deep golden yellow. The flowers are highly fragrant and sticky. Bright red, shiny berries (mildly toxic) are produced in clusters in autumn.

Italian honeysuckle (*L. caprifolium*) has been known to persist near Wolfville, Nova Scotia. Its flowers are also creamy white and fragrant, though often paler; it can be identified by a pair of fused leaves immediately below the flowers.

Top: Oblong leaves are paired; tubular flowers are clustered at stem tips. **Bottom:** Bright red berries are produced in dense clusters.

Disturbed

Introduced Species

Honeysuckle family / Caprifoliaceae

Tartarian honeysuckle
Lonicera tatarica
Shrub honeysuckle

HABITAT: Native to Siberia and eastern Asia, Tartarian honeysuckle has recently become locally naturalized in open forests, roadsides, and pasturelands in southern New Brunswick, Nova Scotia's Annapolis Valley, and a few old homesteads on Prince Edward Island.

CHARACTERISTICS: Tartarian honeysuckle is a bushy, upright shrub. The bark is ash grey and sheds in thin strips. Winter buds are paired, fuzzy, grey, and pointed.

The paired, ovate to elliptical leaves are waxy blue-green on the upper surface and paler on the underside. They have smooth edges and are hairless, with no distinctive fall colour.

Paired white, pink, or crimson flowers grow in the upper leaf axils. They have five petals: four point upward, a fifth points downward. Paired red berries are produced in autumn. **Though birds eat them, they are poisonous to humans.**

Dwarf honeysuckle (*L. xylosteum*) is also naturalized in parts of southern New Brunswick. Though it is similar to Tartarian honeysuckle, its flowers are creamy white to pale yellow, and its leaves have fuzzy undersides. Also naturalized in New Brunswick is Morrow's honeysuckle (*L. morrowii*); it, too, resembles Tartarian honeysuckle but has white flowers.

Top: Red berries are produced in pairs; leaves are hairless. **Middle:** Flowers have five petals, four of which point upward. **Bottom:** Dwarf honeysuckle has pale yellow flowers.

VITAL STATISTICS
Maximum height: 3 metres
Flowering season: May and June

Mixed Forest

Hardwood Forest

Disturbed

Honeysuckle family / Caprifoliaceae

Mountain fly honeysuckle

Lonicera villosa

Northern fly honeysuckle, waterberry

Native Species

VITAL STATISTICS
Maximum height: 1 metre
Flowering season: May to early June

HABITAT: Mountain fly honeysuckle prefers damp to wet sites throughout the Maritimes, such as stream and pond margins, wetlands, and damp, peaty hollows on barrens.

CHARACTERISTICS: This species is a short, upright to sprawling shrub. New twigs are fuzzy and brown; older twigs can be either smooth or flaky.

The winter buds of mountain fly honeysuckle are paired, reddish brown, and pointed. The paired, oblong to elliptical leaves are dark green on the upper surface and distinctly pale on the underside. Both surfaces and leaf edges are covered in fine hairs. When leaves first emerge, they may have a distinct blue-green tint; they turn yellow in autumn.

Leaf axils produce paired, nearly stemless, pale yellow, five-petalled flowers that are slightly funnel- or bell-shaped. The resulting blue berry has a "two-eyed" appearance. The edible berries ripen by late July or early August. Commercialization of the species is being explored in New Brunswick and Nova Scotia.

Top: Mountain fly honeysuckle has paired leaves and flowers. **Middle:** Bell-shaped flowers have five petals. **Bottom:** Berries have a "two-eyed" appearance.

Buckthorn family / Rhamnaceae
European buckthorn
Rhamnus cathartica
Common buckthorn

Introduced Species

VITAL STATISTICS
Maximum height: 8 metres
Flowering season: Mid-May to early June

HABITAT: This European species was traditionally planted in hedges in the Maritimes. Now considered invasive, European buckthorn occasionally grows as a naturalized plant along roadsides and some trails and in open woodlands.

CHARACTERISTICS: European buckthorn is a tall suckering shrub or small tree. Reddish brown twigs have an exfoliating waxy layer; lateral branchlets often end in a spine. Smooth reddish brown young bark becomes dark grey and scaly over time. Winter buds are reddish brown, oval, and pointed.

The opposite or sub-opposite leaves are elliptical to oval, smooth, 5 to 8 centimetres long, and have finely toothed, undulating edges. Dark green on the upper surface, they are much paler below. Fall colour is yellow.

European buckthorn is dioecious. Small, four-petalled, yellow-green flowers are produced in clusters at the base of new twigs. In autumn, the plant produces shiny black drupes; **the berries are mildly toxic** and persist through much of the winter.

The similar glossy buckthorn (*Frangula alnus*) lacks spines and has smooth-edged leaves.

Top: The finely toothed, oval leaves of this species can be opposite or sub-opposite. **Middle:** Green, unripened fruit clustered at stem bases; note the spine-tipped branchlet at lower left. **Bottom:** The shiny black berries are mildly toxic.

Mixed Forest

Hardwood Forest

Disturbed

Twinflower family / Linnaeaceae

Twinflower
Linnaea borealis
Northern twinflower, pink-bells

Native Species

VITAL STATISTICS
Maximum height: 8 centimetres
Flowering season: Late June through July

HABITAT: The twinflower is a predominant wildflower in coniferous and mixed forests, as well as in open areas, throughout the Maritimes.

CHARACTERISTICS: This species is a low, trailing, broad-leaved, evergreen sub-shrub. Twinflower's paired rounded leaves are about 1 centimetre long, have a few rounded teeth, and have scattered hairs on both surfaces.

As its name suggests, twinflower produces a pair of nodding, bell-like flowers atop a thin, wiry, 5- to 8-centimetre-long stalk. Highly fragrant, the blossoms are light pink with dark pink stripes and hairy on inner surfaces.

Twinflower's genus—*Linnaea*—honours Carl Linnaeus, whom many botanists consider the father of modern taxonomy. Some historians say that twinflower was Linnaeus's favourite plant. He took the flower as his personal symbol when he was raised to the Swedish nobility in 1757.

Top: Twinflower has trailing stems that often end in a rosette of leaves. **Middle:** Twinflower forms a groundcover on the forest floor. **Bottom:** The bell-like flowers are highly fragrant.

Muskroot family / Adoxaceae

Smooth arrowwood

Viburnum recognitum
(formerly *V. dentatum*)

Northern arrowwood, southern arrowwood

HABITAT: Smooth arrowwood is a rare species confined to wet thickets and stream and river margins in southwestern New Brunswick near the Maine border. Plants found in Nova Scotia and Prince Edward Island have been introduced.

CHARACTERISTICS: This rounded, suckering shrub has smooth or velvety grey-green twigs. Older bark is mottled grey and finely scaly. Winter buds are paired, pointed, and tan brown.

The smooth, 3- to 9-centimetre-long, glossy leaves vary from rounded to elliptical, with coarsely serrated edges and prominent veins. Fall colour is red-purple. Flat-topped flower clusters are 5 to 10 centimetres across and composed of many small five-petalled flowers. They develop into clusters of dark blue inedible drupes.

Even rarer is maple-leaved viburnum (*V. acerifolium*), which is restricted to dry hardwood forests along the St. Croix River in New Brunswick. Flowers and fruit are similar to smooth arrowwood, but leaves are tri-lobed, more like those of highbush cranberry (*V. opulus* subsp. *trilobum*).

VITAL STATISTICS
Maximum height: 3 metres
Flowering season: June

Top: Leaf edges have very coarse teeth. **Middle:** Five-petalled flowers are produced in flat-topped clusters. **Bottom:** Smooth arrowwood has distinctive clusters of blue fruit.

Muskroot family / Adoxaceae
Hobblebush
Viburnum lantanoides
(formerly *V. alnifolium*)

Alder-leaved viburnum, moosewood, witch hobble

Native Species

VITAL STATISTICS
Maximum height: 3 metres
Flowering season: Mid-May to mid-June

HABITAT: Hobblebush grows throughout moist, mixed forests in New Brunswick. In Nova Scotia it is found primarily in the southwest; it is rare on Prince Edward Island, restricted to southeastern Queens County.

CHARACTERISTICS: The arching branches of this sprawling shrub often root where they touch the ground. Hobblebush twigs are green-brown with pale lenticels; older bark becomes brown-grey, warty, and furrowed. Paired winter buds and terminal overwintering flower buds are tan and scurfy.

Newly emerged leaves are tan green and fuzzy. As leaves age, the hairs become restricted mainly to the undersides. Mature leaves are 10 to 20 centimetres long, dull green, heavily veined, opposite, and coarsely toothed. They are egg- to heart-shaped. Fall colour is shades of red to maroon.

Fragrant, white, flat-topped flower clusters are 7 to 10 centimetres across and have two types of flowers: larger outer sterile blooms and small inner fertile flowers that later develop into inedible elliptical drupes. The berries change from green to red to nearly black as they ripen.

Wayfaring viburnum (*V. lantana*), naturalized in New Brunswick near Lincoln and Saint John, is the European counterpart of hobblebush. Its leaves are more tapered than those of hobblebush and densely hairy on both surfaces. Small fertile flowers appear in clusters; the larger sterile blooms found on hobblebush are absent.

Top: Leaves are heavily veined and coarsely toothed. Flower clusters have large sterile outer flowers and small fertile inner blossoms.
Bottom: Semi-ripe fruit is red.

Native Species

Dogwood family / Cornaceae
Bunchberry
Cornus canadensis
Crackerberry, creeping dogwood, dwarf cornel

HABITAT: Bunchberry, common throughout the Maritimes, occurs in many habitats, including forests, barrens, and wetlands.

VITAL STATISTICS
Maximum height: 25 centimetres
Flowering season: June

CHARACTERISTICS: This sub-shrub often forms large colonies that grow from semi-woody subterranean rhizomes. Bunchberry stems (10 to 25 centimetres tall) are topped by three pairs of closely spaced leaves that initially appear whorled; the lowest pair is largest.

Leaves are mostly ovate to obovate (and sometimes elliptical) with untoothed edges. They are often evergreen through winter, replaced by new shoots in spring.

What appear to be white flowers are sets of four white, petal-like leaves (bracts). The actual flowers are tiny and creamy white, clustered at the bract's centre. By August, flowers develop into a dense cluster of orange-red drupes. The edible fruit has little taste.

Swedish bunchberry (*C. suecica*) is localized in areas of Nova Scotia. It resembles bunchberry but its distinctly paired leaves do not appear whorled, its tiny flowers are purple with white bracts, and red drupes are larger but fewer.

Top: Across the Maritimes, bunchberry is a common and recognizable wildflower on the forest floor. **Middle:** The fruit resembles a large orange-red raspberry and is somewhat crunchy—hence the common name "crackerberry." **Bottom:** The flowers of the similar Swedish bunchberry are purple with white bracts.

Coniferous Forest
Mixed Forest
Hardwood Forest
Wetlands
Barrens

57

Dogwood family / Cornaceae

Round-leaved dogwood
Cornus rugosa

Native Species

VITAL STATISTICS
Maximum height: 3 metres
Flowering season: Late June to mid-July

HABITAT: Round-leaved dogwood prefers dry woodlands and rocky slopes and ravines, especially on limestone substrates. It is found throughout New Brunswick but is localized in Nova Scotia, most commonly along the Bay of Fundy. It is rare on Prince Edward Island, restricted to Prince County.

CHARACTERISTICS: This medium to large shrub has yellow- to red-green stems with purple blotches and a rough texture. Paired winter buds are narrow, pointed, and green.

Leaves are egg-shaped to round, with a rough, veiny upper surface and a paler, woolly underside. Leaf edges are smooth. Leaves range in length from 3 to 13 centimetres. Fall colour is a mix of red tones.

In July, the minute, white, four-petalled flowers are produced in flat-topped clusters. They later develop into loose clusters of pale blue (or occasionally white) drupes. Each drupe has a thin, pin-like extension at its tip. The stems of the fruit are often pink. The fruit is inedible.

Top: Leaves are round, with a rough, veiny upper surface. **Middle:** White, four-petalled flowers are produced in flat-topped clusters. **Bottom:** Loosely clustered pale blue berries have pink stems.

Native Species

Dogwood family / Cornaceae
Red-osier dogwood
Cornus stolonifera
Red-stemmed dogwood

HABITAT: Red-osier dogwood is common in a range of moist to wet habitats throughout the Maritimes.

CHARACTERISTICS: This plant is an upright deciduous shrub. Red-osier dogwood twigs are distinctively smooth and red with many white lenticels. Winter buds are paired, narrow, and remain close to the stems.

Paired leaves are ovate to oblong with smooth edges. Dark green on the upper surface, they are a paler green on the underside. Leaves vary in length from 5 to 12 centimetres. Fall foliage turns shades of yellow, orange, and red.

Flat-topped clusters of small, creamy white, four-petalled flowers are produced in June, becoming white berry-like drupes by September. Each drupe has a thin, pin-like extension at its tip.

The rarer silky dogwood (*C. amomum*) is confined to wet streamside thickets in southwestern New Brunswick. It can be distinguished from red-osier dogwood by silky grey hairs on newest twigs, hair on leaf undersides and along leaf veins, and blue fruit.

VITAL STATISTICS
Maximum height: 2.5 metres
Flowering season: June

Top: The red twigs of red-osier dogwood make them unmistakable, especially in winter.
Middle: Plants produce flat-topped clusters of small, creamy white, four-petalled flowers.
Bottom: The berry-like drupes have a pin-like extension at the tip.

Olive family / Oleaceae

Common lilac

Syringa vulgaris

Purple lilac

Introduced Species

VITAL STATISTICS
Maximum height: 7 metres
Flowering season: June

HABITAT: Common lilac, an introduced species, is still being planted and may also persist on abandoned homesteads. It is native to southeastern Europe, where it grows naturally on rocky slopes. It is found throughout the Maritimes.

CHARACTERISTICS: A deciduous shrub that reaches heights of 3 to 7 metres, common lilac suckers to form large multi-stemmed clumps. Paired and rounded winter buds vary in colour according to the hue of their blossoms: purplish on a purple-flowered plant, and yellow-green on a white-flowered plant.

Leaves are opposite, heart-shaped, and smooth with untoothed margins. They vary in length from 5 to 12 centimetres and have no distinctive fall colour.

Lilacs produce a tight conical-shaped panicle that has many small four-petalled flowers. Highly fragrant, the blossoms are typically purple but can be white. Modern-day variants have single or double flowers and bloom in white and shades of pink, red, purple, blue, and even yellow.

Top: Lilac's paired, heart-shaped leaves are unmistakable. **Middle:** Large dense sprays of purple flowers are produced in June. **Bottom:** Occasionally white-flowered plants are encountered.

Madder family / Rubiaceae
Partridgeberry
Mitchella repens
Running box, two-eyed berry

Native Species

HABITAT: Partridgeberry favours coniferous and mixed forests throughout the Maritimes.

CHARACTERISTICS: A prostrate evergreen sub-shrub, partridgeberry may grow only 1 to 2 centimetres tall. Its opposite, rounded leaves are shiny green, leathery in texture, and hairless. Only about 1 centimetre across, leaves have untoothed or wavy edges and distinctive pale central veins. Stems are smooth.

Small white, four-petalled flowers are produced in pairs at the ends of the stems throughout July. Distinctively, each pair of flowers shares a single ovary. The paired flowers develop into conjoined red berries in September; berries persist through winter.

This species should not be confused with the edible "partridgeberry" of Newfoundland and Labrador, whose correct name is mountain cranberry (*Vaccinium vitis-idaea*).

VITAL STATISTICS
Maximum height: 2 centimetres
Flowering season: July

Top: Rounded, leathery leaves are shiny green and hairless, and have untoothed edges. **Middle:** Small white, four-petalled flowers grow in pairs. **Bottom:** Flowers develop into conjoined berries that appear to be "two-eyed."

Coniferous Forest
Mixed Forest
Hardwood Forest
Barrens

Honeysuckle family / Caprifoliaceae

Common snowberry
Symphoricarpos albus

Northern snowberry, thin-leaved snowberry, waxberry, white coralberry

Introduced Species

VITAL STATISTICS
Maximum height: 2 metres
Flowering season: July and August

HABITAT: Snowberry is native from Quebec west to British Columbia and throughout the eastern USA. It is not native to the Maritimes but has been widely planted in the region as hedging. Snowberry spreads by suckering, which has allowed it to become naturalized in urban fields, scrubland, and abandoned homesteads.

CHARACTERISTICS: Common snowberry grows many thin, dark-barked stems. On older stems, bark tends to shred into thin strips.

Leaves are opposite and oval to round in shape with untoothed or wavy margins (some may be lobed). Leaves vary from 1 to 5 centimetres in length. They are dull green on their upper surface, often with a bluish tint, and paler on the underside. They have no distinctive fall colour.

Pink urn-shaped flowers, 1 centimetre long, are produced in summer in small clusters among the upper leaf axils or as a terminal cluster of blossoms. They are followed in September and October by white globular berries, 1.5 centimetres in diameter.

The fruit is toxic and often persists into early winter.

Top: Leaves are opposite and rounded with untoothed edges. **Middle:** Pink flowers are clustered in upper leaf axils or branch tips. **Bottom:** Globular white berries develop in the fall.

Native Species

Maple family / Aceraceae
Striped maple
Acer pensylvanicum
Moose maple, moosewood

HABITAT: Distributed throughout the Maritimes, striped maple is primarily found in mixed and hardwood forests and along streams and lake margins.

CHARACTERISTICS: Striped maple, a large shrub or small tree, can reach 10 metres in height. Young stems are grey-green to green-brown and smooth with distinct white longitudinal stripes. Older bark becomes red-brown. Winter buds are red and opposite on the stem; most twig tips have a larger, single, pointed bud.

The opposite leaves, green on the upper surface and paler on the underside, are tri-lobed with toothed edges. Emerging spring leaves are often tinted red. When mature, they can be 10 to 20 centimetres long. Fall colour is yellow.

In June, the plant produces a loose pendant cluster of yellow-green, bell-shaped flowers. Female flowers develop into pink or red (and later, brown) winged fruit (called "maple keys" or, botanically, "samaras"). Striped maple samara wings are widely spread.

VITAL STATISTICS
Maximum height: 10 metres
Flowering season: June

Top: Tri-lobed leaves have toothed edges; loose pendant clusters of yellow-green, bell-shaped flowers appear in June. **Middle:** The wings of the samaras are spread at a wide angle. **Bottom:** Young stems have distinct white longitudinal stripes.

Maple family / Aceraceae

Mountain maple
Acer spicatum
Moose maple, white maple

Native Species

VITAL STATISTICS
Maximum height: 8 metres
Flowering season: June

HABITAT: Mountain maple grows in moist, open woodlands, thickets, and rocky slopes throughout the Maritimes.

CHARACTERISTICS: This large shrub or small tree can reach 8 metres in height. Mountain maple winter buds are red and opposite on the stem. Most twigs end in a single bud. Current-season twigs are red to purple and slightly hairy. Older stems and trunk are greyish brown and smooth.

The opposite leaves are tri-lobed, 6 to 13 centimetres long, wrinkled and yellow-green on the upper surface and downy and pale green on the underside. They have coarsely toothed edges. Fall colour is yellow to red.

Mostly upright (sometimes arching) 7- to 15-centimetre-long clusters of 5-millimetre-wide yellow-green flowers are produced after leaves have fully emerged. These tiny flowers develop into pink or red (and later, brown) winged fruit ("maple keys" or, botanically, "samaras"). The angle between the wings is less than 90 degrees.

Top: Rugose yellow-green leaves are palmately tri-lobed and have coarsely toothed edges. **Middle:** Flower sprays generally grow upright from branches. **Bottom:** Samaras are produced in a loose chain.

Muskroot family / Adoxaceae
Squashberry
Viburnum edule
Lowbush cranberry, mooseberry, squashberry viburnum

HABITAT: Squashberry prefers cool, moist woodlands and rocky slopes, especially in upland areas. It is most common in north-central New Brunswick and Cape Breton. It is not native to Prince Edward Island.

CHARACTERISTICS: An upright or sprawling deciduous shrub, squashberry can grow to 2 metres in height but more often barely reaches 1 metre. New twigs are reddish brown with scattered pale lenticels; older twigs and stems are grey. Paired winter buds are shiny red.

The 4- to 8-centimetre-long opposite leaves generally have three short lobes and irregularly toothed edges. Essentially hairless, leaves appear slightly rugose. In autumn, they turn red or a purplish deep red.

Plants produce small, rounded (and often paired) clusters of tiny, five-petalled, creamy white flowers. The edible bright red drupes ripen in September and contain a single, flattened seed.

When not in bloom, the similar highbush cranberry (*V. opulus* subsp. *trilobum*) can be distinguished by the one or two round red glands on each leaf stalk.

VITAL STATISTICS
Maximum height: 2 metres
Flowering season: Mid-May to late June

Top: Paired leaves generally have three lobes and a lightly rugose texture. Note irregularly toothed leaf edges. **Middle:** Five-petalled flowers are produced in small clusters. **Bottom:** The bright red, edible fruit also grows in small clusters.

Muskroot family / Adoxaceae
Highbush cranberry
Viburnum opulus subsp. *trilobum*
(formerly *V. trilobum*)
American bush cranberry, cranberry viburnum

Native Species

VITAL STATISTICS
Maximum height: 4 metres
Flowering season: June to early July

HABITAT: Throughout the Maritimes highbush cranberry grows along stream and pond margins and damp forest edges.

CHARACTERISTICS: Highbush cranberry is a medium-height to tall deciduous shrub that can reach 4 metres. Older bark is grey, and twigs are light reddish brown with rounded, reddish green, opposite buds. The winter buds that will develop flowers in the following spring are larger and rounder than those that develop only leaves.

Tri-lobed leaves are opposite and 6 to 10 centimetres long, and generally have three distinct, elongated, pointed lobes. Leaf edges are irregularly toothed. Leaves have a few hairs on their upper surface; hair is more pronounced on the underside. Each leaf stalk usually has one or two rounded red glands. Fall colour is bright red.

Flat-topped clusters of five-petalled, creamy white flowers are produced in July. Each cluster has two types of flowers: large sterile blossoms on the perimeter and small fertile flowers in the centre. By September, flowers produce loose clusters of bright, shiny red drupes; each contains a single, large, flattened seed. Edible fruit often persists into early winter.

Cranberry viburnum (*V. opulus* subsp. *opulus*) is sometimes encountered near towns and cities in the Maritimes. Its leaf glands are flat-topped or indented rather than rounded, and its fruit is not edible.

Top: Flat-topped flower clusters are composed of large outer sterile flowers and small inner fertile flowers. **Bottom:** Ripe berries are a bright shiny red.

Introduced Species

Maple family / Aceraceae
Norway maple
Acer platanoides

HABITAT: Norway maple, a popular urban tree throughout North America, is native to Europe and southwest Asia. Its copious seed production allows it to spread easily to urban fields, roadsides, and scrubland; it is considered invasive in some areas.

CHARACTERISTICS: In the Maritimes, Norway maple grows 15 to 25 metres tall. Winter buds are relatively large and usually purple- to red-green. The opposite leaves are palmately five-lobed with a few sharply pointed teeth—the iconic maple-leaf shape—and can be 7 to 14 centimetres long. Both surfaces are smooth; the upper side is a little darker than the lower. Spring leaves may have a bronze tint; in autumn they turn brilliant yellow and may have a touch of orange.

Norway maple produces rounded clusters of small yellow-green flowers, before or just as the leaves unfurl. Later they produce loose clusters of samaras, whose wings are widely spread.

Broken leaf stalks exude a milky sap, which easily distinguishes the Norway maple from other maples that grow in the Maritimes.

VITAL STATISTICS
Maximum height: 25 metres
Flowering season: May

Top: Five-lobed leaves have smooth surfaces and a few sharply pointed teeth. **Middle:** Norway maple's rounded clusters of flowers are distinctive. **Bottom:** The wings of a Norway maple samara spread widely.

Mixed Forest

Hardwood Forest

Disturbed

Maple family / Aceraceae
Sycamore maple
Acer pseudoplatanus

Introduced Species

VITAL STATISTICS
Maximum height: 30 metres
Flowering season: June

HABITAT: Native throughout central Europe, sycamore maple was once grown in the Maritimes as an ornamental tree; more recently, Norway maple has become more popular. Sycamore maple's copious seed production has allowed it to spread easily to urban fields, roadsides, and scrubland. It is now considered an invasive species.

CHARACTERISTICS: This tall deciduous tree can reach 30 metres. Trunks have grey, furrowed bark. Winter buds are relatively large and yellow-green.

The opposite leaves have a typical maple-leaf shape: palmately five-lobed with a few larger teeth. The upper leaf surface is dark green and slightly rough-textured; the lower is usually pale green, but on some trees can be purple. Leaves generally are leathery and have no distinctive fall colour.

Sycamore maples produce pendulous chains of small greenish yellow flowers just after the leaves unfurl in spring. Loose chains of samaras appear in September. The angle between the wings of the samaras is less than 90 degrees.

Top: The five-lobed leaves of sycamore maple have a leathery wrinkled texture. **Middle:** Sycamore maple produces a chain of tiny flowers in June. **Bottom:** Sycamore maple samaras are produced in a loose chain.

Native Species

Maple family / Aceraceae
Red maple
Acer rubrum
Scarlet maple, swamp maple

HABITAT: Red maple grows in forested areas of moist valleys, along riversides, and in wetlands throughout the Maritimes.

CHARACTERISTICS: This tree can reach 30 metres in height but is more often much shorter. Red maple's winter buds are opposite and bright red; the single terminal buds are larger. First-year twigs are also bright red but turn light grey in the second year. Bark is smooth and light grey on young trees and darker and rougher on older trees.

New leaves emerge with a red tint but soon turn dark green on the upper surface. Distinctively, leaves are pale green on the underside. The leaf stalk is typically red. Leaves are opposite and palmate with three to five lobes. They vary in size from 5 to 15 centimetres across. Leaf edges are irregularly double-toothed and completely hairless. Their fall colour is predominantly bright scarlet, but individual leaves can vary from bright yellow and orange to dark burgundy.

Trees are mostly monoecious: separate clusters of 5-millimetre-diameter, red to yellow, male or female flowers appear in spring before the trees leaf. Red maple flowers develop into pinkish green and, later, brown samaras; the angle between samara wings is less than 90 degrees.

VITAL STATISTICS
Maximum height: 30 metres
Flowering season: May

Top: Unfurling new red maple leaves have a distinct red tint, as do leaf stalks. **Bottom:** A cluster of male red flowers on a naked stem.

Mixed Forest

Hardwood Forest

Wetlands

Maple family / Aceraceae
Silver maple
Acer saccharinum
River maple, soft maple, white maple

Native Species

VITAL STATISTICS
Maximum height: 30 metres
Flowering season: April to early May

HABITAT: Silver maple prefers rich alluvial flood plains. Native only to New Brunswick, it is most commonly found in the Saint John River valley.

CHARACTERISTICS: Silver maple, which can reach 30 metres in height, has smooth grey bark that becomes flaky with age. New twigs are red-brown, often with a thin, wax-like coating. Branchlets are slightly pendulous and emit a foul odour when crushed. Red winter buds are paired; the terminal bud is larger.

Leaves emerge red-tinted but mature to light green on the upper surface and distinctly silvery green on the underside. Young leaves are hairy on the lower surface. Leaves are 6 to 10 centimetres long, palmately five-lobed, and have deeply cut sinuses and serrated edges. Fall colour is yellow.

Trees are functionally monoecious. The flowers lack petals and form clusters of yellow stamens or red pistils before the trees leaf. Hairy young fruit becomes smooth as it matures into green (then brown) samaras, whose wing spread is less than 90 degrees.

Top: The leaves of silver maple have the most deeply cut outline of any native or naturalized maple in the Maritimes. **Middle:** Female flowers are a cluster of red pistils. **Bottom:** Male flowers form clusters of yellow stamens.

Native Species

Maple family / Aceraceae
Sugar maple
Acer saccharum
Hard maple, rock maple

HABITAT: Sugar maple is common throughout the Maritimes on well-drained sites.

CHARACTERISTICS: This tall maple has furrowed and flaky grey-brown bark. Young twigs are smooth and green to red-brown with pale lenticels. Winter buds are paired and pointed; each twig has a larger single terminal bud.

Leaves are 7 to 15 centimetres in diameter and palmate with three to five lobes. Leaf edges have a few large incisions but are otherwise smooth. Hairless leaves have a green upper surface and paler underside. Fall colour is a mix of yellow, orange, and red.

Clusters of small, petal-less, yellow-green flowers are produced on long hairy stalks as the leaves expand—the overall effect resembles a tassel. They develop into green (later brown) samaras, whose nearly parallel wings form a "U."

Resembling Norway maple (*A. platanoides*), sugar maple can be distinguished by a clear (not milky) sap exuded by broken petioles.

VITAL STATISTICS
Maximum height: 35 metres
Flowering season: Late April to early June

Top: The smooth edges of sugar maple leaves have large incisions. **Middle:** The flowers hang like tassels from the tree. **Bottom:** The wings of the sugar maple samaras are almost parallel.

Willow family / Salicaceae
Cottony willow
Salix eriocephala
Diamond willow, heart-leafed willow, red-tipped willow

Native Species

VITAL STATISTICS
Maximum height: 6 metres
Flowering season: April to early June

HABITAT: Cottony willow occurs throughout the Maritimes along streams and shores, in bottomlands and thickets, and, less commonly, on dunes.

CHARACTERISTICS: This shrubby willow can grow from half a metre to 6 metres tall. Twigs are yellow-brown to reddish brown with or without fine grey hairs. Branches often have a flaky, waxy coating.

The lance-shaped, alternate leaves vary from 3 to 13 centimetres in length and can be hairless or downy; when they first expand, they have a red tint. Leaf edges are finely toothed and often wavy. A key identifier is the pair of relatively large rounded stipules at the base of each leaf.

Cottony willow is dioecious and flowers just before it leafs. Male (yellow) and female (green) catkins are 2 to 4 centimetres long. Female catkins release their cottony white seeds by early summer.

Silky willow (*S. sericea*), which grows in similar habitats, may be mistaken for cottony willow. It is locally common in New Brunswick but rare in Nova Scotia and Prince Edward Island. Its leaves resemble those of cottony willow in shape and size but lack the stipules. In addition, new foliage does not have a purple to red tint, and leaves have finely silky undersides.

Top: Red-tinted new foliage and rounded stipules are identifiers of cottony willow. **Middle:** Silky willow lack stipules and has fine silky hairs. **Bottom:** Silky willow (shown here) and cottony willow both flower before they produce leaves.

Native Species

Willow family / Salicaceae
Shining willow
Salix lucida
Glossy willow

HABITAT: Shining willow is found throughout the Maritimes growing beside streams, on lakeshores, in ditches, and in wet thickets.

CHARACTERISTICS: This large shrub or small tree grows 4 to 6 metres tall. Bark on new stems is yellow to reddish brown and finely hairy; older stems often become glossy. The trunk is grey and furrowed. Winter buds are small and pointed and held close to the stem.

The alternate leaves are lance-shaped or elliptical, 5 to 17 centimetres long, glossy dark green on the upper surface, and only slightly paler (often with a few long hairs) on the underside. Leaves terminate in an elongate, tail-like tip. Their edges have shallow but fine teeth. A pair of rounded stipules is located at the base of each leaf. Foliage turns golden yellow in autumn.

Plants are dioecious. Male and female catkins are produced just as the leaves unfurl. Male catkins are yellow and 2 to 5 centimetres long; female catkins are greener and the same length. Female catkins release their white cottony seeds by midsummer.

VITAL STATISTICS
Maximum height: 6 metres
Flowering season: Early May to June

Top: Narrow leaves have fine teeth and a tail-like tip. **Bottom:** Yellow male catkins bloom just after the first leaves appear.

Wetlands

73

Willow family / Salicaceae
Black willow
Salix nigra
Swamp willow

Native Species

VITAL STATISTICS
Maximum height: 20 metres
Flowering season: May to June

HABITAT: Locally common in southern New Brunswick, black willow is absent elsewhere in the Maritimes. It prefers bottomlands and the shores of lakes, rivers, and streams.

CHARACTERISTICS: One of the tallest willows in the Maritimes, black willow can reach 20 metres in height. Twigs are yellow to orange-brown and smooth; older bark is brown-grey with ridges and furrows. Winter buds are small, pointed, and grow close to the stem.

The lance-shaped alternate leaves grow 7 to 15 centimetres long. Shiny green on both surfaces, they have finely toothed edges and a pair of small rounded stipules at the base. The lower mid-rib is often softly hairy. Fall foliage is bright yellow.

Plants are dioecious. Thin male (yellow) and female (green) catkins grow from 2.5 to 7 centimetres long and flower as the leaves unfurl. Female catkins release white cottony seeds by midsummer.

White willow (*S. alba*) is a European species naturalized near towns and cities throughout the Maritimes. Similar in height, it can be identified by its leaves: few to no stipules, silky-haired undersides (young branchlets are also silky). Also similar is the crack willow (*S. X fragilis*); identify this tall willow by its brittle branchlets and hairless, narrow, stipuled leaves (with pale waxy undersides).

Top: Black willow's very narrow leaves have a pair of rounded stipules at their bases.
Bottom: White willow leaves have silky hairs, especially on the undersides of young leaves.

Introduced Species

Willow family / Salicaceae
Laurel willow
Salix pentandra
Bay willow, wax willow

HABITAT: This willow, native to northern Eurasia, has been planted as an ornamental tree throughout the Maritimes. "Wild" plants can be found along trails in urban areas, at forest edges, and along stream and pond margins.

CHARACTERISTICS: Laurel willow grows as a large shrub or small tree. The bark on new stems is shiny, green, and smooth, but older stems and trunk are grey and furrowed.

The alternate leaves are lance-shaped, 5 to 12 centimetres long, glossy dark green on upper surfaces, and only slightly paler on the undersides. Spring leaves are often distinctly sticky. Leaf edges have shallow, fine teeth. Foliage has no distinctive fall colour.

Plants are dioecious. Male (yellow) and female (greenish yellow) catkins are produced in June after the first leaves appear. Male catkins are 2 to 4 centimetres long, while female catkins are 3 to 6 centimetres long. Female catkins release their seeds in late summer and early fall; this timing helps distinguish laurel willow from the similar shining willow (*S. lucida*), which releases its seeds in early summer.

VITAL STATISTICS
Maximum height: 14 metres
Flowering season: May to June

Top: Few of the Maritimes' naturalized woody plants have leaves as glossy as the laurel willow's. **Bottom:** A female catkin beginning to shed its seeds.

Wetlands

Disturbed

Willow family / Salicaceae
Meadow willow
Salix petiolaris
Basket willow, slender willow

Native Species

VITAL STATISTICS
Maximum height: 6 metres
Flowering season: May and June

HABITAT: Meadow willow occurs in wet meadows and along shorelines throughout the Maritimes. Rare in Nova Scotia and Prince Edward Island, it is more widespread in New Brunswick.

CHARACTERISTICS: This shrubby willow can reach 6 metres but is more commonly less than 3 metres tall. Twigs are yellow-green and often purple-tinted and covered in fine hair. Older stems are yellow-brown to dark brown.

Narrow, lance-shaped, alternate leaves can reach 10 centimetres in length. When they first expand, they are covered in silky hair and can have a purple tint. They become dark green on the upper surface and waxy grey on the underside. Leaf edges are generally smooth but may be finely toothed. Leaves lack stipules and are densely arranged and overlapping.

Plants are dioecious and flower as the leaves expand. Male and female catkins are relatively short (1 to 2 centimetres).

Sandbar willow (*S. interior*) is a similar-sized shrub. Its narrow, lance-shaped leaves have widely spaced teeth and can be up to 14 centimetres long. With little to no stem, they appear to directly join the finely hairy twigs. Sandbar willow also flowers as leaves unfurl, but its catkins are longer (2 to 4 centimetres). In the Maritimes it is found only in New Brunswick, on sandy shorelines.

Top: Meadow willow leaves have pale waxy undersides. Note the female catkins about to release seeds. **Bottom:** Sandbar willow's long narrow leaves appear to attach directly to the branch.

Introduced Species

Willow family / Salicaceae
Purple willow
Salix purpurea
Basket willow, purple osier, purple-osier willow

HABITAT: Purple willow is a European species that has been planted throughout the Maritimes as a hedge plant. It has now become naturalized along roadsides throughout the region.

CHARACTERISTICS: This shrubby willow can grow from 1 to 2.5 metres tall. Twigs are fine, smooth, and purple-red. Older stems are olive-grey and can develop fissures with age.

The narrow, smooth, lance-shaped leaves are 5 to 10 centimetres long and can grow alternate, opposite, or sub-opposite on the branch. Leaves are blue-green above and have silvery undersides; leaf edges are finely toothed. Leaves grow densely on the stems and lack petioles and stipules. Foliage has no distinctive fall colour.

Plants are dioecious. The 2- to 5-centimetre-long catkins are green-yellow, appear with the unfurling leaves, and are often produced in opposite pairs.

Unbranched shoots, called "withies," are used to weave willow baskets. If you see a willow with opposite leaves, it is likely a purple willow.

VITAL STATISTICS
Maximum height: 2.5 metres
Flowering season: April to early May

Top: Purple willow is named for its reddish purple stems, clearly visible here.
Bottom: Catkins are often produced in pairs (male catkins shown).

Disturbed

Wax-myrtle family / Myricaceae

Sweet-fern
Comptonia peregrina

Native Species

VITAL STATISTICS
Maximum height: 1.5 metres
Flowering season: May

HABITAT: Sweet-fern is common throughout much of the Maritimes—open barrens, along roadsides, and in sandy areas.

CHARACTERISTICS: A low suckering shrub, sweet-fern often forms large colonies. Hairy twigs are red-brown. Older bark is coppery to purple-brown.

The fern-like alternate leaves are long and narrow, up to 10 centimetres long and 2 centimetres wide. Large teeth along the leaf margins appear as notches or lobes; leaf edges are often rolled under. Leaves are finely hairy. Light green when they first emerge, they later become dark green above with paler undersides. The upper leaf surface has scattered golden resin droplets. When bruised, leaves emit a sweet fragrance reminiscent of bayberry. Foliage has no distinctive fall colour.

Plants are dioecious or (less common) monoecious. Male catkins are green-brown and up to 5 centimetres long. Produced at stem tips, they are usually arching. Female flowers may grow at branch tips or below male flowers. Small, red, and burr-like, they later develop into green then brown, 2.5-centimetre-long, burr-like husks that surround three to five small nuts.

Sweet-fern has nitrogen-fixing bacteria on its roots, which allow this species to grow in infertile soil.

Top: Sweet-fern's narrow leaves have teeth that appear as notches. **Middle:** Male catkins develop in the fall and persist unopened through the winter. **Bottom:** The female flower's burr-like husk surrounds developing nuts.

Rose family / Rosaceae
Pin cherry
Prunus pensylvanica
Fire cherry

Native Species

VITAL STATISTICS
Maximum height: 10 metres
Flowering season: May to early June

HABITAT: Pin cherry is a common tree in forest clearings and on old burned sites, rocky hillsides, and roadsides throughout the Maritimes.

CHARACTERISTICS: A small tree, pin cherry can reach 10 metres in height. Winter buds are slightly pointed, alternate, and often clustered. Twigs are smooth and reddish brown. Bark has conspicuous horizontal lenticels; shiny and reddish brown to dark brown on younger trees, it may turn grey over time.

The 6- to 10-centimetre-long, lance-shaped leaves have an elongate pointed tip and toothed edges. Hairless, they often fold slightly upward along the mid-rib. They are shiny light green on the upper surface and paler on the underside. **Leaves are toxic if ingested by humans.**

A pair of rounded reddish glands is located at the base of the leaf. Fall colour is an attractive combination of red, orange, and yellow.

Pin cherry produces rounded clusters of white, five-petalled flowers that become shiny, bright red drupes in August. Drupes are produced at the ends of long stalks. The fruit—edible but acidic—makes superb jelly.

Top: Lance-shaped leaves can be folded slightly upward along the mid-rib. Note the developing fall colour. **Middle:** Flowers are produced in rounded clusters. **Bottom:** Shiny red drupes hang from long stalks.

Rose family / Rosaceae
Sand cherry
Prunus pumila
Dwarf cherry

Native Species

VITAL STATISTICS
Maximum height: 2.5 metres
Flowering season: Early June to early July

HABITAT: Sand cherry grows on gravel river shores, sandbars, and occasionally along roadsides, especially where there is limestone-based soil. In the Maritimes, it occurs only in New Brunswick.

CHARACTERISTICS: This species forms small, somewhat sprawling shrubs that are often colonial. Twigs are smooth and red-brown; older stems are grey. The lower stems are often buried beneath sand dunes.

Sand cherry's hairless, leathery leaves are narrow, lance-shaped, and 4 to 7 centimetres long by 1 centimetre broad. The upper surface is dark green and shiny; the underside is paler. The outer half of the leaf (away from the stem) has fine teeth.

Leaves are toxic if ingested by humans.

Small, loose clusters of white, five-petalled flowers develop into stalked, 1-centimetre-wide, purple-black fruit. The fruit is edible but astringent.

Top: Lance-shaped leaves have fine teeth only on outer leaf ends. **Middle:** White flowers are produced in small clusters. **Bottom:** Unripe fruit; fruit becomes purple-black when mature.

Native Species

Willow family / Salicaceae
Sage willow
Salix candida
Hoary willow

HABITAT: Sage willow, a rare species, is found in limestone-based bogs and thickets on Cape Breton Island, in western and northeastern New Brunswick, and on Prince Edward Island (in Prince County).

CHARACTERISTICS: This small deciduous shrub can reach 2 metres but is more commonly shorter than 1 metre. Young sage willow twigs are white and covered in fine dense hairs; older stems are reddish brown and smooth.

The alternate leaves are narrow, lance-shaped to oblong, silvery grey to pale grey-green, and felted on the upper surface. Leaf underside is white and densely felted. Rarely, individual leaves can lose their upper-surface pubescence in the summer and appear relatively shiny and dark green. Leaf edges are smooth, usually revolute, and often undulated. Fall colour is yellow.

Plants are dioecious. Catkins are relatively narrow, densely covered in long white hairs, and 3 to 7 centimetres long. Mature female catkins are silvery green. Male anthers and female stigmas are bright pinkish red. Catkins appear in May and June along with the unfurling leaves.

VITAL STATISTICS
Maximum height: 2 metres
Flowering season: May and June

Top: The white, felted leaves of sage willow are unmistakable. **Middle:** Male catkins have distinctive red stamens. **Bottom:** Mature female catkins are silvery green.

Wetlands

Barrens

Willow family / Salicaceae
Basket willow
Salix viminalis
Osier willow

Introduced Species

VITAL STATISTICS
Maximum height: 8 metres
Flowering season: Late April to early June

HABITAT: Basket willow is native to Europe and western Asia, where it often grows along streams and lakeshores. In the Maritimes, it is an occasional escape or a persistent tree in abandoned homesteads.

CHARACTERISTICS: This willow forms large, multi-stemmed shrubs or small trees that grow 5 to 8 metres tall. New basket willow stems are covered in grey pubescence initially but later become smooth and yellowish brown. Older bark is grey and furrowed.

Basket willow leaves are 10 to 15 centimetres long but often less than 1.5 centimetres wide. They have smooth edges that are frequently rolled. Leaves are quite silvery when they first appear. The upper surface becomes smooth and dark green as they mature; the underside remains silvery grey with dense short hairs. Foliage has no distinctive fall colour.

Plants are dioecious. Catkins are produced before leaves appear. Male catkins are yellow and 2.5 to 3 centimetres long; females are greenish yellow and 3 to 6 centimetres long.

Top: Basket willow leaves are among the longest and narrowest of any regional willow.
Bottom: Young female catkins in spring; note the pubescence on young grey stems.

Mezereum family / Thymelaeaceae

February daphne
Daphne mezereum
Garland flower

Introduced Species

HABITAT: February daphne is a native of the hardwood and mixed forests of Europe. In the Maritimes, it is occasionally found along roadsides near larger communities.

CHARACTERISTICS: This species is an upright shrub. The twigs and bark of February daphne are smooth and golden green-brown. Flower buds form in the fall and can be seen through the winter as clusters of dark rounded buds.

The alternate, lance-shaped leaves are broadest toward their tip. Leaves are smooth and often tinted grey-green. Foliage has no appreciable fall colour.

Stemless clusters of rose pink flowers are produced in April and May, before the plants leaf. They later develop into stemless, shiny red drupes.

All parts of this plant are highly toxic.

VITAL STATISTICS
Maximum height: 1.5 metres
Flowering season: Mid-April to mid-May

Top: February daphne's smooth-edged leaves are widest toward the outer end. **Middle:** Stemless clusters of flowers are produced before the plant leafs. **Bottom:** The stemless, shiny red drupes are highly toxic, as is the entire plant.

Disturbed

Heath family / Ericaceae
Bog rosemary
Andromeda polifolia var. *latifolia*
(formerly *A. glaucophylla*)

Native Species

VITAL STATISTICS
Maximum height: 50 centimetres
Flowering season: June

HABITAT: Throughout the Maritimes, bog rosemary is a common shrub in bog habitats.

CHARACTERISTICS: Bog rosemary is a short, suckering evergreen shrub that grows to 50 centimetres in height.

The alternate leaves are lance-shaped to linear with untoothed, strongly revolute edges. They have a pointed tip, leathery texture, and smooth, waxy coating that gives their upper surface a grey- to blue-green hue. The underside is nearly white and finely hairy. In winter the foliage often turns purple-grey.

Bog rosemary has small, pale pink or white, urn-shaped flowers that are produced in nodding terminal clusters. Seed capsules are pink and globular with five lobes.

Bog rosemary leaves look like those of the culinary rosemary, but they lack the pungent scent and flavour of that species. Their alternate leaf arrangement distinguishes them from bog laurel, whose leaves are opposite.

Top: The leaves' waxy coating gives them a grey-green upper surface and nearly white underside. **Middle:** Small urn-shaped flowers are produced in nodding terminal clusters. **Bottom:** In winter, foliage can be purple-grey.

Native Species

Willow family / Salicaceae
Bebb's willow
Salix bebbiana
Beaked willow, long-beaked willow

HABITAT: This relatively common willow grows in wet and dry thickets and along roadsides throughout the Maritimes.

CHARACTERISTICS: Bebb's willow is a large deciduous shrub or small tree that can reach 10 metres in height. Twigs are yellowish to reddish brown and covered in dense grey pubescence. Older stems are smooth and grey-green with many red lenticels.

The alternate leaves are 5 to 10 centimetres long and vary in shape from elliptical to oblong. The edges may be toothed or appear almost smooth and are often undulated. Leaves are a dull dark green to grey-green on the upper surface, and whitish, densely pubescent, and distinctly net-veined on the underside. Freshly emerging leaves may have a red tint. Robust shoots have a pair of stipules at the base of each leaf. Fall colour is yellow.

Plants are dioecious; 2.5- to 5-centimetre-long catkins bloom primarily in May as the leaves unfurl. The catkins emerge silvery, but during blooming the males appear yellow and the females green. The female catkins release white cottony seeds later in the season.

VITAL STATISTICS
Maximum height: 10 metres
Flowering season: Late April to early June

Top: Leaves are typically grey-green and somewhat wrinkled. Note this specimen's undulate leaf edges and paired stipules. **Middle:** Yellow male catkins blooming with the unfolding leaves. Note the grey pubescent stems. **Bottom:** Catkins bloom in May (females shown).

85

Willow family / Salicaceae
Pussy willow
Salix discolor
Large pussy willow

Native Species

VITAL STATISTICS
Maximum height: 6 metres
Flowering season: April to May

HABITAT: This common willow occupies moist to wet locations, including stream banks, damp thickets, and pond and wetland margins throughout the Maritimes.

CHARACTERISTICS: Pussy willow is a large deciduous shrub that can reach heights of 6 metres. Yellowish to reddish brown twigs are commonly smooth or uncommonly pubescent. Winter buds are shiny and reddish brown. Bark is grey and smooth but can become furrowed with age.

The alternate leaves are 5 to 8 centimetres long, elliptical to lance-shaped, with lightly toothed edges. When they first emerge, the upper surface is pubescent and may have a red tint; later leaves are smooth with a blue-green tint. The underside is waxy and nearly white. Robust shoots have a pair of stipules at the base of each leaf. Fall colour is yellow.

Plants are dioecious. Silvery catkins (2 to 7 centimetres long) bloom several weeks before leaves unfurl. Female catkins produce white cottony seeds by early summer.

Prairie willow (*S. humilis*)—also found throughout the Maritimes—is the region's most densely flowered willow. It blooms when the pussy willow does but has shorter catkins (3 centimetres). Its leaves lack stipules, are never red-tinted, and have a grey, densely hairy underside. Reddish brown twigs are pubescent.

Top: Stems and leaves are generally smooth. Note the red tint and paired stipules on this specimen. **Middle:** Pussy willow catkins (male shown) emerge several weeks before leaves unfurl. **Bottom:** Female catkins are also well-advanced before any leaves appear.

Wax-myrtle family / Myricaceae
Sweet gale
Myrica gale
Bog myrtle

Native Species

VITAL STATISTICS
Maximum height: 1.5 metres
Flowering season: April to May

HABITAT: A common shrub throughout the Maritimes, sweet gale grows in a variety of damp habitats, including bogs and the margins of ponds and streams. Highly flood-tolerant, it often grows with its roots in water.

CHARACTERISTICS: Sweet gale is a low, upright shrub. Stems are shiny, red-brown, and have small, sharply pointed buds.

Alternate, lance- to spoon-shaped leaves have a few teeth at their rounded tips and are distinctly matte grey-green. Leaves, buds, flowers, and seeds are sweetly fragrant when bruised.

Plants are dioecious. Male catkins are brown but in bloom are yellow (with reddish brown scales) and about 1 centimetre long. Female flowers are a tiny cluster of red styles. Flowers of both sexes are crowded at branch tips and bloom before leaves appear.

The fruit is small and cone-like, with tiny yellow-green to brown nutlets. It can be used sparingly as a spice.

Top: The matte grey-green leaves are spoon-shaped; note the few rounded teeth at leaf ends. **Middle:** The fruit of sweet gale is small and cone-like, with tiny nutlets. **Bottom:** In bloom, yellow male catkins have reddish brown scales.

Wetlands

Barrens

Birch family / Betulaceae
Eastern hop-hornbeam
Ostrya virginiana
Hop-hornbeam, ironwood, leverwood

Native Species

VITAL STATISTICS
Maximum height: 12 metres
Flowering season: April to May

HABITAT: Eastern hop-hornbeam grows on riversides and among rich hardwood forests throughout the Maritimes; it is considered rare on Prince Edward Island.

CHARACTERISTICS: This small tree rarely reaches its potential height (12 metres). Eastern hop-hornbeam twigs are reddish brown, smooth or slightly hairy, with pale lenticels. Older bark becomes grey and appears shredded. Winter buds are oval and slightly hairy. Eastern hop-hornbeam timber is considered the hardest of any Canadian woody plant.

Alternate, elliptical to oval leaves are 7 to 12 centimetres long. They have smooth upper surfaces and lightly hairy undersides; leaf edges are double-toothed. Autumn foliage is yellow.

Plants are monoecious and flower just as leaves unfurl. Male catkins are 1.5 to 5 centimetres long, reddish brown before opening, yellow-brown in bloom. Female catkins are green with extruding red stigmas and reach 1.5 centimetres in length. They develop nutlet clusters, each enclosed in an inflated, oval-shaped bract, similar to those of American hop (*Humulus lupulus*).

Top: Elliptical leaves have double-toothed edges. **Middle:** Maturing female catkins (green) and spent male catkins (brown). **Bottom:** The bark is distinctly shredded.

Beech family / Fagaceae
American beech
Fagus grandifolia
Common beech

Native Species

VITAL STATISTICS
Maximum height: 25 metres
Flowering season: May

HABITAT: In the Maritimes, American beech generally grows in hardwood forests.

CHARACTERISTICS: A tall tree with light grey, smooth bark, American beech in the Maritimes often has dark, corky wounds and blighted branches caused by a canker disease. Twigs often have a zigzag pattern. The long pointed winter buds resemble thorns.

Leaves are covered in long silky hairs when young. They become smooth over time, retaining hair only along lower veins. Elliptical to oval with coarsely toothed edges, they can be 5 to 15 centimetres long. Fall colour is yellow then light brown. Young trees often retain some brown leaves through the winter.

Plants are monoecious. Yellow-green male flowers consist of a rounded cluster of stamens at the tips of 2.5-centimetre-long, pendulous stalks. The green female flowers—stigmas surrounded by a hairy calyx—are almost insignificant. Both flower as leaves emerge. Female flowers later produce one to three triangular, shiny brown nuts enclosed in a woody husk covered in soft spines. The nuts are edible but bitter (but bears are fond of them).

Mixed Forest

Hardwood Forest

Top: American beech's elliptical leaves are coarsely toothed. **Middle:** Female fruit has a hairy husk. **Bottom:** Male flowers—a cluster of stamens—hang at the end of a long stalk.

89

Rose family / Rosaceae
Bartram's serviceberry
Amelanchier bartramiana

Bartram's chuckleypear, Bartram's shadbush, mountain juneberry, mountain serviceberry

Native Species

VITAL STATISTICS
Maximum height: 2.5 metres
Flowering season: May

HABITAT: This shrub grows in a variety of habitats—both moist and dry—including open coniferous forest, roadsides, old burned sites and barrens, and stream and pond margins. It occurs throughout the Maritimes.

CHARACTERISTICS: Bartram's serviceberry varies greatly in height from 50 centimetres to 2.5 metres. Stems are slender, smooth, and reddish brown, with a scaly, white, waxy coating. Buds are narrow, pointed, and purple-red.

The alternate leaves are elliptical to oval with finely toothed edges. When they first unfurl, they have a distinct bronze tint. In autumn they turn a mixture of yellow, orange, and red.

The 1- to 2-centimetre-wide, white, five-petalled flowers are produced in May. They appear singly or in clusters of two to four. When in a cluster, one flower is at the branch tip and the others grow from the upper leaf axils. No other native serviceberry in the Maritimes has this feature.

The purple berry-like fruit ripens by early August. It has a persistent calyx, which gives it a terminal "crown" similar to a blueberry's. The fruit of Bartram's serviceberry is sweet and juicy.

Top: Elliptical to oval leaves have finely toothed edges. **Middle:** Flowers are mainly produced in pairs or groups of three. Note the bronze tint of these spring leaves. **Bottom:** The calyx leaves a "crown" on the purple fruit.

Rose family / Rosaceae

Serviceberry: shrub species

Amelanchier species

Juneberry, shadblow

HABITAT: Several shrubby serviceberry species (native and hybridized) grow in forests and disturbed areas, on barrens, and by streams and ponds across the Maritimes; they vary little so are discussed as a group. Dwarf (*A. spicata*) and Fernald's (*A. fernaldii*) serviceberry grow in all three provinces. Round-leaved (*A. sanguinea*) and Gaspé (*A. gaspensis*) serviceberry are rare (on limestone substrates in New Brunswick). A rare Nova Scotian Atlantic Coastal Plain species—Nantucket serviceberry (*A. nantucketensis*)—strongly resembles dwarf serviceberry, but its flowers produce pollen ("andropetaly").

CHARACTERISTICS: Shrub serviceberry species are 1 to 3 metres tall, upright to sprawling, and form suckers. Twigs are smooth and reddish brown; older stems have smooth, grey bark. Winter buds are narrow and pointed.

Alternate leaves are oval to elliptical with finely toothed edges. Leaves emerge green with fine hair on the underside (Fernald's serviceberry has smooth leaves). Fall colour is a mixture of yellow, orange, and red.

Loose, mostly pendulous sprays of three to eight, five-petalled white flowers appear in late spring. Sweet but mealy purple-black fruit (with a calyx-remnant "crown") ripen in late July and August.

Top: Oval leaves are finely toothed (dwarf serviceberry shown). **Middle:** Shrubby serviceberry species have flower clusters of up to eight blossoms. **Bottom:** Fruit clusters are relatively small.

VITAL STATISTICS

Maximum height: 3 metres
Flowering season: Mid-May to early June

Rose family / Rosaceae
Serviceberry: tree species
Amelanchier species
Juneberry, shadblow

Native Species

VITAL STATISTICS
Maximum height: 14 metres
Flowering season: May

HABITAT: In the Maritimes, tree-like serviceberry species grow in forests and beside roads, streams, and ponds. Inland (*A. interior*), purple (*A. intermedia*), smooth (*A. laevis*), and shadblow (*A. canadensis*) serviceberry are in all three provinces; downy (*A. arborea*) is absent from Prince Edward Island.

CHARACTERISTICS: Tree-like serviceberries—difficult to tell apart—share many traits. They reach 9 to 14 metres in height but do not sucker. Twigs are red-brown, smooth, or slightly hairy. Ash grey bark has dark streaks; it may furrow with age. Winter buds are yellow-brown, narrow, and pointed.

Alternate, finely toothed, oval to elliptical leaves are 4 to 7.5 centimetres long. The underside is finely hairy (smooth serviceberry is hairless). New leaves of smooth, purple, and inland serviceberry are bronze-tinted (green on shadblow and downy serviceberry). All become dark green above and pale below. Fall colour is a mix of yellow, orange, and red.

Flowers form in upright to arching, elongate clusters; white and five-petalled, they open when leaves are half-grown. Mealy fruit hangs in clusters, ripens to purple, and tastes sweet.

Top: Smooth serviceberry's typical purple-tinted foliage; flowers on taller serviceberries form elongate clusters. **Bottom:** Fruit on these serviceberries hangs in clusters. Note the "crown" formed by calyx remnants.

Native Species

Rose family / Rosaceae
Black chokeberry
Aronia melanocarpa

HABITAT: Black chokeberry is commonly found in moist to wet sites throughout the Maritimes, such as wetlands, wet forest edges, and stream and pond margins.

CHARACTERISTICS: This is a deciduous, upright, suckering shrub that rarely reaches its potential height of 3 metres. Black chokeberry twigs are reddish brown and smooth. Lateral winter buds are small and reddish brown; terminal buds are narrow and pointed.

The 3- to 7-centimetre-long leaves are alternate, elliptical to spoon-shaped, and have a blunt tip and gradually tapering base. The upper leaf surface is dark green and shiny; the underside is paler without hairs, a feature that helps distinguish it from the similar purple chokeberry. Leaf edges are finely toothed. Autumn colour is orange to purple-red.

Small flat-topped clusters of white, five-petalled flowers appear in June. Flower/fruit stalks are smooth, unlike those of the similar purple chokeberry (next entry), whose stalks are pubescent. Flowers, whose stamens are often conspicuously pink, later develop into clusters of black, berry-like pomes in September and October. The fruit often persists well into winter. It is edible but very bitter.

VITAL STATISTICS
Maximum height: 3 metres
Flowering season: June

Top: Leaves have blunt tips and finely toothed edges. **Middle:** Stamens are conspicuously pink. **Bottom:** Black, berry-like pomes hang from smooth stalks.

93

Rose family / Rosaceae
Purple chokeberry
Aronia X *prunifolia*
(formerly *A. floribunda*)

Native Species

VITAL STATISTICS
Maximum height: 2 metres
Flowering season: Late May to June

HABITAT: Throughout the Maritimes, purple chokeberry is commonly found in moist to wet sites such as wetlands, thickets, stream and pond margins, and sandy areas.

CHARACTERISTICS: A deciduous, upright, suckering shrub that rarely exceeds 1.5 metres, purple chokeberry is considered a self-perpetuating hybrid of red chokeberry (*A. arbutifolia*) and black chokeberry (*A. melanocarpa*). Twigs and flower/fruit stalks have fine hairs. Older stems are grey and smooth. Lateral winter buds are small and reddish brown; terminal buds are narrow and pointed.

The 3- to 7-centimetre-long leaves are alternate and obovate to oblanceolate, with a blunt tip and gradually tapering base. The upper leaf surface is dark green and shiny; the underside is paler with hair. Leaf edges are finely toothed. Autumn colour is bright scarlet to purple-red.

Small, flat-topped clusters of white, five-petalled flowers appear late May to June. Flowers, whose stamens are often conspicuously pink (see black chokeberry, p. 93), develop into single or loose clusters of purple-black, berry-like pomes in September and October. The fruit often persists into winter; it is edible but very bitter.

Red chokeberry may be encountered in southwestern Nova Scotia. Taller than purple chokeberry, it can reach 4 metres. Its fruit is red.

Top: The underside of the spoon-shaped leaves and new stems are pale with fine hairs. **Middle:** The black fruit is in small clusters. Note the pubescent stems. **Bottom:** Stamens are conspicuously pink

Introduced Species

Rose family / Rosaceae
Common apple
Malus pumila
(formerly *M. domestica*)
Crabapple

HABITAT: "Wild" apples grow along roadsides throughout the Maritimes where seeds from tossed apple cores have germinated. They also survive on abandoned homesteads.

CHARACTERISTICS: The common apple tree is often wider than it is tall and rarely exceeds 10 metres in height. Stems are thick and have many short, spur-like branchlets. Winter buds are pointed and often have white hairs.

The alternate leaves are elliptical with a toothed edge. On most trees, leaves emerge covered in white hairs. These hairs are generally lost on the upper leaf surface over time but remain on the underside. The upper leaf surface is usually dull and rough-textured, and leaf petioles are distinctly hairy. Leaves have no appreciable fall colour.

From late May through early June, apple trees produce rounded clusters of white to pink, fragrant flowers, each with five petals. The small edible green to red fruit ripens in October.

"Wild" pear (*Pyrus communis*) also occurs sporadically in southern Nova Scotia. It has a pyramidal shape, spiny branches, shiny hairless leaves, and white flowers.

VITAL STATISTICS
Maximum height: 10 metres
Flowering season: Late May to early June

Mixed Forest

Hardwood Forest

Top: Elliptical leaves have toothed edges. Note the pubescent petioles. **Middle:** Showy flowers make common apple one of the Maritimes' most attractive naturalized trees. **Bottom:** Edible (but sometimes sour) fruit ripens in October.

Disturbed

Rose family / Rosaceae
Sweet cherry
Prunus avium
Mazzard cherry

Introduced Species

VITAL STATISTICS
Maximum height: 16 metres
Flowering season: May

HABITAT: "Wild" sweet cherry is occasionally encountered along roadsides and on abandoned homesteads throughout Nova Scotia and New Brunswick.

CHARACTERISTICS: A medium-sized tree, sweet cherry has smooth, grey-brown bark with narrow, horizontal lenticels. Twigs are light grey-brown and smooth. Winter buds are reddish brown and rounded. Flowering spurs often have winter buds in clusters.

The 6- to 14-centimetre-long leaves are alternate and egg-shaped to elliptical with sharply toothed edges. The upper surface is shiny green; the underside is paler and has hairs on the lower veins. The upper portion of the leaf stalk has one to three shiny, rounded, red glands. Fall colour is yellow and brown.

Clusters of three to five white, five-petalled flowers develop into sweet-tasting, long-stalked, dark purple-red drupes.

Sour cherry (*P. cerasus*) is occasionally found "wild" in Nova Scotia and New Brunswick. It can be distinguished by its leaves: stiffer, smaller, hairless, with rounded teeth. It also lacks red glands on its leaf stalks. The bright red fruit tastes sour.

Top: Red glands on leaf stalks are a key identifier.
Middle: Flowers are produced in showy clusters.
Bottom: The sweet-tasting, dark purple-red fruit hangs on long stalks.

Rose family / Rosaceae
Black cherry
Prunus serotina
Rum cherry

HABITAT: Black cherry grows in moist to dry woodlands and thickets. It is most common in southern New Brunswick and along Nova Scotia's Fundy coast but uncommon on Prince Edward Island.

CHARACTERISTICS: A medium-sized to large tree, black cherry has smooth, dark grey bark; young trees have horizontal lenticels. With age, bark becomes flaky. Young twigs are smooth and reddish brown with a thin, flaking, waxy coating. Winter buds are small, rounded, and shiny red-brown.

The alternate leaves are 5 to 12 centimetres long, elliptical to lance-shaped, with finely toothed edges. They are smooth and glossy green on the upper surface; the paler underside has fine hairs along the mid-rib. Fall colour is yellow to orange.

Fragrant, small, white, five-petalled flowers are produced in arching chains up to 15 centimetres long. They develop hanging clusters of shiny purple-black drupes. The fruit tastes bittersweet. **All parts of this plant are toxic except for the fruit pulp and skin.**

The similar chokecherry (*Prunus virginiana*), which often suckers to form clumps, has rounded leaves that are broadest above the midpoint and narrow abruptly to a pointed tip.

Top: Flowers grow in arching sprays. Note the glossy, finely toothed leaves. **Middle:** The glossy black fruit is produced in chains. **Bottom:** Bark becomes flaky over time.

VITAL STATISTICS
Maximum height: 30 metres
Flowering season: June

Holly family / Aquifoliaceae

Inkberry

Ilex glabra

Gallberry

Native Species

VITAL STATISTICS
Maximum height: 2.5 metres
Flowering season: July

HABITAT: In the Maritimes, inkberry is found only in Nova Scotia, where it is most common in the southwestern Atlantic Coastal Plain region. It grows in wet and dry sites, such as swamps, barrens, and coniferous forest.

CHARACTERISTICS: A suckering, broad-leaved evergreen shrub, inkberry rarely reaches its potential height of 2.5 metres. Young twigs are smooth and green. Older bark is pale grey, often flaking to reveal dark, green-brown bark below. Plants become bare-stemmed and spindly with age.

The alternate leaves are evergreen, elliptical to spoon-shaped, smooth, and shiny. Dark green on the upper surface, they have a pale underside and can be 3 to 6 centimetres long. Leaves have a few teeth along their outer edges and often gain a purple tint in winter.

Plants are dioecious. Tiny white male (clustered) and female (solitary) flowers are produced among the upper leaf axils, often hidden beneath the leaves. Female flowers develop into short-stalked, black, shiny drupes that persist through winter.

Top: The outer edges of the spoon-shaped leaves are toothed. Note the nearly stemless black fruit. **Bottom:** Solitary female flowers are produced among the leaf axils.

Holly family / Aquifoliaceae
Common winterberry
Ilex verticillata
Black alder, Canada holly, winterberry holly

Native Species

VITAL STATISTICS
Maximum height: 2 metres
Flowering season: July

HABITAT: Common winterberry grows throughout the Maritimes in moist to wet sites, such as bogs and swamps, stream and pond margins, and wet thickets.

CHARACTERISTICS: Although deciduous, common winterberry is a true holly. It forms a shrub with pale grey stems that grows to 2 metres in height.

The alternate leaves are elliptical to oval with a pointed tip and finely toothed edges. The upper leaf surface is hairless, glossy, and somewhat rugose; the underside is paler, with a few fine hairs along the veins. Fall colour is a mixture of yellow and brown.

Plants are dioecious. The small white flowers have five to eight petals and are produced in nearly stemless clusters at the leaf axils. Male flowers, also small, have yellow stamens. Female plants produce orange to red, short-stalked, berry-like drupes that ripen in October but can persist well into winter. Each berry has four to nine small nutlets.

Top: Edges of elliptical leaves are finely toothed. Note flower bud clusters in leaf axils. **Middle:** Small male flowers have yellow stamens. **Bottom:** Common winterberry is easily identified when leaves have fallen and the fruit is clearly visible.

White alder family / Clethraceae
Coastal sweet pepperbush
Clethra alnifolia
Coast pepperbush, summersweet

Native Species

VITAL STATISTICS
Maximum height: 2 metres
Flowering season: August to early October

HABITAT: A rare shrub in Canada, coastal sweet pepperbush is found only in a few sites on the Atlantic Coastal Plain in southwestern Nova Scotia. It grows along lakeshores, in wet thickets, on swampy ground, and in sandy, open woodlands.

CHARACTERISTICS: Coastal sweet pepperbush is a suckering shrub with light brown, rough stems. Older bark is grey and may peel in long strips.

The alternate leaves are 3.5 to 7 centimetres long and are elliptical, oval, or spoon-shaped. Leaf edges are sharply toothed on the outer half of the leaf but smooth or finely toothed close to the leaf base. Leaves are shiny green and smooth on the upper surface and somewhat paler on the underside. Leaf stems are slightly hairy.

This shrub blooms later than any other in the Maritimes. Plants produce white, upright, terminal racemes up to 15 centimetres long; each flower in the cluster has five petals. Flowers are highly fragrant; stems are slightly hairy. The fruit consists of long clusters of small, rounded, brown capsules.

Top: The leaves' sharp teeth are more noticeable on the outer leaf than near the stem. **Bottom:** Flowers are produced in upright terminal racemes.

Heath family / Ericaceae
Eastern teaberry
Gaultheria procumbens
Checkerberry, creeping wintergreen, wintergreen

HABITAT: Eastern teaberry is common throughout the Maritimes, growing in dry forests and barrens.

CHARACTERISTICS: Teaberry is an evergreen sub-shrub with trailing, subterranean stems and upright, leafy stems that reach 5 to 15 centimetres in height.

The alternate leaves emerge reddish purple but soon become dark green, stiff, and shiny. Leaves are elliptical to rounded, and hairless. The serrations on their toothed edges can be so narrow and pointed as to appear almost hair-like. Leaves are clustered near the top of upright stems, appearing whorled; they have a wintergreen scent when bruised. In winter, leaves may regain a purple tint.

Nodding, white, urn-shaped flowers are produced from the axils of short leafy stems. Flowers are either solitary or in a small cluster; each has five lobes. By October, they produce red, berry-like fruit that tastes of wintergreen. Calyx remnants often form a "crown" on the tip of the fruit. The pistil also remains as a short, thread-like extension in the centre of this "crown." The edible fruit often persists through winter into spring.

VITAL STATISTICS
Maximum height: 15 centimetres
Flowering season: Late July to August

Top: Leaf edges have sharp, hair-like teeth; white flowers are urn-shaped with five small lobes. **Middle:** Berries can be hidden under leaves. **Bottom:** Calyx remnants may form a "crown" on the fruit tip.

Heath family / Ericaceae
Early lowbush blueberry
Vaccinium angustifolium
Low sweet blueberry, lowbush blueberry

Native Species

VITAL STATISTICS
Maximum height: 50 centimetres
Flowering season: Late May to mid-June

HABITAT: Early lowbush blueberry (the most common Maritimes blueberry) grows on coastal headlands, peaty or sandy barrens, and in newly burned areas.

CHARACTERISTICS: A deciduous, suckering, twiggy shrub, early lowbush blueberry can grow 50 centimetres tall. Current-season twigs are green; older stems are reddish brown.

The alternate leaves are elliptical to lance-shaped, 1 to 3.5 centimetres long, with finely toothed edges. New leaves often have a bronze tint; mature leaves are hairless, shiny green on upper surfaces, and paler on the undersides. The main veins on lower surfaces are often finely haired. Fall colour is brilliant scarlet.

Terminal clusters of white or pink-tinted, urn- to bell-shaped flowers appear late May to mid-June. Each five-lobed blossom is 5 to 6 millimetres long. Sweet-tasting berries—blue to black with a waxy bloom—ripen in August and September. Calyx remnants give them a terminal "crown."

Northern blueberry (*V. boreale*) is a dwarf version (10 centimetres) found mainly on the highest hills of Cape Breton and New Brunswick and in Prince County, Prince Edward Island. Its new twigs are warty; emerging leaves have no red tint. Highbush blueberry (*V. corymbosum*) is found in southwest Nova Scotia and, rarely, in southern New Brunswick. It can reach 3 metres in height.

Top: Plants produce terminal clusters of urn-shaped, white or pink-tinted flowers.
Bottom: Elliptical leaves are hairless and shiny; clustered blueberries often have a waxy bloom.

Heath family / Ericaceae
Dwarf bilberry
Vaccinium caespitosum
Dwarf blueberry, dwarf huckleberry, dwarf whortleberry

Native Species

HABITAT: Dwarf bilberry grows on rocky cliffs, ledges, and barrens. It is uncommon in both Nova Scotia and New Brunswick and absent from Prince Edward Island.

CHARACTERISTICS: This dwarf deciduous shrub reaches only from 5 to 30 centimetres in height. New twigs are yellow-green, often with spare hairs; older stems are red to brown and hairless.

The alternate leaves, 1 to 4 centimetres long, are oblanceolate to spatulate, hairless, shiny, and net-veined, with finely toothed edges. They turn scarlet in autumn.

Solitary, deep pink, urn-shaped flowers are produced from the leaf axils in July. The flowers are 4 to 6 millimetres long and end in five lobes. Edible blue berries with a waxy bloom ripen in August and September. The remnants of the calyx become a small "crown" at the end of the berry.

VITAL STATISTICS
Maximum height: 30 centimetres
Flowering season: July

Top: Leaves are spoon-shaped with finely toothed edges. **Middle:** Solitary, pink, urn-shaped flowers are produced from the leaf axils. **Bottom:** The calyx remnants form a small "crown" at the berry tip.

Barrens

Wax-myrtle family / Myricaceae
Northern bayberry
Morella pensylvanica
(formerly *Myrica pensylvanica*)

Bayberry, candleberry, waxberry, wax-myrtle

Native Species

VITAL STATISTICS
Maximum height: 2 metres
Flowering season: June

HABITAT: Throughout the Maritimes, northern bayberry grows on sand dunes and coastal headlands.

CHARACTERISTICS: Upright northern bayberry grows to 1.5 metres. Stems are grey-brown with small rounded buds. Leaves are shiny, alternate, and elliptical to obovate, with somewhat rounded ends and slightly undulating edges. They are reddish when they first emerge.

Northern bayberry is semi-evergreen: leaves remain on plants well into the winter months. All parts are sweetly fragrant when bruised—bayberry candles get their distinct fragrance from this plant's berries.

Plants are dioecious. Male catkins are small and green, while females are merely tiny green nubs. Catkins are produced after plants have leafed, in late June through July. Female plants produce blue-grey, rounded "berries" (actually a rounded cluster of hard nutlets) in autumn. These may remain on the tree for several years.

Northern bayberry can grow in very nutrient-poor soil thanks to nitrogen-fixing bacteria on its roots.

Top: Shiny elliptical leaves have somewhat blunt tips and slightly undulating edges.
Middle: Immature female catkins appear as tiny green nubs. **Bottom:** These blue-grey, rounded "berries" are actually a cluster of hard nutlets.

Holly family / Aquifoliaceae

Mountain holly
Ilex mucronata
(formerly *Nemopanthus mucronata*)
Catberry

Native Species

VITAL STATISTICS
Maximum height: 3 metres
Flowering season: May and June

HABITAT: Mountain holly is a common shrub in damp woodlands, barrens, bogs, and occasionally coastal headlands throughout the Maritimes.

CHARACTERISTICS: This deciduous shrub can reach 3 metres. Young twigs are purplish brown and smooth, with scattered, tiny white lenticels; older stems are pale grey. Winter buds are purplish brown. Terminal buds are pointed, lateral buds more rounded.

Thin leaves are alternate, mostly elliptical to obovate, and usually have untoothed edges. A matte light green to grey-green, they are hairless with a purplish stalk. Fall colour is a mix of yellow and brown.

Plants are dioecious. Both sexes have small, greenish yellow flowers that have four or five petals. They are produced at the ends of relatively long flower stems and bloom in June. In late August through September, female plants produce dull red, long-stalked, berry-like drupes that contain four or five nutlets.

The contrast between young purple twigs and older pale grey stems make this shrub particularly easy to identify in winter.

Top: Purplish brown young twigs clearly contrast with older grey stems. Note the long stalks on fruit. **Middle:** The elliptical leaves generally have untoothed edges. **Bottom:** A tiny green flower is produced at the end of a long stalk.

105

Dogwood family / Cornaceae

Alternate-leaved dogwood
Cornus alternifolia
Green osier, pagoda dogwood

Native Species

VITAL STATISTICS
Maximum height: 8 metres
Flowering season: Mid-June to mid-July

HABITAT: Throughout the Maritimes, alternate-leaved dogwood is found in well-drained forests and shaded ravines.

CHARACTERISTICS: Alternate-leaved dogwood is a deciduous shrub that can reach 8 metres in height. Twigs are smooth and reddish green to purple, with alternate, narrow, pointed buds. Older stems are green, often with white streaks. Lateral branches are noticeably horizontal.

The alternate, ovate to elliptical leaves are shiny green on the upper surface and whitish green on the underside, with untoothed, often undulating edges. Leaves are often crowded at the ends of the stems, appearing whorled. Leaf arrangement—alternate on the branch and somewhat whorled—helps distinguish this dogwood from the other species in the Maritimes. Fall colour is in purple tones.

Flat-topped clusters of small, creamy white, four-petalled flowers are produced in July. They develop into blue-black, berry-like drupes in September.

Top: The smooth-edged leaves are slightly undulating. **Middle:** Shrubs produce flat-topped clusters of small four-petalled flowers. The crowded leaves below appear almost whorled. **Bottom:** Ripe berries are distinctly dark blue.

Native Species

Heath family / Ericaceae
Leatherleaf
Chamaedaphne calyculata
Cassandra, dwarf Cassandra

HABITAT: Leatherleaf is a common shrub in wetlands, in damp barrens, and along lakeshores throughout the Maritimes.

CHARACTERISTICS: This evergreen grows about 1 metre tall. Leatherleaf twigs are covered in tawny scales but older stems are smooth.

Leaves are alternate, somewhat spoon-shaped, and 1 to 4 centimetres long. They have revolute edges and often overlap on the stem. Scurfy on both surfaces, they are leathery in texture. The upper surface is green; the underside is pale brownish green. In winter, leaves turn brown to rusty red.

Small, white, nodding, urn-shaped flowers are produced from the leaf axils of short side-branches. The brilliant white of the petals contrasts sharply with the tawny calyx. Flowers are single but with the leaves form a one-sided, leafy raceme. They bloom in May and June. Seed capsules are rounded and upright on short stalks. The remnants of the stigma form a hair-like extension.

VITAL STATISTICS
Maximum height: 1 metre
Flowering season: Early May to mid-June

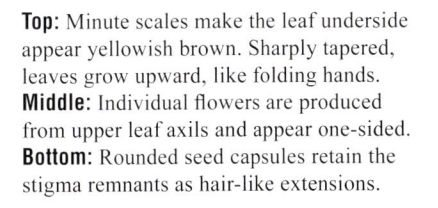

Top: Minute scales make the leaf underside appear yellowish brown. Sharply tapered, leaves grow upward, like folding hands.
Middle: Individual flowers are produced from upper leaf axils and appear one-sided.
Bottom: Rounded seed capsules retain the stigma remnants as hair-like extensions.

Wetlands

Barrens

Heath family / Ericaceae
Black huckleberry
Gaylussacia baccata

Native Species

VITAL STATISTICS
Maximum height: 1 metre
Flowering season: June to early July

HABITAT: Black huckleberry is a common shrub in open woodlands, barrens, and bogs throughout the Maritimes.

CHARACTERISTICS: This deciduous shrub reaches only 1 metre in height. Black huckleberry's young twigs are covered in white down; older stems are brownish grey with flaking bark. New branches are covered in resinous glands, which make leaves and stems quite sticky.

Leaves are smooth, bright green, 3 to 5 centimetres long, and elliptical to oval. Close inspection reveals fine, golden glands that make leaves sticky. The untoothed leaf edges have a fringe of hair. Fall colour is brilliant scarlet.

Black huckleberry produces a one-sided raceme of red to coral pink, nodding, urn-shaped flowers in June. Each flower has five lobes. The fruit is a shiny black, edible, berry-like drupe that ripens in October.

Top: Oval leaves have smooth edges; ripe fruit is shiny and black. **Bottom:** Pink urn-shaped flowers are produced in nodding clusters.

Heath family / Ericaceae

Dwarf huckleberry

Gaylussacia bigeloviana
(formerly *G. dumosa*)

Bog huckleberry

HABITAT: Less common in the Maritimes than black huckleberry, dwarf huckleberry occurs in bogs and barrens near the coast. It is an Atlantic Coastal Plain species.

CHARACTERISTICS: Dwarf huckleberry is a suckering, deciduous shrub that is generally shorter than 60 centimetres. Reddish green twigs are covered in white down; older stems are brownish grey and smooth.

The alternate leaves are dark green, leathery, oblong to ovate, and 3 to 5 centimetres long, with untoothed, hair-fringed edges and a conspicuously pointed tip. Both leaf surfaces are shiny; many tiny resinous spots make them a little sticky, especially on the underside. Foliage turns brilliant scarlet in autumn.

The white-pink flowers of dwarf huckleberry are produced individually from upper leaf axils, forming a slightly one-sided raceme. Nodding and bell-shaped, they have five lobes. By October, they produce shiny black, berry-like drupes that have a few sticky hairs. Though considered edible, the fruit is rather tasteless.

VITAL STATISTICS
Maximum height: 60 centimetres
Flowering season: June to mid-July

Top: Spoon-shaped leaves are blunt at the tip and tapered at the base. **Middle:** The five-lobed flowers are distinctly bell-shaped. **Bottom:** Mature black fruit has a few short hairs.

Heath family / Ericaceae

Rhodora
Rhododendron canadense

Native Species

VITAL STATISTICS
Maximum height: 1.2 metres
Flowering season: May to mid-June

HABITAT: Throughout the Maritimes, rhodora is a common shrub on barrens and peatlands, in moist thickets, and on rocky slopes.

CHARACTERISTICS: An erect deciduous shrub, rhodora can reach 1.2 metres. Twigs are yellow-brown; older stems are brown to grey. Winter buds are purplish brown.

The alternate leaves are elliptical, grey-green to blue-green, and 3 to 6 centimetres long. Upper and lower leaf surfaces are covered in fine hairs. Leaf edges are revolute, untoothed, and fringed in hair. In autumn, leaves turn purplish red. **All parts of this plant are toxic.**

Deep rose-purple or (rarely) white, 2- to 3-centimetre-long flowers are produced in terminal clusters in late May and June. Flowers have five fused petals: three on the upper side, two on the lower. Flowers appear as the leaves unfurl. Oval seed capsules are purple-brown and quite hairy.

Lapland rosebay (*R. lapponicum*), a dwarf evergreen rhododendron, is restricted to the Corney Brook Gorge on Cape Breton Island. It has small, smooth-edged, elliptical leaves with scurfy surfaces and small clusters of saucer-shaped purple-pink flowers.

Top: Rhodora's revolute leaf margins are clearly visible here. **Middle:** Rhodora in bloom on open barrens. **Bottom:** Lapland rosebay produces purple saucer-shaped flowers in terminal clusters.

Native Species

Heath family / Ericaceae
Common Labrador tea
Rhododendron groenlandicum
(formerly *Ledum groenlandicum*)
Labrador tea

Coniferous Forest

VITAL STATISTICS
Maximum height: 1 metre
Flowering season: June

HABITAT: Common Labrador tea is found on wet barrens and in wet, open forests and wetland areas throughout the Maritimes.

CHARACTERISTICS: An upright, broad-leaved, evergreen shrub, common Labrador tea usually does not reach its 1-metre potential height. Twigs are covered in white to rusty red hairs; older stems are reddish brown and flaky.

New leaves are densely covered in white hairs. As leaves mature, most upper-surface hair is lost, leaving a dark green, rugose leaf top. Leaf undersides remain hairy, but the hair becomes rusty red and felt-like. Leaves are alternate, elliptical, and 1.5 to 5 centimetres long with untoothed, revolute edges. They often turn reddish brown to greenish brown in winter.

The leaves are highly aromatic when bruised and can be steeped to make a tea; **do not boil them—high temperatures release a toxin.**

Rounded terminal buds become small, white, five-petalled flowers from mid-June through July. Oval seed capsules are produced at the ends of slender, often twisted stalks.

Top: Labrador tea growing in barrens habitat next to common juniper (*Juniperus communis*), at left. **Middle:** Leaves have revolute edges and a felted underside. **Bottom:** Flowers grow in a rounded terminal cluster.

Wetlands

Barrens

111

Heath family / Ericaceae
Large cranberry
Vaccinium macrocarpon
American cranberry, cranberry

Native Species

VITAL STATISTICS
Maximum height: 10 centimetres
Flowering season: July

HABITAT: Wetlands—especially coastal wetlands—are the preferred habitat for large cranberry, which is fairly common throughout the Maritimes.

CHARACTERISTICS: Large cranberry is a trailing, broad-leaved evergreen with brown, flaking bark. The alternate, 5- to 10-millimetre, elliptical leaves are crowded on the stems. Shiny green on the upper surface, they have whitened undersides and untoothed, slightly revolute edges. New leaves often have a reddish tint; in winter, they may be tinted purple.

Nodding pink flowers are composed of four backward-curving petals and eight fused stamens that point downward, appearing beak-like. Produced in July, flowers are usually in twos or threes and sub-terminal; leafy stems extend beyond the blossoms.

Flowers develop into relatively large, deep red to dark purple berries that ripen in October and November. Large cranberry's tart berries are prized for jams and preserves, sauces, and desserts.

The similar small cranberry (*V. oxycoccus*) can be distinguished from the large cranberry by its flowers and berries, which are located at the ends of the stems.

Top: Leaves have pale undersides and untoothed, slightly revolute edges. Note the red tint on edges, typical in spring. **Middle:** Flowers have four backward-curving petals. Leafy stems extend beyond the flowers. **Bottom:** In winter, leaves are tinted purple. Berries are dark red when ripe.

Heath family / Ericaceae
Velvet-leaved blueberry
Vaccinium myrtilloides
Canada blueberry, sourtop, sourtop blueberry

Native Species

VITAL STATISTICS
Maximum height: 60 centimetres
Flowering season: June

HABITAT: Throughout the Maritimes, velvet-leaved blueberry grows in recently burned areas, barrens, open coniferous woodlands, and peat bogs.

CHARACTERISTICS: Velvet-leaved blueberry forms a low, 20- to 60-centimetre in height, deciduous shrub. Young twigs are green and densely covered in fine hairs. Older stems are reddish brown and warty.

The alternate leaves are elliptical to lance-shaped, covered in fine hairs, and have hairy, untoothed edges. Leaves turn burgundy red in the fall.

Terminal clusters of 4- to 6-millimetre, greenish white, urn- to bell-shaped flowers are produced in July after leaves appear. Each flower ends in five lobes. The blue berries ripen in August and September and have a waxy bloom.

This edible blueberry tastes rather sour. Its finely hairy leaves will distinguish it from any of the Maritimes' other "blueberries."

Top: Leaves appear dull because they are covered in fine hairs. **Middle:** Plants produce terminal clusters of greenish white, urn-shaped flowers. **Bottom:** These ripe berries are typical of a blueberry. Note the fine white hairs on the leaf underside (to the left of the berries).

Willow family / Salicaceae
Balsam poplar
Populus balsamifera
Balm of Gilead, black cottonwood

Native Species

VITAL STATISTICS
Maximum height: 30 metres
Flowering season: May

HABITAT: Balsam poplar is most common along rich, moist bottomlands and the edges of larger streams, rivers, and lakes. It is found throughout the Maritimes.

CHARACTERISTICS: A deciduous tree, balsam poplar can reach 30 metres when mature. Twigs are shiny reddish brown with longitudinal ridges; they bear pointed, dark reddish brown, sticky buds that have a strong balsamic odour (particularly noticeable during warm humid weather). Trunks have grey bark with deep furrows.

The alternate leaves are ovate, 6 to 12 centimetres long, and somewhat heart-shaped. The upper surface is shiny olive green; the underside is paler with a metallic sheen. Newly emerged leaves are often an even shinier, golden green. Leaf edges are finely toothed. Foliage turns yellow in autumn.

Plants are dioecious with greenish, 6- to 10-centimetre-long catkins produced on male and female trees. Flowers appear in May, before leaves emerge. Mature female catkins release pale brown to white, cottony-plumed seeds from late June to early July.

Jack's hybrid poplar (*P. X jackii*) is a naturalized hybrid derived from balsam poplar. It has similar characteristics but can be distinguished by its heart-shaped leaves and slightly hairy twigs, leaf stalks, and leaf mid-rib. It is found occasionally on or near old homesteads throughout the Maritimes.

Top: In spring, leaves are so shiny they appear burnished. **Bottom:** These female catkins are just starting to release their fuzzy white seeds.

Native Species

Willow family / Salicaceae
Large-toothed aspen
Populus grandidentata
Big-toothed aspen, whitewood

HABITAT: Large-toothed aspen is most common in recently burned areas and on disturbed sites and dry woodlands throughout the Maritimes. It is uncommon on Cape Breton Island.

CHARACTERISTICS: This deciduous tree can grow to 20 metres in height. Large-toothed aspen twigs are reddish to greyish brown and covered with white hairs, especially when young. Winter buds are dark reddish brown, pointed, and covered in grey hairs. The smooth bark is pale green on younger trees but becomes grey-brown and furrowed as trees mature. Plants will send up new shoots from their roots to form large clumps.

Leaves are alternately arranged, ovate, abruptly pointed, 4 to 12 centimetres long, and coarsely toothed. New foliage is covered in white hairs. Mature leaves are smooth on the upper surface but whitened with hairs on the underside. Leaves move in the slightest breeze—appearing to tremble—and make a distinct rustling sound. Their fall colour is bright yellow.

Plants are dioecious, with catkins 5 to 7.5 centimetres long that bloom before the trees leaf. Male catkins are grey-brown and hairy; females are much less hairy and appear greener. Mature female catkins release white, cottony-plumed seeds in early July. Large-toothed aspen usually grows on drier sites than the similar trembling aspen (*P. tremuloides*) does.

Top: The rounded leaves have large teeth.
Bottom: Hairy, grey-brown male catkins, which have bloomed before the tree has leafed.

VITAL STATISTICS
Maximum height: 20 metres
Flowering season: Mid-April to mid-May

Mixed Forest

Hardwood Forest

Disturbed

Willow family / Salicaceae
Trembling aspen
Populus tremuloides
Aspen, quaking aspen

Native Species

VITAL STATISTICS
Maximum height: 25 metres
Flowering season: Mid-April to mid-May

HABITAT: Trembling aspen grows on moist but well-drained sites throughout the Maritimes. It is particularly common in recently burned areas.

CHARACTERISTICS: A deciduous tree, trembling aspen reaches between 15 and 25 metres in height. Twigs are slender and shiny reddish brown to greyish brown. Winter buds are shiny, dark reddish brown, and pointed, but not sticky like those of the balsam poplar. The smooth bark is pale green on younger trees but becomes silver grey to white as trees mature. Plants will sucker to form large clumps.

Leaves are alternately arranged, ovate to rhombic, abruptly pointed, 3 to 8 centimetres long, and finely toothed. The upper surface is dark green and the underside quite pale. Leaves move in the slightest breeze—appearing to tremble—and make a distinct rustling sound. Their fall colour is bright yellow.

Plants are dioecious, with 3- to 6-centimetre-long catkins. Male catkins are distinctly grey and hairy; females are much less hairy and appear greener. Mature female catkins release white, cottony-plumed seeds in early July.

Trembling aspen usually prefers wetter sites than the similar large-toothed aspen; its finely toothed leaf edges will easily distinguish it from that species.

Top: Almost round, the leaves are abruptly pointed and finely toothed. **Middle:** Young trees have smooth greenish bark. **Bottom:** Catkins (female shown) bloom before the trees leaf.

Native Species

Willow family / Salicaceae
Balsam willow
Salix pyrifolia

HABITAT: Balsam willow grows in bogs and wet thickets throughout the Maritimes.

CHARACTERISTICS: This willow is a shrubby plant with smooth, glossy, reddish purple to yellow-brown stems. Balsam willow's larger stems become grey or brown.

The 3- to 8-centimetre-long leaves are alternate, elliptical to oval, hairless, and shiny on the upper surface but pale and waxy on the underside. Leaf edges are finely toothed. The tapered leaf tips end abruptly, but the bases are rounded. Newly emerging leaves are often tinted red and have a translucent quality. The leaves emit a balsamic fragrance when bruised.

Plants are dioecious. Catkins are 2 to 6 centimetres long and bloom just as the leaves unfurl.

VITAL STATISTICS
Maximum height: 4 metres
Flowering season: Mid-May to early June

Top: This specimen has oval foliage and smooth reddish purple stems. **Bottom:** These mature female catkins are beginning to release seeds.

Wetlands

Birch family / Betulaceae

Speckled alder
Alnus incana subsp. *rugosa*
(formerly *A. rugosa*)
Swamp alder

Native Species

VITAL STATISTICS
Maximum height: 5 metres
Flowering season: Late March to May

HABITAT: Speckled alder grows in a variety of wet habitats, including swamps, thickets, forest hollows, stream edges, riverbanks, and lake and pond margins. It is a common shrub throughout the Maritimes.

CHARACTERISTICS: An upright deciduous shrub, speckled alder can reach 5 metres in height. Twigs are reddish brown, usually smooth, and have a few pale lenticels. Winter buds are reddish brown and rounded, with narrow stalks.

The alternate leaves are ovate to round, with a coarse, double-toothed edge that is often undulating. Leaves generally have at least 10 pairs of lateral veins. Deep green and wrinkled on the upper surface, they are paler and somewhat hairy on the underside. Foliage has no appreciable colour change in autumn.

Plants are monoecious. Male catkins are 6 to 8 centimetres long, pendulous, and yellow-brown. They bloom early, before the leaves unfurl and often while snow is still on the ground. Small female catkins appear on stems that arch downward. They are greener than male catkins and have red stigmas. They develop into loose clusters of hard, rounded, 1- to 2-centimetre-long, green "cones" that become dry and brown in autumn and can remain attached for several years.

Top: The round leaves are double-toothed with 10-plus pairs of lateral veins and wavy edges.
Bottom: Male catkins bloom before leaves appear, often while snow is still on the ground.

Native Species

Birch family / Betulaceae
Smooth alder
Alnus serrulata
Brookside alder, hazel alder

HABITAT: Smooth alder grows most commonly beside lakes or large rivers but may be found in drier, open woodlands. It is rare in New Brunswick (only along the Eel and St. Croix rivers), localized in southwestern Nova Scotia, and absent from Prince Edward Island.

CHARACTERISTICS: This upright deciduous shrub can reach 5 metres in height. Its reddish brown twigs are covered in grey fuzz. Winter buds are reddish brown, rounded, and pubescent with narrow stalks. Older bark is smooth and grey-brown.

The alternate leaves are obovate, widest above mid-leaf; their finely toothed edge are often undulated. Leaves generally have 10 or fewer pairs of lateral veins. The upper surface is deep green; the paler underside is somewhat hairy. New spring leaves are sticky. Foliage has no appreciable fall colour change.

Plants are monoecious. Male catkins— 6 to 8 centimetres long, pendulous, and yellow-brown—bloom before leaves unfurl (snow may still cover the ground). Small female catkins grow on stems that arch upward. Greener than males, with red stigmas, they develop into loose clusters of hard, rounded, 1- to 2-centimetre-long, green "cones" that become dry and brown in autumn (may not fall for several years). Obovate leaves distinguish this species from the other two Maritimes alders.

Top: Leaves have fewer than 10 pairs of lateral veins. Note unopened male catkins.
Bottom: Male catkins in bloom are pendulous; females grow on upward-arching stems.

VITAL STATISTICS
Maximum height: 5 metres
Flowering season: Late March to May

Mixed Forest

Hardwood Forest

Wetlands

Birch family / Betulaceae
American green alder
Alnus viridis subsp. *crispa*
(formerly *A. crispa*)
Green alder, mountain alder

Native Species

VITAL STATISTICS
Maximum height: 3 metres
Flowering season: May to June

HABITAT: Throughout the Maritimes, American green alder is a common shrub, growing beside streams and rivers, at pond margins, in wet ditches and disturbed areas, and on exposed headlands, barrens, cliffs, and rocky slopes.

CHARACTERISTICS: The deciduous American green alder can reach 3 metres in height. Twigs are brown and smooth with scattered pale brown lenticels. Winter buds are pointed, shiny reddish brown, and sticky.

The alternate leaves are ovate to somewhat cordate, with finely toothed edges and a distinctly wrinkled appearance. Generally, each leaf has fewer than 10 pairs of lateral veins. Leaves are dark green on their upper surface and a pale, shiny green on the underside, often with fine rusty hairs along the veins. Spring leaves can be sticky when pinched. Foliage has no appreciable fall colour change.

Plants are monoecious. Male catkins are 6 to 8 centimetres long, pendulous, and yellow-brown; they bloom in May and June as leaves unfurl. Female catkins are quite small, more erect and greener than males, and have red stigmas. Female catkins develop into loose clusters of hard, rounded, 1- to 2-centimetre-long, green "cones" that become dry and brown in autumn.

Top: Leaves are rounded with finely toothed margins. Note that paired veins number fewer than 10. **Middle:** Mature female catkins of all alder are brown, woody, and cone-like. **Bottom:** Male catkins bloom as leaves appear.

Native Species

Birch family / Betulaceae
Yellow birch
Betula alleghaniensis
(formerly *B. lutea*)

HABITAT: Yellow birch grows in moist, rich woodlands and on hillsides throughout the Maritimes; it is especially common near the Bay of Fundy.

CHARACTERISTICS: A deciduous tree, yellow birch can reach 30 metres in height. Twigs are slender and light brown; when broken, they have a distinctive wintergreen fragrance and flavour. Bark is reddish to yellowish brown and smooth, although it often peels into papery shreds.

Leaves are alternate and 6 to 12 centimetres long. Dark green on the upper surface, they are paler on the underside and have hairs along the lower veins. They are oval to cordate with irregularly toothed edges and nine or more pairs of veins. The base is more gradually tapered than on leaves of the other tall birches in the Maritimes. Fall colour is bright yellow.

Plants are monoecious. Male catkins are drooping, brownish yellow, and 3 to 5 centimetres long. Female catkins are narrow, erect, green-brown, and only 1.5 centimetres long. They flower from May to June, then develop an upright, 2- to 4-centimetre-long, brown, cone-like form that releases seeds in fall.

VITAL STATISTICS
Maximum height: 30 metres
Flowering season: May and June

Top: Leaves are coarsely toothed and taper toward the base. **Middle:** Elongate male catkins hang from branchlet tips. **Bottom:** Bark is a distinctive golden brown.

121

Birch family / Betulaceae
Heart-leaved birch
Betula cordifolia
Mountain paper birch, mountain white birch

Native Species

VITAL STATISTICS
Maximum height: 20 metres
Flowering season: May and June

HABITAT: Heart-leaved birch grows in a variety of moist but well-drained habitats throughout the Maritimes.

CHARACTERISTICS: A deciduous tree that can reach 20 metres, heart-leaved birch is more shrub-like in exposed areas. Young twigs are reddish brown and hairless. Smooth bark—which varies from reddish brown to white—peels in thin strips.

The 6- to 12-centimetre-long, alternate leaves are cordate with a tapering tip and heart-shaped base. Resin glands on young leaves make them slightly sticky. Most leaves have at least nine pairs of veins and irregularly toothed edges. Fall colour is bright yellow.

Plants are monoecious. Male catkins are drooping, 3 to 9 centimetres long, and brownish green. Females—upright, green, and only 1.5 centimetres long—bloom through May and June; they become brown and lengthen to 2 to 4 centimetres in late summer.

Until recently, heart-leaved birch was considered a variety of paper birch (*Betula papyrifera*), and it is difficult to tell the two apart. To identify heart-leaved birch, look for the heart-shaped leaf base and hairless young twigs. In addition, heart-leaved birch leaves have twice as many teeth (averaging 47 per side) as paper birch (23 per side). Blue birch (*B.* X *caerulea-grandis*)—a common hybrid of heart-leaved and grey birch—has the reddish brown bark of the former and the foliage of the latter.

Top: This species' leaves are distinctly heart-shaped. **Bottom:** Male catkins hang; smaller female catkins are erect.

Native Species

Birch family / Betulaceae
Paper birch
Betula papyrifera
Canoe birch, white birch

HABITAT: A common species in the Maritimes, paper birch occurs on forested slopes and burned sites as well as along shorelines.

CHARACTERISTICS: Paper birch is a deciduous tree that can reach 20 metres. Young twigs are reddish brown and covered in short, dense hairs and many small white lenticels. The smooth bark can vary in colour from reddish brown (young trees) to white (older, larger trees); older bark generally peels in sheets.

The alternate leaves are 6 to 12 centimetres long, ovate to oblong, with a tapering pointed tip. They are irregularly toothed, dark green on the upper surface and paler below, with fewer than 10 pairs of lateral veins. Fall colour is bright yellow.

Plants are monoecious. Male catkins are pendulous, 3 to 9 centimetres long, and brownish green to yellow-brown. They appear at branch ends; shorter female catkins (1.5 centimetres long) grow on lateral branchlets. Green female catkins develop into drooping, light brown, 2- to 4-centimetre-long, cone-like forms that release seeds in late autumn.

VITAL STATISTICS
Maximum height: 20 metres
Flowering season: Mid-April to May

Top: Ovate leaves are irregularly toothed with a tapering pointed tip and usually seven pairs of veins. **Middle:** Male catkins are at branch ends, and smaller, thinner female catkins on lateral branchlets. **Bottom:** White bark on older trees will peel in sheets.

123

Birch family / Betulaceae
Weeping birch
Betula pendula
European weeping birch, European white birch, silver birch

Introduced Species

VITAL STATISTICS
Maximum height: 20 metres
Flowering season: May

HABITAT: Native to much of Europe, weeping birch is locally naturalized along roadsides and on scrubland across the Maritimes.

CHARACTERISTICS: Weeping birch is a deciduous tree that can grow as tall as 20 metres. Young bark is generally smooth and bright white. As trees age, bark at the trunk base develops rough dark grey areas that gradually merge, creating a strong contrast to the smooth white bark above. Smaller stems are reddish brown and slender. On older trees, the tips of the outermost branches often droop, hence this species' common name. "Weeping" branch tips easily distinguish it from other tall Maritimes birches.

The alternate leaves, 3 to 7 centimetres long, are somewhat triangular (deltoid-ovate) with coarsely toothed edges. Essentially hairless, they are particularly shiny when they first emerge. Fall colour is yellow.

Plants are monoecious. Male and female catkins appear in May as the leaves unfurl. Male catkins are 4 to 9 centimetres long and often produced in groups of two or three; solitary females are 2 to 4 centimetres long and appear cone-like when mature.

Downy birch (*B. pubescens*) is an occasional escape in Nova Scotia. Its leaves resemble those of weeping birch but branchlets do not droop and young stems are downy.

Top: Triangular leaves have coarsely toothed edges. **Bottom:** The bark at the base of the trunk of older trees is dark grey and rough.

Native Species

Birch family / Betulaceae
Grey birch
Betula populifolia
Fire birch, old-field birch

HABITAT: Grey birch is considered a "pioneer" species; it grows on dry sandy soil in forests, burned sites, scrubland, and barrens throughout the Maritimes (though it is uncommon on Cape Breton Island).

CHARACTERISTICS: A bushy tree, grey birch grows to 15 metres. Young trees have smooth, reddish brown bark, which becomes chalky white over time. The bark generally does not peel. Twigs are slender and reddish brown; raised lenticels make them feel rough. Winter buds are slender, smooth, and red to green-brown.

The alternate, 5- to 8-centimetre-long leaves are triangular, with long tail-like tips. Smooth and shiny green on the upper surface, they are slightly paler on the underside and have double-toothed edges. Spring foliage is often sticky. Fall colour is yellow.

Plants are monoecious. Male catkins, usually produced individually, are pendulous and grow 5 to 8 centimetres long. Females are more erect and shorter (1 to 2.5 centimetres). Mature female catkins appear cone-like.

VITAL STATISTICS
Maximum height: 15 metres
Flowering season: Mid-April to May

Top: Triangular leaves have a long tapering tip.
Bottom: Pendulous male catkins (lower right) are often solitary; smaller female catkins grow upright (at left of photo).

Birch family / Betulaceae
Bog birch
Betula pumila
Swamp birch

Native Species

VITAL STATISTICS
Maximum height: 2.5 metres
Flowering season: June

HABITAT: Bog birch prefers open wet habitats, especially calcareous wetlands. Uncommon to rare in the Maritimes, it can be found flanking the Cumberland Strait and in the Cape Breton Highlands.

CHARACTERISTICS: This deciduous shrub grows upright or prostrate; stems can reach 2.5 metres. Bog birch twigs are often densely pubescent; older stems are smooth with shiny, reddish brown bark.

The alternate leaves are oval, obovate, reniform, or round, with round-toothed edges. Leaves are dark green on top, pale with fine hairs below. Fall colour is red.

Plants are monoecious. Nondescript male and female catkins appear in June as leaves unfurl. Mature, cone-like female catkins are 1 to 1.5 centimetres long.

Glandular birch (*B. glandulosa*) is restricted to Nova Scotia's Ingonish Barrens and the highest mountains of New Brunswick's Northumberland County. It has sticky stems and hairless, sticky leaves about 2 centimetres in diameter. Newfoundland dwarf birch (*B. michauxii*) is scattered throughout Nova Scotia and found in one location in eastern New Brunswick. Its small, hairless, fan-shaped leaves often overlap on the stems. The rare dwarf white birch (*B. minor*) is restricted to the Cape Breton Highlands and New Brunswick's Restigouche County. New leaves and twigs are slightly sticky (like those of glandular birch—but twice as big).

Top: Oval leaves have paler undersides. Note the stubby mature female catkins and pubescent stems.
Bottom: The fan-shaped leaves of Newfoundland dwarf birch often overlap along the stem.

Native Species

Birch family / Betulaceae
Beaked hazelnut
Corylus cornuta
Beaked filbert, beaked hazel

HABITAT: Beaked hazelnut grows in forests, on forest edges and rocky slopes, and along stream banks throughout the Maritimes (except southwestern Nova Scotia).

VITAL STATISTICS
Maximum height: 2.5 metres
Flowering season: April to May

CHARACTERISTICS: A rounded shrub, beaked hazelnut can reach 2.5 metres in height. Twigs are yellow-brown; older bark is rough and brown. Winter buds are small and rounded.

The alternate rugose leaves are ovate with sharp, double-toothed edges. The upper leaf surface is sparsely hairy; the underside is covered in downy hair. Fall colour is bright yellow.

Plants are monoecious. Male catkins are 2.5 centimetres long and yellowish green. The small female catkins are spider-like in appearance; they bloom from April to May, before leaves appear. The fruit is a small, edible nut covered by a hairy husk shaped like a tubular "beak"; it ripens in October.

Beaked hazelnut can be easily misidentified as an alder; however, its leaves are brighter green and thinner. As well, unlike alder, beaked hazelnut does not produce cones and its leaves turn bright yellow in autumn.

Top: Ovate leaves have sharp, double-toothed edges and a rugose texture. **Middle:** A mature male catkin. **Bottom:** The fruit is enclosed in a hairy husk with a long tubular "beak" (hence its common name).

Elm family / Ulmaceae
White elm
Ulmus americana
American elm, water elm

Native Species

VITAL STATISTICS
Maximum height: 25 metres
Flowering season: April to early May

HABITAT: White elm prefers moist deciduous woodlands as well as the flood plains of larger rivers. It is found throughout the Maritimes (though in recent years Dutch elm disease has drastically reduced its population) and has been extensively planted as an ornamental.

CHARACTERISTICS: This tree has a rounded crown and drooping branchlets. White elm twigs can be smooth or hairy, are reddish brown, and have a slight zigzag shape. Older bark is dark grey, ridged, and flaky. Winter buds are egg-shaped, reddish brown, and smooth.

The alternate leaves are oval, 7 to 15 centimetres long, and uneven at the base; leaf edges are double-toothed. Slightly rough on the upper surface, they have a few downy hairs on the underside. Foliage turns yellow in the fall.

White elm is monoecious. It flowers in early spring before leaves appear. Flowers are produced along the branches and consist of drooping clusters of anthers or pistils. Female flowers develop into rounded, flat, papery samaras that have hairy edges.

Siberian elm (*U. pumila*) is a Eurasian elm species naturalized around Fredericton and Kouchibouguac National Park. More shrubby than white elm, it has leaves that are smooth, elliptical to lance-shaped, symmetrical at the base, and shorter than 7 centimetres. Additionally, leaves have simple serrated edges.

Top: Leaves have double-toothed edges. **Middle:** Developing female samaras have hairy edges—a key identifier. **Bottom:** Male flowers are simply clusters of stamens.

Introduced Species

Elm family / Ulmaceae
English elm
Ulmus procera
Common elm

HABITAT: English elm is a European native. Planted extensively throughout the Maritimes, it is now naturalized along roads, on scrubland, and in forests next to towns and cities.

CHARACTERISTICS: This large tree has a broad crown and upright branches. English elm twigs are reddish brown and covered in fine hairs. Older twigs develop corky ridges. Bark is dark grey, ridged, and flaky. Winter buds are oval, brown, and slightly hairy.

The alternate leaves are oval to elliptical, 4 to 10 centimetres long, uneven at the bottom, and have double-toothed edges. The upper surface is slightly rough and the underside is covered in soft hair. Fall colour is yellow.

English elm is monoecious. Flowers appear before leaves emerge; lacking petals, they consist of clusters of stamens or pistils. Female blossoms develop into rounded, flat, papery samaras that have hairy edges.

Wych elm (*U. glabra*) occurs occasionally in the Maritimes. Its leaves have a very rough upper surface; the underside is densely covered in fine hair. Its oval leaves are widest beyond the centre point, and mature female fruit lack hair along the edges. They flower later than other Maritime elms, in May and early June. Both species are highly susceptible to Dutch elm disease.

Top: The leaves of English elm (shown) are much smaller than those of American elm.
Bottom: Typically, these wych elm samaras lack hair along their edges.

VITAL STATISTICS
Maximum height: 40 metres
Flowering season: April and May

Barberry family / Berberidaceae
Common barberry
Berberis vulgaris
European barberry

Introduced Species

VITAL STATISTICS
Maximum height: 3 metres
Flowering season: May and June

HABITAT: Native to Europe, common barberry was originally planted as an ornamental throughout the Maritimes. Though many have been removed (the plant hosts wheat rust), some naturalized shrubs are occasionally seen in pastures or roadside thickets.

CHARACTERISTICS: Common barberry is a spiny, upright shrub. Reddish green young twigs become grey-brown with longitudinal ridges as they age. Older bark is smooth and grey with darker patches. Spines are produced in groups of three at the base of leaf clusters. Winter buds are small, oval, and reddish brown.

Leaves are produced in alternate clusters of two to five. Round to spoon-shaped, they are 2 to 5 centimetres long and have sharply toothed edges. Fall colour is a mix of yellow, orange, and red.

Flowers hang in chains from the axil of the leaf clusters. Individual blossoms are bright yellow with six petaloid sepals and six petals. They later develop into hanging chains of bright red, elliptical berries that are edible but very sour.

Top: Rounded leaves have sharply toothed edges. **Middle:** Flowers hang in chains. **Bottom:** Fruit is also produced in hanging chains.

Native Species

Witch-hazel family / Hamamelidaceae
American witch-hazel
Hamamelis virginiana
Common witch-hazel

VITAL STATISTICS
Maximum height: 4 metres
Flowering season: Mid-Sept. to Nov.

Mixed Forest

Hardwood Forest

HABITAT: American witch-hazel is locally common in dry to moist, mixed or hardwood forests in the Maritimes. Uncommon on Cape Breton Island, it is absent from northwestern New Brunswick.

CHARACTERISTICS: This species is a large non-suckering shrub. American witch-hazel twigs are light brown and finely pubescent, while older bark is smooth and grey-brown. Winter buds are scurfy and shaped like a hoof.

The alternate leaves are 5 to 15 centimetres long and oval; they have undulating, round-toothed edges. The leaf stalks are finely hairy, yet the upper surface of the leaves is smooth and the underside has only a few hairs along the main veins. Leaves turn yellow or gold in autumn.

Round flower buds usually hang in small clusters. In autumn, they open into spider-like yellow flowers with four 1.5- to 2-centimetre-long, narrow petals. In the following months, plants produce pubescent, woody, brown capsules that contain a pair of shiny black seeds, which are forcibly expelled once fully ripe.

Top: Oval leaves have round teeth and undulating edges. **Middle:** These shrubs produce yellow spider-like flowers in the fall. **Bottom:** The woody fruit is covered in fine pubescence.

Rose family / Rosaceae
Hawthorn species
Crataegus species

Native Species

VITAL STATISTICS
Maximum height: 8 metres
Flowering season: May to June

HABITAT: Though uncommon, at least a dozen species of hawthorn can be found in thickets, along shorelines and streams, and in open woods, old fields, and clearings throughout the Maritimes. Because the various hawthorns are difficult to tell apart, they are discussed here as a group.

CHARACTERISTICS: Hawthorn usually develops as a large shrub; it can reach 3 to 8 metres in height, depending on the species. Twigs are shiny, yellowish to reddish brown, and have a few 2- to 6-centimetre-long thorns (as do branches). Rounded winter buds are reddish brown; older bark is grey and scaly.

The 2- to 5-centimetre-long leaves alternate on the stems. Mostly oval—but sometimes elliptical—they generally have three or four pairs of lobes and large teeth. Mature leaves are smooth on the upper surface and duller below; leaves on some species have hair. Fall colour is bright yellow.

In June, five to ten white, 1.3- to 1.6-centimetre, five-petalled flowers are produced in rounded clusters. They develop into 1-centimetre-long red fruit in September and October. Each berry-like pome contains three (occasionally four) relatively large seeds. The calyx persists to "crown" the fruit tip. Though edible, fruit is mostly used to make teas, juice, syrup, and jelly.

Top: Typically, hawthorn leaves are oval with three or four (as here) pairs of lobes and large teeth. **Middle:** Five-petalled white flowers are produced in clusters. **Bottom:** Hawthorn branches have broadly spaced long thorns.

Species identification is based on anther colour and number, fruit size, and leaf shape. In addition to the introduced English hawthorn, species found in the Maritimes include:
- Big-fruit hawthorn (*C. macrosperma*): Nova Scotia and New Brunswick
- Brainerd's hawthorn (*C. brainerdi*): common in some Nova Scotia and New Brunswick locations
- Cockspur hawthorn (*C. crus-galli*): Nova Scotia
- Copenhagen hawthorn (*C. intricata*): Nova Scotia
- Dotted hawthorn (*C. punctata*): Nova Scotia and New Brunswick
- Downy hawthorn (*C. mollis*): Nova Scotia
- Fan-leaved hawthorn (*C. flabellata*): Nova Scotia and commonly in New Brunswick
- Fireberry hawthorn (*C. chrysocapa*): the most common Maritimes species, found in all three provinces
- Fleshy hawthorn (*C. succulenta*): all three provinces
- Jones' hawthorn (*C. jonesiae*): all three provinces
- Quebec hawthorn (*C. submollis*): Nova Scotia and New Brunswick
- Rough hawthorn (*C. scabrida*): Nova Scotia and New Brunswick

Top: A persistent calyx crowns the end of each fruit (fireberry hawthorn shown). **Middle:** Distinctively, cockspur hawthorn has elliptical leaves. **Bottom:** Fleshy hawthorn has fan-shaped leaves.

Rose family / Rosaceae
English hawthorn
Crataegus monogyna

Common hawthorn, European hawthorn, one-seed hawthorn, single-seed hawthorn

Introduced Species

VITAL STATISTICS
Maximum height: 6 metres
Flowering season: June

HABITAT: This introduced species is native to Europe and western Asia, where it grows on rocky slopes. In the Maritimes it has occasionally become naturalized along roadsides and in old pastures.

CHARACTERISTICS: English hawthorn is a small tree that generally does not reach its full height of 6 metres. Young stems have 1- to 1.5-centimetre-long thorns and a grey waxy coating that reveals reddish brown bark when shed. Older bark is dull brown, often with vertical orange cracks.

The alternate leaves are 2 to 6 centimetres long and primarily ovate, with three to seven deep lobes and toothed edges (they resemble small maple leaves). Leaves are a glossy dark green on their upper surface and paler on the underside. Foliage turns yellow in the autumn.

Many small clusters of fragrant, white, five-petalled flowers are produced in June, followed by 1-centimetre-long, dark red fruit that contains a single seed. The calyx is persistent, making a distinct rounded hollow at the fruit tip. Fruit often persists through most of the winter.

Top: With their five lobes and toothed edges, the oval leaves resemble those of a maple tree. **Middle:** Fragrant, white, five-petalled flowers appear in many small clusters. **Bottom:** The persistent calyx leaves a rounded hollow at the fruit tip.

Rose family / Rosaceae

Canada plum
Prunus nigra

Native Species

Black plum, horse plum

VITAL STATISTICS
Maximum height: 10 metres
Flowering season: Mid-May to early June

HABITAT: Scattered through New Brunswick (native) and Nova Scotia (introduced), Canada plum is absent from Prince Edward Island. It grows along fence rows, in old pastures, and on abandoned homesteads.

CHARACTERISTICS: Canada plum, a tall shrub or bushy tree, can reach 10 metres in height. Bark is grey and shaggy; twigs are smooth and dark brown-grey with scattered spines and pale lenticels. Winter buds are brown and pointed.

The oval, 5- to 12-centimetre-long leaves are generally widest above the middle, with narrow pointed tips and blunt double-toothed edges. The upper surface of the smooth leaves is dull green; the underside is pale. Fall colour is yellow.

Flowers are produced in small clusters on short lateral branchlets that often have a spiny tip. Lightly fragrant, the white, five-petalled blossoms can become pink-tinted over time. They bloom as leaves unfurl. The fruit—sour but edible—is a fleshy, reddish orange, oval drupe.

Canada plum, along with pin cherry and common chokecherry, is prone to black knot disease, a fungal infection that creates lumpy black growths on branches.

Top: The oval leaves, widest above the middle, quickly taper to a pointed tip. **Middle:** Flowers grow on short lateral branchlets. **Bottom:** The fruit is a reddish orange drupe.

Disturbed

Rose family / Rosaceae
Chokecherry
Prunus virginiana
Eastern chokecherry, red chokecherry

Native Species

VITAL STATISTICS
Maximum height: 7 metres
Flowering season: Late May to June

HABITAT: Throughout the Maritimes, chokecherry grows along roadsides and at the edges of dry woodlands.

CHARACTERISTICS: Chokecherry—a large shrub or small tree—commonly suckers to form clumps. Winter buds are alternate and quite pointed. Twigs are smooth and reddish grey with many pale brown lenticels. Bark is smooth and grey.

The alternate leaves can be oval, ovate, or somewhat elliptical but are broadest above the centre point. They are hairless, narrow abruptly to a pointed tip, and 4 to 12 centimetres long. The upper surface is dark green; the underside is a paler green. The leaf stalk can have one or more rounded glands. Fall colour is yellow.

Cylindrical, often pendant, 6- to 12-centimetre-long clusters of small, white, five-petalled flowers are produced from late May through June. By late August, plants produce chains of red to purplish black drupes. The fruit, edible but astringent, is best used in jellies and syrup.

All other plant parts are highly toxic.

Top: Leaves are oval and, typically, broader above their centre point. Note the fine teeth and abruptly pointed tip. **Middle:** Small, white, five-petalled blossoms form clusters. **Bottom:** The sour fruit grows in small chains.

136

Native Species

Rose family / Rosaceae

Broad-leaved meadowsweet

Spiraea latifolia

Meadowsweet, white meadowsweet

HABITAT: Broad-leaved meadowsweet grows in a variety of habitats, both wet and dry. Common throughout the Maritimes, it is found most often in disturbed sites—old pastures and roadsides—and alongside streams or ponds.

CHARACTERISTICS: A deciduous, upright, suckering shrub, broad-leaved meadowsweet can reach 1.5 metres. Stems are reddish to golden brown, smooth, and often ridged.

Leaves are 5 to 7 centimetres long, oval to obovate, alternate, hairless, and coarsely toothed. Fall colour is yellow to gold.

Dense, 10- to 15-centimetre-long, pyramid-shaped clusters of many small five-petalled flowers are produced through July and August. Generally, flowers are white but may also be pale pink. Dense clusters of small star-like seed capsules persist through winter and are helpful in identifying this shrub.

Meadowsweet can form dense colonies, especially in the flood plains and deltas of larger streams and rivers.

VITAL STATISTICS
Maximum height: 1.5 metres
Flowering season: July to August

Top: Leaves are oval, hairless, and coarsely toothed. **Middle:** Small five-petalled flowers are arranged in a dense pyramidal cluster. **Bottom:** Dense clusters of small star-like seed capsules help identify this shrub.

Rose family / Rosaceae
Steeplebush
Spiraea tomentosa
Hardhack

Native Species

VITAL STATISTICS
Maximum height: 1.2 metres
Flowering season: August to September

HABITAT: Steeplebush grows in old pastures and along wet ditches, rivers, and lakeshores. It is most common in central Nova Scotia, in southern New Brunswick, and throughout Prince Edward Island.

CHARACTERISTICS: This low shrub has upright, mostly unbranched stems. Young stems are densely pubescent but later become hairless and brown. Steeplebush winter buds are very tiny.

The alternate leaves are 5 to 7 centimetres long, oval to elliptic, with coarsely toothed edges. They are rugose, dark green, and hairless on the upper surface but paler with white to tawny pubescence on the underside. Fall colour is yellow.

Dense, 10- to 20-centimetre-long, pyramid-shaped clusters of many small five-petalled flowers are produced primarily in August. Blossoms are deep pink or, more rarely, white. Dense upright clusters of small star-like seed capsules persist through winter.

Top: Leaves are rugose and dark green on the upper surface. **Middle:** Flowers are produced in tall pyramidal clusters. **Bottom:** The leaf underside is distinctly pale and pubescent.

Staff-tree family / Celastraceae
Oriental bittersweet
Celastrus orbiculatus
Asian bittersweet, Japanese bittersweet

Introduced Species

VITAL STATISTICS
Maximum length: 18 metres
Flowering season: June

HABITAT: Oriental bittersweet is an Asian species that was planted in the Maritimes as an ornamental vine. It is now naturalized in New Brunswick and, to a lesser degree, Nova Scotia and Prince Edward Island, where it is aggressive and considered an invasive species.

CHARACTERISTICS: This vine twines around neighbouring trees and shrubs. Oriental bittersweet twigs are light brown with distinct round leaf scars and small winter buds. Older stems are silvery brown, and the trunk is often finely scaly.

The alternate leaves are oval to round, 5 to 10 centimetres long, with round-toothed edges. Hairless, they are green on the upper surface and paler on the underside. Fall colour is yellow.

Plants are dioecious. Tiny male and female flowers—star-like, five-petalled, and yellow-green—are produced in small clusters among the leaf axils. Fruit becomes golden yellow capsules that split and recurve to reveal red seeds. Seeds often remain through most of the winter.

All parts of this plant are toxic if ingested.

Top: Oval leaves have rounded teeth. **Middle:** Small greenish yellow flowers are produced in small clusters. **Bottom:** The golden yellow fruit capsules split to reveal red seeds.

Mixed Forest

Hardwood Forest

Disturbed

Buckthorn family / Rhamnaceae
Alder-leaved buckthorn
Rhamnus alnifolia
Swamp buckthorn

Native Species

VITAL STATISTICS
Maximum height: 1 metre
Flowering season: Mid-May to mid-June

HABITAT: Alder-leaved buckthorn grows in swampy woods and boggy meadows, primarily over limestone substrates. It is scattered throughout the Maritimes.

CHARACTERISTICS: A deciduous, suckering shrub, alder-leaved buckthorn can reach 1 metre in height. Twigs are smooth with green to red bark; on older stems, bark becomes grey.

The alternate leaves are oval and have finely toothed edges. They are hairless on upper and lower surfaces; the upper is somewhat shiny.

Flowers are quite small and have five greenish yellow petals. Short-stalked and star-shaped, they appear among the leaf axils singly or in small clusters from mid-May to mid-June. Plants produce solitary or small clusters of red to purple-black berry-like drupes in August. The fruit, which is not edible, is often hidden beneath the leaves. **All parts of this plant are toxic if ingested.**

Top: Oval and slightly shiny leaves have finely toothed edges. **Middle:** Yellow-green star-shaped flowers are produced in small clusters among leaf axils. **Bottom:** Small clusters of red to purple-black fruit are often concealed by leaves.

Native Species

Mallow family / Malvaceae
Basswood
Tilia americana
American basswood, American linden

HABITAT: An uncommon species in the Maritimes, basswood is restricted to the hardwood forests of southwestern New Brunswick.

VITAL STATISTICS
Maximum height: 25 metres
Flowering season: July to August

CHARACTERISTICS: Basswood is a large tree with grey-brown fissured bark. Twigs are smooth and reddish green in year one, then turn grey. They often have a zigzag pattern. Shiny, reddish brown, rounded winter buds have a lopsided bulge.

The alternate 12- to 20-centimetre-long leaves are egg- to heart-shaped and asymmetrical: one side of the base has a larger bulge. The upper leaf surface is hairless; the lower has tufts of hairs at vein axils. Leaf edges are sharply toothed. Fall colour is yellow.

Sweetly fragrant flowers are produced in nodding clusters midway along a narrow, curving, papery bract. Individual flowers are small, greenish to yellowish white, with five petals. The tan, woody, globular fruit is produced in a loose cluster and is finely pubescent.

Little-leaved linden (*T. cordata*) is a naturalized European species occasionally found near communities. Its smaller leaves (5 to 10 centimetres) are hairless and its fruit is ribbed. Large-leaved linden (*T. platyphyllos*) is another occasional escape. It is even more similar to basswood but has slightly pubescent twigs and leaf stalks, and fewer flowers per cluster.

Top: All linden leaves are typically asymmetrical (basswood shown). Note the yellow-green flowers above the leaf. **Bottom:** Tan pubescent fruit hangs in loose clusters; ribs identify this as little-leaved linden. Note the elongate papery bract.

Hardwood Forest

Aster family / Asteraceae
Eastern baccharis tree
Baccharis halimifolia
Consumption weed, groundsel tree, sea myrtle

Native Species

VITAL STATISTICS
Maximum height: 3 metres
Flowering season: August to September

HABITAT: This rare Atlantic Coastal Plain species grows in transitional zones where forest meets salt marsh. It is found in Nova Scotia (only in Shelburne County) but nowhere else in Canada.

CHARACTERISTICS: Eastern baccharis tree is a bushy semi-deciduous shrub. The bark is light grey to reddish brown, flaky, and ridged. Glandular-sticky stems are green, angular in cross-section, and smooth.

Leaves are alternate, grey-green, and obovate (spoon-shaped) or diamond-shaped. They can be 6 centimetres long. Smaller leaves are smooth-edged; larger ones have a few large teeth on outer ends. The leaf underside is often sticky. Leaves stay green (sometimes with a plum tint) through much of winter.

Plants are dioecious. Tufted flowers are produced in branching clusters at stem tips. Male flowers are dull yellow; female flowers are creamy white. Individual blossoms are mainly a dense head of stamens or pistils—both flower sexes have nondescript, narrow, hair-like petals. Seeds are produced in a dense head. When mature, they form a crown of downy hair similar to a mature dandelion's (making this species easy to identify).

Top: Larger leaves have a few large teeth at their outer end. **Bottom:** Flowers are composed of tufts of pistils (as seen in these female flowers) or stamens.

Greenbrier family / Smilacaceae
Common greenbrier
Smilax rotundifolia

Bullbriar, common catbrier, horsebriar, round-leaved carrionflower

HABITAT: Common greenbrier is an Atlantic Coastal Plain species. In the Maritimes it grows only in southwestern Nova Scotia, in thickets along lakes and rivers.

CHARACTERISTICS: A suckering, vining woody plant, common greenbrier can reach 10 metres (when supported). Unsupported, it grows as a forbiddingly tangled thicket. Branchlet stems are often square. Young stems are smooth and green with scattered stiff prickles; stems become brown over time.

The alternate leaves are round to cordate, 5 to 12 centimetres long, and leathery in texture, with smooth edges. The upper surface is shiny green, the underside paler. One or two tendrils at the leaf stalk base help the plant "climb." Leaves are semi-evergreen, lasting into early winter.

Plants are dioecious. Fetid, pale yellow-green flowers are produced in small clusters along upper leaf axils. Each flower has six tepals. Female flowers develop into clusters of smooth blue-black berries (often with a waxy bloom) that persist through much of the winter.

VITAL STATISTICS
Maximum height: 10 metres
Flowering season: May and June

Top: The smooth-edged leaves are distinctly rounded. **Middle:** Flowers grow in rounded clusters (male flowers shown). **Bottom:** Fruit is produced in rounded clusters.

143

Barberry family / Berberidaceae
Japanese barberry
Berberis thunbergii

Introduced Species

VITAL STATISTICS
Maximum height: 1.5 metres
Flowering season: May

HABITAT: Native to Asia, Japanese barberry is a popular ornamental. It is now found as a naturalized shrub in scattered locations throughout the Maritimes, mainly in thickets, pastures, and open woods.

CHARACTERISTICS: Japanese barberry is a spiny, bushy, upright shrub. Its smooth reddish green young twigs become brown and gain longitudinal ridges. Older bark is smooth and light grey with darker patches. Solitary spines are at the base of each leaf cluster. Winter buds are small, reddish brown, and oval.

The foliage is produced in alternate clusters of two to five leaves. They are 1.5 to 3.5 centimetres long, round to spoon-shaped, with smooth edges. Fall colour is a mix of orange and red.

Flowers are produced singly or in small clusters from the axil of the leaf clusters. Pale yellow, they have six petal-like sepals and six petals. They develop into elliptical, glossy red berries, which often persist into the winter. The edible fruit has a sharp taste.

Unlike common barberry, Japanese barberry is not an alternate host to wheat rust disease.

Top: Leaves are produced in clusters. **Middle:** Each flower has six sepals and six petals. **Bottom:** The glossy elliptical fruit often persists into the winter.

Buckthorn family / Rhamnaceae

Glossy buckthorn
Frangula alnus
(formerly *Rhamnus frangula*)
European alder buckthorn

Introduced Species

HABITAT: A European species, glossy buckthorn was introduced to the Maritimes as a hedge plant. An invasive species, it is now rapidly spreading along roads and in pastures, open woodlands, and thickets throughout the region.

CHARACTERISTICS: Glossy buckthorn is a deciduous upright shrub or small tree. Bark is dark brown with pale, raised lenticels. Twigs are light grey-brown with fine hairs. Tan-coloured buds are covered in fine hairs. Despite what its name suggests, it has no thorns.

The alternate, 5- to 10-centimetre-long leaves are elliptical to egg-shaped, with smooth (and often undulating) edges. The upper surface is shiny green; the underside is paler with hairs along the veins. Foliage turns yellow in autumn.

Tiny, pale yellow-green flowers cluster in the leaf axils. Bell- to star-shaped with five petals, they turn red then form black drupes, which remain attached well into the winter.

The drupes are mildly toxic to humans. The berries are popular with overwintering fruit-eating birds, however, who inadvertently spread the seeds of this invasive species.

VITAL STATISTICS
Maximum height: 6 metres
Flowering season: June

Top: Oval leaves are glossy and have smooth edges. **Middle:** The pale green flowers are star-shaped. **Bottom:** The black fruit grows in the leaf axils.

Mixed Forest

Hardwood Forest

Wetlands

Disturbed

Mezereum family / Thymelaeaceae

Eastern leatherwood
Dirca palustris

Leatherwood, moosewood, ropebark, wicopy

Native Species

VITAL STATISTICS
Maximum height: 3 metres
Flowering season: May

HABITAT: Eastern leatherwood grows in rich mixed and hardwood forests. Rare in Nova Scotia, it is restricted to Hants County's Avon peninsula. It is rare and localized in New Brunswick and absent from Prince Edward Island.

CHARACTERISTICS: This shrub rarely attains its potential height of 3 metres. Bark is a smooth greyish brown. Younger twigs are smooth and green (later brown); twigs have a characteristic jointed appearance. Winter buds are fuzzy and purplish brown.

Eastern leatherwood's alternate leaves are 5 to 10 centimetres long, elliptical to oval, with smooth edges and blunt tips. Young leaves have scattered downy hairs. Mature leaves are dark green and smooth on the upper surface, paler on the underside. Fall colour is yellow.

Fragrant flowers are produced in small nodding clusters in early spring as leaves appear. Flowers have no petals—their yellow-green sepals are fused into a tube. Stamens extend distinctly beyond the sepals. Flowers later develop oval-shaped, yellow to orange drupes.

This plant is toxic if ingested; even skin contact can cause dermatitis in some people.

Top: Elliptical to oval leaves have blunt tips.
Bottom: Yellow-green flowers are distinctly tubular.

Native Species

Heath family / Ericaceae
Common bearberry
Arctostaphylos uva-ursi

Bearberry, kinnikinnik

HABITAT: Throughout the Maritimes, common bearberry grows on exposed barrens and coastal headlands, in sandy soils, on rocky slopes, and in open forests.

CHARACTERISTICS: Common bearberry is a trailing, mat-forming, broad-leaved evergreen. Its flexible stems can extend more than 1 metre in length. New twigs are somewhat sticky and pubescent but later become smooth. Older stems are reddish brown to grey with peeling bark.

The alternate spoon-shaped leaves are 1 to 3 centimetres long, leathery, and have untoothed edges. Leaves are smooth; their upper surface is dark green and shiny, the underside paler. Leaves often gain a purple tint in winter. Dead leaves turn black and often remain attached to the shrub.

Bearberry produces terminal nodding clusters of two to seven urn-shaped flowers in late May and June. Flowers can be white, pink, or white with pink tips. The red berries they develop ripen in September; they are edible but tasteless.

VITAL STATISTICS
Maximum height: 10 centimetres
Flowering season: Late May to June

Top: Leaves are spoon-shaped, smooth, and shiny. Note the untoothed edges. **Middle:** Pink urn-shaped flowers are produced in terminal nodding clusters. **Bottom:** Mature berries are dull red.

Coniferous Forest

Mixed Forest

Barrens

Dunes

147

Heath family / Ericaceae
Trailing arbutus
Epigaea repens
Mayflower

Native Species

VITAL STATISTICS
Maximum height: 10 centimetres
Flowering season: Early April to May

HABITAT: Trailing arbutus is a common forest-floor species but can also occur on open barrens. It occurs throughout the Maritimes.

CHARACTERISTICS: This species is a prostrate, broad-leaved, evergreen sub-shrub. Trailing arbutus branches are green to reddish brown and quite hairy.

The alternate leaves are reticulated, oval, and 2.5 to 7 centimetres long. Stiff hairs cover upper and lower surfaces and leaf edges (especially on youngest leaves). Leaf edges are untoothed; leaf bases are distinctly cordate. Rich green in colour, leaves become an increasingly lighter yellow-green with exposure to the sun.

Clusters of 1.5-centimetre-diameter flowers grow at the ends of trailing stems. The five petals of each blossom fuse at the base to form a tube. Spicily fragrant, flowers can be white or pink; they bloom from early April through May.

Trailing arbutus is the provincial floral emblem of Nova Scotia. Flowers are sold commercially in farmers' markets throughout the Maritimes—let us hope zealous picking does not deplete populations here, as has occurred elsewhere.

Top: Trailing arbutus creeping along a mossy forest floor alongside the much smaller twin-flower (*Linnaea borealis*). **Middle:** Leaves are generally somewhat shiny and leathery, with heart-shaped bases. **Bottom:** The flower's five petals fuse at the base to form a tube.

Native Species

Heath family / Ericaceae

Creeping snowberry
Gaultheria hispidula
Capillaire, magna-tea berry

VITAL STATISTICS
Maximum height: 5 centimetres
Flowering season: June

HABITAT: Creeping snowberry, found throughout the Maritimes, grows in shady, mossy, coniferous to mixed forests or, less commonly, on open barrens, bogs, and headlands.

CHARACTERISTICS: This plant is a broad-leaved, trailing, evergreen sub-shrub. The thin stems of creeping snowberry are brown with short stiff hairs. Its ovate leaves are alternate and stiff with smooth revolute edges. The leaves' upper surface is glossy, bright green, and hairless; the underside is pale with a few short stiff hairs.

Throughout June, plants produce tiny, bell-shaped, white or almost transparent, solitary flowers with four petals. The blossoms are usually hidden under the foliage. In August and September, solitary, white, egg-shaped berries are produced. The berries have a few short brown hairs and are edible; the flavour is distinctly wintergreen.

Creeping wintergreen is sometimes confused with twinflower (*Linnaea borealis*)—but twinflower's leaves are opposite (not alternate) on the stem, and twinflower lacks the wintergreen fragrance when leaves are crushed.

Top: Creeping snowberry can form a solid evergreen mat; ovate leaves are glossy with smooth edges. **Middle:** Tiny bell-shaped flowers have four petals; note the hairy stems. **Bottom:** Egg-shaped berries have a scattering of short brown hairs.

Heath family / Ericaceae
Small cranberry
Vaccinium oxycoccus
Marshberry

Native Species

VITAL STATISTICS
Maximum height: 5 centimetres
Flowering season: Mid-June to July

HABITAT: Throughout the Maritimes, small cranberry grows in wetlands and on damp barrens.

CHARACTERISTICS: Small cranberry is a trailing, broad-leaved evergreen with small, 3- to 8-millimetre, alternate, ovate to triangular leaves on thread-like stems. The widely spaced leaves are shiny green on the upper surface and whitened on the underside, with untoothed revolute margins. They often become purple-tinted in winter.

Nodding pink flowers have four recurved petals and eight fused stamens that point downward, appearing beak-like. They are produced singly or in clusters of up to four at the ends of the trailing stems. They bloom mid-June through July and produce round to egg-shaped berries that change from speckled purple-brown to bright red. The edible berries, prized for preserves, are fully ripened by October. Fruit often overwinters and tastes even better in the spring.

The widely spaced, somewhat triangular leaves, the thread-like stems, and the position of the fruit at the ends of those stems distinguish this plant from large cranberry (*V. macrocarpon*).

Top: Small cranberry has small ovate leaves widely spaced on thread-like stems. **Middle:** Nodding pink flowers have four recurved petals. **Bottom:** These brownish purple, speckled berries are not quite ripe.

Heath family / Ericaceae
Alpine bilberry
Vaccinium uliginosum
Bog bilberry, bog blueberry

Native Species

VITAL STATISTICS
Maximum height: 30 centimetres
Flowering season: June

HABITAT: Rare throughout the Maritimes (and found mainly in Cape Breton), alpine bilberry grows on peaty coastal headlands and subalpine slopes and summits.

CHARACTERISTICS: Alpine bilberry is a low, sprawling to prostrate, deciduous shrub. It can reach 30 centimetres but more often is less than 10 centimetres. Twigs are reddish brown; older branches are brown with exfoliating bark.

The alternate, somewhat leathery leaves are 0.5 to 2 centimetres long, oval to oblong, with untoothed edges. They are hairless and dull grey- to blue-green on the upper surface; the paler underside has distinct reticulated veins. Foliage turns purplish red in autumn.

One to three white or pink, urn-shaped flowers (5 millimetres long) appear at branch tips in June. Each ends in four small lobes. In August and September, blossoms develop into blue to black berries with a waxy bloom; calyx remnants form a "crown." The dried pistil also remains attached, forming a short, thread-like "bill."

Even rarer, oval-leaved blueberry (*V. ovalifolium*) may be found in the cool coniferous forests of northern Cape Breton. It grows to 1.5 metres and has round, smooth-edged leaves and solitary, pale pink, urn-shaped flowers. Its blue berries have a round scar at the tip.

Top: Oval leaves are dull grey-green with smooth edges and noticeable net veins; fruit has a waxy bloom. **Bottom:** Pink urn-shaped flowers are produced at branch tips.

Barrens

Heath family / Ericaceae
Mountain cranberry
Vaccinium vitis-idaea

Foxberry, lingonberry, partridgeberry, rock cranberry

Native Species

VITAL STATISTICS
Maximum height: 10 centimetres
Flowering season: June

HABITAT: Mountain cranberry grows on coastal headlands, barrens, and sand dunes throughout the Maritimes.

CHARACTERISTICS: This species forms a broad-leaved evergreen sub-shrub that grows up to 10 centimetres tall. Plants are suckering and somewhat trailing in habit. Stems are reddish brown and shiny.

Alternate oval leaves are crowded on the stems. The thick leaves have a leathery to almost plastic-like texture. Dark shiny green on the upper surface, they have a paler underside and smooth edges. Leaves often curve downward. They may emerge with a red tint and can become purple-tinted in winter.

Terminal clusters of nodding, pink, bell-shaped flowers are produced in June. Each blossom terminates in four somewhat reflexed lobes. They develop shiny red to purplish berries in late September. The remnants of the calyx form a "crown" at the berry tip. Berries are tart but highly prized for jams, jellies, and syrup.

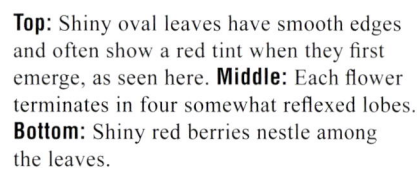

Top: Shiny oval leaves have smooth edges and often show a red tint when they first emerge, as seen here. **Middle:** Each flower terminates in four somewhat reflexed lobes. **Bottom:** Shiny red berries nestle among the leaves.

Beech family / Fagaceae
Northern red oak
Quercus rubra
American red oak, red oak

HABITAT: Throughout the Maritimes, northern red oak grows in mixed and deciduous woodlands on well-drained sites.

CHARACTERISTICS: Northern red oak is a tall tree with furrowed grey bark. Young twigs are smooth and green in their first summer but become dark grey by autumn. Winter buds are often clustered at branch tips. They are reddish brown and pointed, with a frosty pubescence.

The alternate leaves are 12 to 20 centimetres long and roughly oval with seven to eleven bristle-tipped lobes. Early spring foliage has pink pubescence; mature leaves are green and hairless on the upper surface and paler on the underside, with tufts of hairs at the axis of the veins. Fall colour is primarily red but may be simply brown; young trees often retain dead leaves through much of the winter.

Plants are monoecious. The male catkins are in hanging yellow-green clusters; the green female flowers are in short axillary spikes. Female flowers develop into rounded 2- to 2.5-centimetre-long acorns. The cap is flat, like a beret.

VITAL STATISTICS
Maximum height: 30 metres
Flowering season: Mid-May to mid-June

Top: Leaves have bristle-tipped lobes. **Middle:** Typical of all the Maritime oaks, male flowers are yellow-green pendulous catkins. **Bottom:** The acorn has a flat beret-like cap.

Beech family / Fagaceae
Burr oak
Quercus macrocarpa
Blue oak, mossy-cup oak

Native Species

VITAL STATISTICS
Maximum height: 30 metres
Flowering season: Mid-May to mid-June

HABITAT: In the Maritimes, burr oak grows only in southern New Brunswick in swampy woods and along the margins of larger rivers and lakes.

CHARACTERISTICS: Burr oak is a tall tree with brownish grey, scaly, and narrowly ridged bark. Twigs are yellow-brown and pubescent when young but become hairless and grey, often developing corky ridges. Winter buds, often clustered at twig tips, are rounded and covered in grey pubescence.

The alternate leaves are 15 to 30 centimetres long, roughly oval, and widest above the middle, with many rounded lobes. New leaves are pubescent; once mature, they become shiny dark green on the upper surface but remain fuzzy and paler on the underside. Leaves turn yellow-brown in autumn.

Plants are monoecious. Male flowers are hanging yellow-green catkins; the green female flowers are located in short axillary spikes. Female flowers develop into rounded acorns that are 3 to 4 centimetres long. The cup-like, hairy-fringed cap covers half the nut.

Top: Leaves have many rounded lobes.
Bottom: A hairy-fringed cap covers half the nut.

Introduced Species

Beech family / Fagaceae
English oak
Quercus robur

HABITAT: A European native, English oak has been extensively planted in the Maritimes as an ornamental. Naturalized trees are now sometimes seen in the region.

CHARACTERISTICS: English oak is a tall, broad tree with deeply fissured grey-brown bark. Smooth yellow-brown twigs have an exfoliating waxy coating. Winter buds are rounded and light brown with pale-edged scales; they often are clustered at branch tips.

The alternate leaves are 10 to 15 centimetres long, roughly oval, hairless, and leathery. They have three to seven pairs of rounded lobes and very short stalks. The base of each leaf has a pair of ear-like lobes. The upper leaf surface is dark green, the underside paler. Leaves have no distinctive fall colour; younger trees often hold on to dead leaves for much of the winter.

Plants are monoecious. Male catkins hang in yellow-green clusters; the green female flowers are in short axillary spikes. Female flowers develop into narrow 1.5- to 2.5-centimetre-long acorns. A cup-like cap covers a quarter to a third of the nut.

VITAL STATISTICS
Maximum height: 30 metres
Flowering season: Mid-May to mid-June

Top: The round-lobed leaves have very short stalks. **Middle:** Male catkins bloom shortly after the leaves unfurl. **Bottom:** The cap covers up to a third of the nut.

Nightshade family / Solanaceae

Bittersweet nightshade
Solanum dulcamara
Climbing nightshade

Introduced Species

VITAL STATISTICS
Maximum length: 3 metres
Flowering season: June to September

HABITAT: Native throughout Europe and Asia, this introduced species is now widely naturalized in North America, where it is considered invasive. It typically grows in disturbed urban areas in the Maritimes.

CHARACTERISTICS: Bittersweet nightshade is a woody climbing vine. Its twining stems can reach 3 metres in length. Young stems are green to purple; older wood becomes grey-brown.

The 4- to 12-centimetre-long, smooth-edged leaves have two shapes: some are ovate; others have two large lobes at the base, making the leaves look almost trifoliate. Plants smell rank when bruised and have no distinctive fall colour.

The 1-centimetre-diameter purple flowers have five strongly recurved petals. Yellow anthers form a central beak-like extension in the blossom. Flowers are produced in loose clusters of three to twenty blossoms throughout the summer; they develop into 1-centimetre-long, egg-shaped, shiny red berries in autumn.

The fruit may look like a tiny tomato (which *is* a related species), but **the berries are mildly poisonous to humans.**

Top: An example of the leaf type with two lobes at leaf base. **Middle:** Distinctive purple flowers have five reflexed petals and a yellow, fused, beak-like stamen. **Bottom:** Ripe berries are shiny red and egg-shaped.

Introduced Species

Rose family / Rosaceae
Eastern ninebark
Physocarpus opulifolius
Common ninebark

HABITAT: Native to Ontario and Quebec, eastern ninebark is considered naturalized in New Brunswick and Nova Scotia, where it is occasionally found at the edges of roads and woodlands, especially near towns and cities. It is not considered naturalized on Prince Edward Island, where it generally grows on or near old or abandoned homesteads.

CHARACTERISTICS: Eastern ninebark is a large shrub with yellow- to red-brown bark that exfoliates in long strips. Twigs are smooth and reddish brown with thin longitudinal ridges.

The alternate leaves are roughly round, 4 to 9 centimetres long, and tri-lobed. Hairless, they are green on the upper surface and paler on the underside, with blunt-toothed edges. They have no marked fall colour.

Five-petalled white flowers, produced in hemispherical clusters, have distinctive extruding stamens. They bloom throughout June. Blossoms develop into a cluster of reddish brown, star-like seed capsules.

VITAL STATISTICS
Maximum height: 3 metres
Flowering season: June

Mixed Forest

Hardwood Forest

Top: Leaves are tri-lobed and vaguely maple-like. **Middle:** Flowers are produced in round clusters. Note the extruding stamens. **Bottom:** The seed capsules (unripe shown) are somewhat star-shaped.

Disturbed

Willow family / Salicaceae

White poplar
Populus alba
Silver poplar

Introduced Species

VITAL STATISTICS
Maximum height: 25 metres
Flowering season: April to early May

HABITAT: White poplar is native throughout Europe and east to central Asia. Extensively planted in the Maritimes as an ornamental, it has naturalized on roadsides and old homesteads and is considered invasive.

CHARACTERISTICS: This fast-growing tree often suckers, producing groves or clumps. Young twigs and winter buds are greyish white with down-like hair. Young bark is smooth and grey to greenish white, with darker diamond-shaped markings. Trunks are often furrowed and cracked.

Leaves are palmately lobed; the three to five blunt lobes have a few teeth. Young leaves are densely covered in white felt-like hair. The upper surface may become smooth, but the upper-surface veins and leaf undersides retain the hair, appearing white. Leaves (5 to 15 centimetres long) have hints of yellow to no distinctive fall colour.

Plants are dioecious. From April through early May, before leaves appear, trees produce pinkish grey to pale yellow catkins (up to 8 centimetres long). They release silvery white, cottony seeds in July and August.

Grey poplar (*P.* X *canescens*) looks similar but has toothed—not lobed—leaves.

Top: White poplar leaves have five lobes; note the white veins. **Middle:** Grey poplar leaves (shown here) are toothed, have white felted undersides and are not lobed. **Bottom:** As trees mature, bark becomes furrowed and cracked.

Disturbed

Currant family / Grossulariaceae
Wild black currant
Ribes americanum
American black currant

HABITAT: Wild black currant grows in moist, deciduous woodlands and thickets and beside streams—especially in limestone regions. Native to New Brunswick, it is probably introduced in the other two Maritime provinces.

CHARACTERISTICS: This low shrub has smooth, reddish black bark. Wild black currant twigs are finely pubescent, often slightly ridged, and spineless. Winter buds are narrow and pointed.

The alternate, 3- to 8-centimetre-long leaves are palmately three- or five-lobed, with coarsely double-toothed edges. The upper surface is green with sticky resinous dots; the underside is slightly hairy. Foliage turns red in autumn.

Flowers are produced in narrow hanging clusters. Blossoms are creamy white to yellow; five petal-like sepals and five petals form a tube around the stamens and pistils. They develop into loose hanging clusters of smooth black berries. Often, the calyx remnants form a small beak at berry tips. The edible but tart fruit is used for jams and jellies.

Eurasian black currant (*R. nigrum*), an occasional escape in the Maritimes, can be distinguished from American black currant by its pubescent (not smooth) calyx and smaller bracts at the base of each fruit stalk. Both species are alternate hosts for white pine blister rust.

VITAL STATISTICS
Maximum height: 1.5 metres
Flowering season: Late May to mid-June

Top: Sticky resin dots the leaves (see upper left); note the diagnostic narrow bract at the base of flower at top left. **Bottom:** Fruit are black and hang in loose clusters.

Currant family / Grossulariaceae
Skunk currant
Ribes glandulosum
Fetid currant

Native Species

VITAL STATISTICS
Maximum length: 2 metres
Flowering season: Mid-May to mid-June

HABITAT: Skunk currant grows in a range of wet and dry habitats throughout the Maritimes, including woodlands and clearings, as well as on burned sites and rocky slopes.

CHARACTERISTICS: This low, sprawling, deciduous shrub is generally shorter than 1 metre but stems can reach 2 metres or more. Twigs are smooth, grey to brown, and have reddish brown buds. The plant emits a skunk-like odour.

Skunk currant is among the earliest Maritimes shrubs to leaf. Leaves are alternate, palmate with five lobes, and 5 to 8 centimetres across. Leaf edges are coarsely toothed. The upper leaf surface is smooth; the paler underside has fine hairs. Fall colour is red to purple.

Narrow upright clusters of small white to pale pink flowers appear from mid-May through June. Each blossom has five petal-like sepals and five minute inset petals; stalks and calyx are sticky. Flowers develop into loose chains of bristly—but edible—red berries in August. The calyx remnants form a small beak at the tip of each berry.

Top: The palmate leaves have five lobes and are coarsely toothed. **Middle:** Flowers have five white petal-like sepals separated by five tiny pink petals. **Bottom:** The bright red fruit is very shiny.

Currant family / Grossulariaceae
Swamp gooseberry
Ribes hirtellum
Northern gooseberry, smooth gooseberry, wild gooseberry

Native Species

HABITAT: Throughout the Maritimes, swamp gooseberry grows in moist thickets, along woodland edges, on rocky slopes, and in clearings.

CHARACTERISTICS: Swamp gooseberry is an upright or sprawling shrub. New twigs are brownish grey with a few 3- to 8-millimetre-long spines at the leaf nodes. Older stems are reddish brown with exfoliating bark.

The 2.5- to 6-centimetre-long, coarsely toothed, alternate leaves are palmately three- to seven-lobed. Lobes are shallower than those on bristly black currant. Both leaf surfaces are smooth; the underside can be lightly hairy, especially along veins. Leaf stalks often have a few long hairs. Fall colour is red to bronze.

In June, clusters of one to four bell-shaped flowers appear among the upper leaves. Each bloom has five greenish white to dull purple, petal-like sepals. Flowers develop into smooth green berries that turn reddish purple by September. The calyx remnants give the berry a beak-like extension. The fruit looks and tastes like cultivated gooseberry.

Eastern prickly gooseberry (*R. cynosbati*) grows in western New Brunswick; it can be distinguished by its bristly fruit.

VITAL STATISTICS
Maximum height: 1 metre
Flowering season: Late May to mid-June

Top: Leaf stalks usually have a few long hairs.
Middle: A pair of greenish white, bell-shaped flowers emerging from a leaf axil.
Bottom: Ripe fruit is reddish purple.

Currant family / Grossulariaceae
Bristly black currant
Ribes lacustre
Bristly currant, swamp black currant, swamp currant

Native Species

VITAL STATISTICS
Maximum height: 1.5 metres
Flowering season: June

HABITAT: Throughout the Maritimes, bristly black currant grows in moist forests, on rocky slopes, in damp hollows, and at swamp edges, especially in limestone areas.

CHARACTERISTICS: This upright deciduous shrub can reach 1.5 metres. Bristly black currant twigs are yellowish brown to yellowish grey and densely covered in bristly prickles and a few spines.

The alternate, 3- to 4-centimetre-wide leaves are palmate with three or five deep lobes with toothed edges. The terminal lobe is often much longer than the others. Leaves are mostly hairless, but the stalk often has a few long hairs. Leaves give off a skunk-like odour when bruised. Fall colour is red to purple.

Bristly black currant produces a loose drooping cluster of small greenish white to pale pink-purple flowers that have five petal-like sepals and five inset true petals. In August, they produce edible, bristly, purple-black fruit. The calyx remnants form a flattened cap on the berries.

Like all currants, this species is an alternate host to white pine blister rust.

Top: Palmate leaves have five deep lobes and toothed edges; the terminal lobe is longest.
Middle: Flowers are produced in drooping clusters. Note the bristly stem. **Bottom:** The fruit has conspicuous bristles; calyx remnants form a cap.

Currant family / Grossulariaceae

Swamp red currant
Ribes triste
American red currant, wild red currant

Native Species

VITAL STATISTICS
Maximum height: 80 centimetres
Flowering season: May and June

HABITAT: Swamp red currant inhabits damp woods, thickets, and rocky slopes. It is widespread in New Brunswick but more restricted in the other two Maritime provinces.

CHARACTERISTICS: A low, sprawling, deciduous shrub, swamp red currant reaches only 80 centimetres in height. Stems are smooth and grey.

The alternate leaves are mostly palmate with three (sometimes five) lobes, which are shallower than those of skunk currant. Smooth on the upper surface, leaves are finely hairy on the underside and 3 to 8 centimetres across. Fall foliage turns red and purple.

In June, narrow drooping clusters of small smoky purple flowers emerge on sticky stalks. Each flower has five petal-like sepals; they develop into smooth red edible berries in August. Calyx remnants form a beak-like extension on the berry; fruit hangs in loose chains.

The similar European red currant (*R. rubrum*) is naturalized throughout the Maritimes. It is distinguished by its yellow-green flowers. Also similar are skunk currant (*R. glandulosum*), which smells foul when bruised, and squashberry (*Viburnum edule*), which has opposite—not alternate—leaves.

Top: Leaves are most often tri-lobed, as shown here. **Middle:** Small flowers are dull pinkish green and hang in loose chains. **Bottom:** Translucent red berries also hang in chains.

Rose family / Rosaceae
Cloudberry
Rubus chamaemorus
Bakeapple, salmonberry

Native Species

VITAL STATISTICS
Maximum height: 25 centimetres
Flowering season: June to early July

HABITAT: Cloudberry grows in acidic bogs and, less commonly, on rocky coastal headlands throughout the Maritimes.

CHARACTERISTICS: This plant is a low deciduous sub-shrub. Growing from subterranean and semi-woody rhizomes, unbranched stems can be 10 to 25 centimetres tall. Non-flowering stems often have a solitary leaf; flowering stems may have two or three alternate leaves.

The leaves—palmate with five lobes and sharply toothed edges—resemble a cloak in shape. Leathery and rugose, they are somewhat glossy, often bronzy green (especially in exposed locations), and turn bronzy purple in autumn.

Plants are dioecious. Separate male and female plants bloom in June and early July. Solitary white flowers (2 to 4 centimetres across) have four to seven petals and many stamens. The calyx tightly encloses developing fruit. Upon ripening (August and September), it curls back to reveal the solitary, orange to amber, raspberry-like fruit, which is edible and prized for jams and jellies.

Top: Rugose leaves are palmately five-lobed (female flower shown). **Middle:** The male flower's many stamens can be seen in this close-up. **Bottom:** Solitary orange fruit resembles raspberries.

Rose family / Rosaceae

Purple-flowering raspberry

Rubus odoratus

Flowering raspberry, thimbleberry

Introduced Species

VITAL STATISTICS

Maximum height: 2 metres
Flowering season: June and July

HABITAT: Purple-flowering raspberry was introduced to New Brunswick from further west. Some authorities believe it is native to Nova Scotia (others disagree); considered rare, it is found mainly near and on old homesteads.

CHARACTERISTICS: A rambling shrub with peeling light brown bark, purple-flowering raspberry has spineless canes covered in somewhat sticky, bristly hairs. Unlike other shrubby *Rubus* species, its canes are perennial (not biennial), although some dieback may occur in severe winters.

The alternate, 12- to 25-centimetre-long leaves are often velvety on both surfaces, palmately lobed, and coarsely toothed. Undistinguished fall colour is yellowish green at best.

Flower buds are covered in sticky red hairs. They open to reveal fragrant, 3- to 5-centimetre-diameter, showy purple flowers, which are saucer-shaped and have five petals—reminiscent of a wild rose. Produced in clusters, they develop into somewhat flattened, red, raspberry-like fruit that is dry and tasteless.

Top: Leaves are palmately lobed and coarsely toothed. **Middle:** Purple flowers are saucer-shaped. **Bottom:** The fruit resembles a flattened raspberry.

Mixed Forest

Hardwood Forest

Disturbed

Grape family / Vitaceae
Riverbank grape
Vitis riparia
Frost grape

Native Species

VITAL STATISTICS
Maximum length: 7 metres
Flowering season: June to early July

HABITAT: Riverbank grape grows in thickets beside streams and rivers. It is native to New Brunswick; isolated populations in Nova Scotia are introduced.

CHARACTERISTICS: A tall vine with twining tendrils, riverbank grape has brown bark that often peels in long thin strips.

Alternate leaves are rounded and palmately lobed, 10 to 25 centimetres long, and coarsely toothed with hairs along the edges. The upper leaf surface is smooth; the lower often has hairs along the veins. Fall colour is yellow.

Sprays of fragrant, minute, green flowers are produced opposite the leaves. They develop into clusters of small blue-black berries that taste sour but are edible and make delicious jelly.

Northern fox grape (*V. labrusca*), native to New England, is now naturalized in Nova Scotia and New Brunswick. Its branchlets and new leaves are densely pubescent. Mature leaves may lose upper surface hair but remain pale and felted on the underside.

Top: Rounded leaves are coarsely toothed. **Middle:** The fruit resembles commercial grapes but is smaller. **Bottom:** Northern fox grape leaves have pale felted undersides, as seen on the upper central leaves.

Native Species

Heath family / Ericaceae

Common pipsissewa
Chimaphila umbellata
Common prince's pine, pipsissewa

HABITAT: Common pipsissewa grows in dry, mossy, coniferous or mixed forest. It is widespread in New Brunswick but uncommon in Nova Scotia and on Prince Edward Island.

CHARACTERISTICS: This low, colonial, evergreen sub-shrub has unbranched stems that reach from 10 to 30 centimetres in height.

Common pipsissewa leaves are spoon-shaped, dark green, and glossy. They have a leathery texture and toothed edges, can be 3 to 7 centimetres long, and are produced in whorls of three or four.

In July, a single flower stem arises at the tip of leafy stems. Five-petalled, nodding, white or pink blooms appear in an umbel of three to eight flowers. Petals often bend backward. The fruit is a globular capsule that often persists through winter.

VITAL STATISTICS
Maximum height: 30 centimetres
Flowering season: July

Top: Teeth on the spoon-shaped leaves are mainly on outside edges. Note whorls of three or four leaves. **Middle:** This white-flowered specimen has recurved petals. **Bottom:** Globular fruit grows on erect stalks.

Coniferous Forest

Mixed Forest

167

Heath family / Ericaceae
Sheep laurel
Kalmia angustifolia
Lambkill, dwarf laurel

Native Species

VITAL STATISTICS
Maximum height: 1.5 metres
Flowering season: Late May to mid-July

HABITAT: Throughout the Maritimes, sheep laurel grows on barrens, rocky pastures, recently burned sites, and dry bogs.

CHARACTERISTICS: Sheep laurel is a broad-leaved, evergreen, suckering shrub that can reach 1.5 metres in height. Stems are smooth and reddish brown.

Leaves are hairless and oblong to elliptical. Generally produced in whorls of three, they are 2 to 5 centimetres long with untoothed, somewhat revolute edges. New leaves are often tinted bronze, becoming green to blue-green; in winter, leaves can take on red to brown tints.

Flowers appear in lateral clusters below the newest set of leaves. Rose pink and saucer-shaped, they have five lobes. Each stamen is set into a cup on the corolla and springs outward when touched. Blossoms appear from late May through mid-July. The fruit is a small rounded capsule at the end of a wiry stalk; old capsules may persist all winter.

Sheep laurel roots produce phytotoxins (making this plant "allelopathic"), which can suppress the growth of nearby species.

This species is highly toxic to livestock and humans.

Top: Untoothed elliptical leaves are produced in whorls of three. **Middle:** Sheep laurel flowers grow in clusters. **Bottom:** The globular seed capsules grow on wiry stalks.

Native Species

Loosestrife family / Lythraceae
Swamp loosestrife
Decodon verticillatus
Water-willow

HABITAT: Swamp loosestrife, an Atlantic Coastal Plain species, grows in shallow bog pools and along lakeshores. It is rare in New Brunswick (known only in a few southwestern locations). In Nova Scotia it is mainly found in the counties of Digby, Shelburne, and Queens; it is not native to Prince Edward Island.

CHARACTERISTICS: Swamp loosestrife resembles an herbaceous perennial with a somewhat woody base. It is usually rooted in water or saturated soil. Bark at the plant base feels spongy.

Herbaceous upper stems die back in winter. Summer stems are smooth with longitudinal ridges; they are green with a red tint in early summer and redden more as the season progresses. Very flexible, they often arch to touch the soil, where they can root into new plants.

Leaves are paired or in a whorl of three or four. Lance-shaped, they are 5 to 15 centimetres long with smooth edges. In fall, they turn bright pink-red.

Five-petalled pink flowers are produced in clusters among the upper leaf axils. Stamens and pistil are longer than the petals, giving the flower a pincushion-like appearance. Flowers bloom in late summer; globular, pink-tinted capsules with a star-like crown (calyx remnants) follow.

VITAL STATISTICS
Maximum height: 3 metres
Flowering season: July and August

Top: Swamp loosestrife's flexible stems reflect their other common name: water-willow.
Bottom: Flowers are produced in clusters among the upper leaf axils.

Wetlands

Buttercup family / Ranunculaceae
Purple clematis
Clematis occidentalis
Northern blue clematis, western blue clematis

Native Species

VITAL STATISTICS
Maximum length: 3 metres
Flowering season: May to June

HABITAT: Purple clematis is an uncommon species in New Brunswick, very rare in Nova Scotia (one known location), and absent in Prince Edward Island. It grows on rocky slopes and in open woods, primarily in limestone regions.

CHARACTERISTICS: A climbing or sprawling vine, purple clematis has smooth, thin, brown stems. Somewhat angled in cross-section, stems have longitudinal ridges and swollen "joints" where paired buds or leaves are located. New stems are fuzzy and purple-tinted.

The opposite leaves are trifoliate with 3- to 6-centimetre-long, heart-shaped leaflets. The leaflet edges may be smooth or shallowly toothed. New leaves are fuzzy but become smooth as they mature.

Flowers are solitary and nodding, held atop 5- to 15-centimetre-long stalks. The four purple-blue petals are actually petal-like sepals. Their outer surfaces are sparsely fuzzy. Each measures 3.5 to 6 centimetres long. They later develop into tufted clusters of seeds with long feathery tails.

Top: Each leaf is composed of three heart-shaped leaflets. **Middle:** The four "petals" of each flower are actually petal-like sepals. **Bottom:** Each seed has a long plumose "tail."

Native Species

Buttercup family / Ranunculaceae

Virginia clematis
Clematis virginiana
Virgin's-bower

HABITAT: Virginia clematis grows on rocky slopes, along streams and rivers, in ravines and thickets, and at the edge of woodlands throughout the Maritimes.

CHARACTERISTICS: A climbing or tangled vine, Virginia clematis has smooth, thin, brown stems. Somewhat angled in cross-section, the stems have longitudinal ridges and swollen "joints" where paired buds or leaves are located. Young stems are often slightly hairy and tinted purple.

Trifoliate leaves are opposite on the stems. Each leaflet is heart- to egg-shaped and has coarsely jagged teeth. New leaves are pubescent, older leaves are smooth (with scattered hairs on the underside). New foliage may be bronze-tinted.

Plants are dioecious. Fragrant flowers are produced in compact axillary clusters of many 1.5- to 3-centimetre-diameter creamy white flowers. Each bloom has four petal-like sepals, which are hairy on the outside, and a starburst of stamens. Female flowers develop silky clusters of seeds that have feathery tails.

VITAL STATISTICS
Maximum length: 5 metres
Flowering season: August

Mixed Forest | Hardwood Forest | Wetlands

Top: Each leaflet is egg-shaped with coarsely toothed edges. **Middle:** Flowers are produced in clusters; the four "petals" are actually petal-like sepals. **Bottom:** Seeds with feathery tails are produced in silky clusters.

Maple family / Aceraceae
Manitoba maple
Acer negundo
Box elder

Introduced Species

VITAL STATISTICS
Maximum height: 18 metres
Flowering season: May

HABITAT: Manitoba maple is native to western North America but has been planted as an ornamental throughout the Maritimes. It is now established in the wild, as well, and is considered an invasive species.

CHARACTERISTICS: This medium-sized deciduous tree has an irregular crown and, often, multiple trunks. Manitoba maple bark is dark grey and furrowed. Young stems are green with a purple tint but frequently become shiny reddish brown. The white waxy coating on the stems is easily rubbed off. Older stems are smooth and light grey. Winter buds are rounded and covered in white hairs.

The opposite hairless leaves are pinnately compound with three to seven leaflets. They can be 15 to 40 centimetres long. Leaflets are elliptical and coarsely toothed or lobed along their edges. They are green on the upper surface and paler on the underside. Leaves turn yellow in autumn.

Plants are dioecious. Tiny yellow-green petal-less male and female flowers are produced in hanging clusters at the ends of the branchlets. Female trees develop hanging clusters of paired samaras; the wings form a narrow V-like angle. Seeds often remain attached to the tree well into the winter months, providing food for overwintering evening grosbeaks and pine grosbeaks.

Top: On this specimen, each leaf has five leaflets. **Middle:** Tiny yellow-green flowers hang in clusters. **Bottom:** Samaras have a V-like angle and remain on the trees after leaves have fallen.

Native Species

Olive family / Oleaceae
White ash
Fraxinus americana
American ash

HABITAT: White ash occurs in rich, moist, hardwood forests. It is fairly common in New Brunswick and Nova Scotia but rare on Prince Edward Island.

VITAL STATISTICS
Maximum height: 25 metres
Flowering season: Mid- to late May

CHARACTERISTICS: This tall deciduous tree generally has a narrow pyramidal shape and a single trunk. Young branches are stout, hairless, and light brown to grey-olive green. Older bark is light brown-grey and furrowed with ridges. The terminal winter bud resembles a light brown chocolate chip. Lateral buds are small and rounded; the leaf scar is U-shaped (on other Maritime ash species leaf scars are round).

White ash has opposite pinnate leaves composed of seven hairless oval leaflets with finely toothed or smooth (more common) edges. The upper leaf surface is dark green; the underside is pale. Each leaflet is attached to the main leaf stalk by its own stalk—unlike any other native or naturalized ash in the Maritimes. Leaves are 20 to 40 centimetres in length; fall colour is yellow, often with a purple tint.

Plants are dioecious. Male or female flowers—tiny, petal-less, and yellow to purple—generally grow from side or auxiliary (not terminal) buds on hairless stalks. The flower clusters appear as leaves unfurl. Female flowers develop into hanging clusters of paddle-shaped samaras; the wing is attached near the top of the seed.

Top: Each leaflet has its own distinct stalk joining it to the main leaf stalk. **Bottom:** The wing of each samara is attached at the top of the seed.

Mixed Forest

Hardwood Forest

Olive family / Oleaceae
European ash
Fraxinus excelsior
Common ash

Introduced Species

VITAL STATISTICS
Maximum height: 25 metres
Flowering season: May

HABITAT: European ash, native in Europe and western Asia, has been planted throughout the Maritimes as an ornamental. It can persist after a homestead disappears and self-seed on roadsides and in other disturbed areas.

CHARACTERISTICS: This wide-crowned deciduous tree can reach 25 metres. Smooth and greenish brown thick stems end in a relatively large black winter bud shaped like a chocolate chip. Lateral buds are smaller and rounded. Older bark on European ash is light grey-brown with vertical fissures.

Leaves are opposite, 20 to 35 centimetres long, and pinnately compound with seven to thirteen elliptical to lance-shaped and shallowly toothed leaflets. The upper leaf surface is dark green, hairless, and relatively shiny; the underside is paler. Leaves have no distinctive fall colour.

Plants are mostly dioecious—male and female flowers are generally on separate trees—but sometimes a single tree has flowers of both sexes or can be a different sex in different years. Tiny yellowish green flowers appear at branch ends and bloom as leaves unfurl. The fruit is a cluster of paddle-shaped samaras; the wing is often twisted.

The black winter buds and relatively shiny foliage distinguish this ash from others in the Maritimes.

Top: This specimen's compound leaves have 11 to 13 shallowly toothed leaflets. **Middle:** The wings of European ash samaras often have a twist, as here. **Bottom:** Tiny flowers are packed into dense clusters (males shown).

Native Species

Olive family / Oleaceae
Black ash
Fraxinus nigra
Swamp ash

HABITAT: Black ash grows in rich, damp to wet forests or beside lakes and larger rivers. Common in New Brunswick, it is scattered in Nova Scotia and rare on Prince Edward Island.

CHARACTERISTICS: A narrow, short, deciduous tree, black ash has smooth, stout, greyish green twigs with opposite, rounded, dark brown buds and a single relatively large terminal bud. Older bark is light grey and scaly.

Leaves are opposite and pinnately compound, with seven to eleven oval to lance-shaped leaflets. The leaf is 20 to 35 centimetres long; leaflets are shorter (7 to 12 centimetres), finely toothed, and taper to a narrow tip. Leaves are dark green and largely hairless, but small tufts of rusty hair grow on the underside where the leaf joins the main stalk, a feature that distinguishes black ash from the other ash species in the Maritimes. Fall colour is bright yellow.

Clusters of minute, purple to yellow, petal-less flowers are produced at the end of 1-centimetre-long hairless stalks as leaves unfurl. Male and female flowers can appear on separate trees, but usually trees produce male, female, and hermaphroditic flowers. The fruit is a brownish, green paddle-shaped samara, which grows in loose clusters. The wing extends the length of the seed and may be twisted.

VITAL STATISTICS
Maximum height: 15 metres
Flowering season: May to early June

Top: The hairless leaflets are finely toothed and taper to a narrow tip. **Bottom:** This species' samaras are typical of ash trees. Older bark is scaly, as here.

175

Olive family / Oleaceae
Red ash
Fraxinus pennsylvanica
Downy ash, green ash

Native Species

VITAL STATISTICS
Maximum height: 15 metres
Flowering season: May

HABITAT: Red ash grows on the edges and flood plains of large rivers and lakes. Uncommon in the Maritimes, it is native only to central Nova Scotia and near southwestern rivers of New Brunswick.

CHARACTERISTICS: Red ash is a small to medium-sized tree with an irregular rounded crown. Lower branches often swing down then back up at the tips. Bark is grey-brown and ridged. Younger grey to green-brown twigs are stout with a few downy hairs, a feature that distinguishes red ash from other ash species. Reddish brown terminal winter buds resemble fuzzy chocolate chips; lateral buds are smaller and rounder.

The opposite pinnate leaves (15 to 30 centimetres long) have seven (rarely, nine) oval to elliptical, 7- to 13-centimetre-long leaflets with smooth or finely toothed edges and no stalks. The upper leaf surface is light green and smooth; the paler underside may have downy hairs. Fall colour is yellow.

Plants are dioecious. Tiny yellow to purple petal-less male or female flowers are produced in loose clusters as leaves unfurl. Flower stalks are hairy, unlike those of other Maritime ash species. Female flowers develop into clusters of paddle-shaped samaras; the wing is attached at the narrow seed's midpoint.

Top: Leaves have seven leaflets that attach directly to the main leaf stalk. **Middle:** Hairy stems are a key diagnostic feature (female flowers shown). **Bottom:** Samaras are long and thin; bark is ridged.

176

Muskroot family / Adoxaceae

Common elderberry

Sambucus canadensis

American black elderberry, American elder, Canada elderberry

HABITAT: Common elderberry grows in open woods, old pastures, and damp thickets, as well as along shorelines throughout the Maritimes.

CHARACTERISTICS: This species is a multi-stemmed deciduous shrub. Common elderberry bark is brown, furrowed, and rough. Twigs are silvery grey and smooth with warty lenticels, and winter buds are small, pointed, and reddish brown.

The opposite leaves are pinnately compound and 12 to 28 centimetres long. Each leaf is composed of five to eleven elliptical to lance-shaped leaflets with finely toothed edges. Smooth on the upper surface, leaves are often hairy along the underside veins. They have no distinctive fall colour.

Flowers are produced in flat-topped clusters up to 20 centimetres across. Individual five-petalled blossoms are tiny, fragrant, and white. They become clusters of small red, then purple-black, juicy drupes. Fruit stalks are usually bright purple-red. (The berries are not eaten raw but can be used to make jellies, pies, or wine, if you can get to them before the birds do.)

Common elderberry leaves are toxic if ingested.

VITAL STATISTICS
Maximum height: 4 metres
Flowering season: Early July to August

Top: The leaves of this specimen are composed of 11 narrow leaflets. **Middle:** Flowers are produced in flat-topped clusters. **Bottom:** Black berries are attached by purple-red stalks.

Muskroot family / Adoxaceae
Red elderberry
Sambucus racemosa var. *pubens*
(formerly *S. pubens*)
Red-berried elder

Native Species

VITAL STATISTICS
Maximum height: 4 metres
Flowering season: May to June

HABITAT: Throughout the Maritimes, red elderberry grows in open woodlands, on rocky slopes and streamsides, and in disturbed areas such as roadsides and meadows.

CHARACTERISTICS: A deciduous shrub, red elderberry can reach 4 metres in height. Twigs are light brown to reddish brown; older stems have many raised warty lenticels. The trunk has scaly light brown bark. Winter buds are relatively large, globular, and green to purple.

Red elderberry is among the earliest shrubs to leaf in spring. Leaves are opposite and pinnately compound, with five or seven lance-shaped, sharply toothed leaflets. The upper leaflet surface is smooth; the underside is somewhat downy. Foliage has no distinctive fall colour.

Red elderberry produces a conical head of numerous small, five-petalled, creamy yellow to greenish yellow flowers in June, which are followed by loose clusters of small, bright red, berry-like drupes in July and August. It is one of the earliest-ripening shrubs in the Maritimes.

The leaves (if ingested) and fruit of this elderberry are toxic to humans but appreciated by fruit-eating birds.

Top: The leaves of this specimen are composed of five leaflets. Flowers appear in a dense conical head. **Bottom:** Small bright red fruit is produced in distinct clusters.

Rose family / Rosaceae
Dewberry
Rubus pubescens
Dwarf raspberry

HABITAT: Dewberry is a common woodland plant in the Maritimes. It prefers damp forests but also grows on damp rocky slopes, at wetland edges, and along shorelines.

CHARACTERISTICS: A sub-shrub with short slender stems, dewberry can be either flowering or vegetative. It appears to be herbaceous, but look closer: the loosely upright, flowering stems (10 to 25 centimetres long) are somewhat woody at the base. Trailing vegetative stems can grow to a metre or more; their tips often root to create new plants. Both stem types are softly hairy.

The alternate thin leaves are palmately compound with double-toothed edges and three or (less often) five leaflets. Leaves may have a few hairs and, in full sun, a bronze tint.

Dewberry produces five-petalled flowers that are white or pale pink. The petals, held at right angles to the calyx, meet at the tips or can be recurved; flowers appear singly or in a loose cluster of two to five blossoms. They develop into small, sweet-tasting, translucent, shiny red, raspberry-like fruit.

VITAL STATISTICS
Maximum height: 25 centimetres
Flowering season: June

Top: Leaves are palmately compound. **Middle:** Dewberry has modest white flowers. Bronzy leaves indicate this specimen grows in full sun. **Bottom:** The solitary translucent fruit resembles a raspberry.

Rose family / Rosaceae
Bristly dewberry
Rubus hispidus
Swamp dewberry, trailing blackberry

Native Species

VITAL STATISTICS
Maximum height: 2 metres
Flowering season: July

HABITAT: Bristly dewberry grows in damp hollows in open woods, in bogs, on barrens, and along roadsides throughout the Maritimes.

CHARACTERISTICS: A trailing shrub, bristly dewberry has canes up to 2 metres long that are covered in fine bristles (stems on the *obovalis* variety, however, are nearly smooth). Bark and bristles are pinkish red.

The alternate leaves are trifoliate with evergreen, leathery, sharply toothed, oval-shaped leaflets. Hairless, the leaves are shiny dark green on the upper surface and duller and often purple-tinted on the underside.

Flowers are produced in an elongate spray. Individual blossoms, white with five petals, develop into small, red to purple-black, raspberry-like fruit, which tastes sour and is not particularly juicy.

Northern dewberry (*R. flagellaris*, previously known as *R. recurvicaulis* or *R. plicatifolius*) is uncommon in the Maritimes. It has trailing stems and mostly trifoliate leaves, but foliage is deciduous. Canes have stout curved prickles. It blooms in June; the black fruit is juicy and sweet.

Top: Smooth shiny trifoliate leaves are evergreen. **Middle:** Flowers are produced in an elongate spray. **Bottom:** The small red to purple-black berries resemble raspberries.

Cashew family / Anacardiaceae
Poison ivy
Toxicodendron radicans
(formerly *Rhus radicans*)

HABITAT: Poison ivy frequents rocky woodland slopes, cliff bases, and talus but also occurs in damp thickets and on flood plains along rivers and lakes. It is found throughout the Maritimes, most often on calcareous substrates.

CHARACTERISTICS: It is now generally accepted that there are two subspecies of poison ivy: *T. radicans* subsp. *rydbergii* and *T. radicans* subsp. *radicans*. The former grows as a low shrub to 1.5 metres tall; the latter has vining stems that can reach 10 metres and grow along the ground or up tree trunks using aerial roots. Young poison ivy twigs are smooth and silvery grey-green. Winter buds are small, pointed, and scurfy. Aerial roots make older stems appear hairy.

Alternate leaves are trifoliate and 15 to 25 centimetres long. Each oval leaflet has irregularly toothed edges. The upper leaf surface is a smooth shiny green; the underside is pale and may have hairs along the veins. Spring foliage is bronzy red; leaves turn bright scarlet, yellow, or orange in the fall.

Tiny yellow-green, five-petalled flowers are produced in dense clusters. They develop into hanging clusters of small greenish white drupes that often persist through winter.

All parts of the plant are toxic and can cause severe, itchy dermatitis.

VITAL STATISTICS
Maximum length: 10 metres
Flowering season: Late June to mid-July

Top: This photo illustrates the folk rhyme for avoiding poison ivy's toxic foliage: "Leaves of three, leave it be." **Bottom:** Small yellow-green flowers are produced in a dense cluster.

Pea family / Fabaceae

Scotch broom
Cytisus scoparius

Common broom, English broom

Introduced Species

VITAL STATISTICS
Maximum height: 2.5 metres
Flowering season: June to July

HABITAT: This European shrub was planted throughout the Maritimes as an ornamental. Now occasionally naturalized, especially in coastal areas of southern Nova Scotia, Scotch broom is considered an invasive species.

CHARACTERISTICS: Scotch broom is a deciduous upright shrub that appears tangled. Bark is greenish brown with shallow fissures. Younger stems are green; twigs are smooth, green, and angled, with longitudinal grooves.

The alternate oval leaves—trifoliate or simple—have smooth edges and measure only 1 to 2.5 centimetres long. The upper surface is green and smooth; the underside is pale and fuzzy. Leaves turn yellow in the fall.

Solitary or paired flowers, yellow and pea-like, are produced along upper stems—a wand-like arrangement. They develop into fuzzy-edged, brown pea-pods that are 2.5 to 4 centimetres long.

A second naturalized pea relative—Siberian peashrub (*Caragana arborescens*)—is found in Fredericton and St. Andrew's, New Brunswick. An upright shrub (to 4 metres), it has smooth golden green bark, small pinnate leaves, scattered spines, and loose clusters of yellow flowers (June).

Top: Scotch broom has tiny leaves, grooved green stems, and masses of yellow pea-like flowers. **Middle:** Seedpods are fuzzy; note the small trifoliate leaves on upper twigs. **Bottom:** Siberian peashrub has pinnate leaves and small clusters of yellow pea-like flowers.

Grape family / Vitaceae

Virginia creeper
Parthenocissus quinquefolia
Woodbine

Introduced Species

HABITAT: Virginia creeper is native to eastern North America but introduced in the Maritimes (as an ornamental vine). It is occasionally found in disturbed areas, such as roadsides and scrubland near towns and cities.

CHARACTERISTICS: This deciduous vine clings by aerial roots and tendrils that end in rounded pads. Virginia creeper bark is brown and hairy (a result of aerial roots). Twigs are smooth and grey-brown; pale lenticels and tendrils are opposite the leaves. Winter buds are pointed and orange-red.

Hairless alternate leaves—palmately compound with five leaflets—are 10 to 20 centimetres across. The oval leaflets have coarsely toothed edges; the upper surface is shiny green and the underside is paler. New leaves are often bronze-tinted. In autumn foliage turns bright red.

Minute, green, five-petalled flowers are produced in elongate clusters at the ends of long stems. They develop into tiny (5- to 7-millimetre) blue-back berries that resemble miniature grapes. **The fruit is mildly toxic to humans.**

Thicket creeper (*P. inserta*) is a similar species but its tendrils lack the adhesive rounded pads and actually twine around other vegetation. Leaf undersides are finely hairy, and flowers are produced in loose rounded (not elongate) clusters.

VITAL STATISTICS
Maximum length: 20 metres
Flowering season: June and July

Top: Hairless leaves have five coarsely toothed leaflets. **Bottom:** The fruit resembles tiny grapes.

Rose family / Rosaceae
Blackberry species
Rubus species

Native Species

VITAL STATISTICS
Maximum height: 2 metres
Flowering season: Mid-June to July

HABITAT: Several species of blackberries grow throughout the Maritimes in open woods and damp thickets and along roadsides and shorelines. Because the various species share similar traits, they are described here as a group.

CHARACTERISTICS: All blackberries form thick colonies of suckering, upright to arching canes. Canes live for two years; they are unbranched the first year and grow short side branches, which produce flowers and fruit, in the second. Canes die after fruit production.

Canada blackberry (*R. canadensis*) canes reach 2 metres in height and are mostly smooth or have scattered prickles. Pennsylvanian blackberry (*R. pensilvanicus*) and Alleghaney blackberry (*R. alleghiensis*) canes are a similar size but have more bristles. Bristly blackberry (*R. setosus*) canes are shorter (under 1 metre) and have many hairs or soft bristles.

Leaves of all species are alternate and palmately compound with (usually) five coarsely toothed leaflets. Both the upper and lower leaflet

Top: Palmately compound leaves have leaflets with coarsely toothed edges (Canada blackberry shown). **Bottom:** Blackberry fruit growing on short side branches on second-year canes (Canada blackberry shown).

surfaces are essentially hairless on the Canada blackberry, hairy only along the lower veins on bristly blackberry, and finely hairy on the undersides of Pennsylvanian and Alleghaney blackberry. The latter species is distinguished by sticky, hairy glands on flower and fruit stalks. Fall foliage is generally unremarkable on all species; plants are sometimes partially evergreen, although some years leaves may turn red to purple depending on fall frost.

Older literature cites *R. elegantulus* and *R. vermontanus* in the Maritimes, but these are now considered synonyms of *R. canadensis* and *R. setosus* respectively.

Blackberries produce clusters of up to 25 white, 2- to 4-centimetre-diameter, five-petalled flowers. The edible fruit is an aggregate of small, attached, black drupes that ripen in September and October.

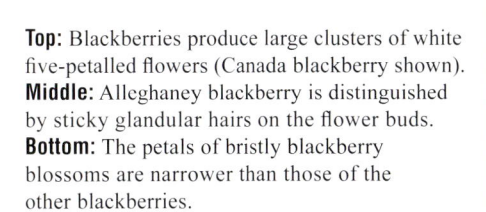

Top: Blackberries produce large clusters of white five-petalled flowers (Canada blackberry shown).
Middle: Alleghaney blackberry is distinguished by sticky glandular hairs on the flower buds.
Bottom: The petals of bristly blackberry blossoms are narrower than those of the other blackberries.

Walnut family / Juglandaceae
Butternut
Juglans cinerea
White walnut

Native Species

VITAL STATISTICS
Maximum height: 20 metres
Flowering season: Mid-May to mid-June

HABITAT: In the Maritimes, butternut is native only to New Brunswick, where it occurs in rich hardwood forests mainly in the Saint John and Miramichi river valleys.

CHARACTERISTICS: Butternut is a small to medium-sized deciduous tree with ash grey, ridged and furrowed bark. Older stems are stout, grey-brown, and smooth with many fine lenticels. New branchlets are covered in downy hair. Winter buds are rounded and fuzzy, covered in yellow-brown hair. Leaf scars are distinctly three-lobed.

The alternate leaves are pinnately compound with seven to seventeen elliptical leaflets. Leaves are 40 to 70 centimetres long—the longest of any native Maritimes tree. Finely toothed leaflets attach directly to the main leaf stem—except the terminal one, which is distinctly stalked. New leaves are yellow-green and rugose; they turn dark green but become yellow in autumn. Leaves are finely hairy, especially on the underside.

Plants are monoecious. Male flowers—long yellow-green catkins—are at the base of new spring growth. Female flowers are clusters of red fuzzy pistils at the ends of new spring growth. They develop into a cluster of one to five green, lemon-shaped, sticky, fuzzy husks up to 5 centimetres wide. The fruit contains a single large edible nut, which resembles a brain.

Butternut canker, a deadly disease, may limit this species' distribution in the future.

Top: Butternut leaflets have finely toothed edges. **Bottom:** The fruit takes the form of fuzzy green husks.

Rose family / Rosaceae
Wild red raspberry
Rubus idaeus

Raspberry, red raspberry

Native Species

HABITAT: Throughout the Maritimes, wild red raspberry grows in disturbed sites and shrubby thickets, and at forest edges.

CHARACTERISTICS: Wild red raspberry forms colonies of suckering canes that can be 2 metres tall. Each cane lives for two years. In the first year they have no branches; in the second they grow short side branches that produce flowers and fruit. Canes are covered in prickles and bristles.

The alternate leaves are compound with three to seven oval leaflets that narrow to a pointed tip. The hairless leaflets are darker green on the upper surface and densely hairy and paler on the underside. Leaf edges have coarse teeth, and the entire leaflet looks wrinkled. Foliage has no distinctive fall colour.

Clusters of 1.5-centimetre-long, whitish green, five-petalled flowers are produced mostly in July. The almost indiscernible petals are short-lived. The calyx is bristly. The fruit is an aggregate of small, attached, red drupes that ripen through August. They are edible and popular for pies and preserves or eating fresh.

VITAL STATISTICS
Maximum height: 2 metres
Flowering season: Late June to July

Top: Pinnate leaves have five rugose, toothed leaflets. **Middle:** Greenish white flowers have almost indiscernible petals. Note the bristly calyx on the unopened flower (lower right). **Bottom:** The "berry" is actually many small red drupes joined to make a single fruit.

Rose family / Rosaceae
Smooth rose
Rosa blanda
Meadow rose

VITAL STATISTICS
Maximum height: 2 metres
Flowering season: June to early August

HABITAT: Smooth rose grows on rocky shores and gravelly slopes. It is common in New Brunswick, known only in Queens County on Prince Edward Island, and rare in Nova Scotia (found only in the Sydney area).

CHARACTERISTICS: A suckering deciduous shrub, smooth rose varies in height from 70 centimetres in windswept locations to 2 metres in sheltered sites. Cane bases have needle-like prickles, which are scattered or absent elsewhere on the stems.

The alternate leaves are pinnately compound with five to seven elliptical, toothed leaflets. Dull and smooth on the upper surface, leaflets are fine and densely hairy on the underside.

Flowers—solitary or in clusters—are 4 to 6 centimetres in diameter, have five pink petals, and are highly fragrant. They develop into 1- to 1.5-centimetre, globular to oval, red hips, which can be used to make jelly or rosehip tea. The fruit often persists through much of the winter.

Top: Leaves have a dull finish on the upper surface. **Middle:** The five-petalled flowers are often solitary. **Bottom:** Stem prickles are nearly absent.

Native Species

Rose family / Rosaceae
Carolina rose
Rosa carolina
Pasture rose

HABITAT: Carolina rose grows throughout the Maritimes on open rocky and sandy areas, in dry pastures, and along roadsides.

CHARACTERISTICS: This low suckering deciduous shrub rarely reaches 1 metre in height. The lower section of a Carolina rose cane has a few prickles; the upper section has a pair of straight, narrow prickles at the base of each leaf, and a few more between the leaves. The smooth stems are green or purple-tinted.

The alternate, pinnately compound leaves have five to nine hairless leaflets, which are coarsely toothed with five to fifteen teeth on each edge above the middle. Note that the similar swamp rose (*R. palustris*) has more teeth (12 to 25) above the leaflet centre. The dull green leaves turn red or orange in autumn.

Fragrant pink flowers are mostly solitary and are 4 to 5.5 centimetres in diameter. They develop into globular red hips, which can be used to make jelly, and often persist through much of the winter.

VITAL STATISTICS
Maximum height: 1 metre
Flowering season: Late June to July

Top: Each leaflet edge has 5 to 15 teeth beyond the midpoint. **Middle:** Flowers usually appear singly on this wild rose species. **Bottom:** Straight prickles grow near the base of each leaf.

Rose family / Rosaceae
Shining rose
Rosa nitida
Northeastern rose, swamp rose

VITAL STATISTICS
Maximum height: 1 metre
Flowering season: July to August

HABITAT: Shining rose occurs throughout the Maritimes in a variety of moist habitats, including acid wetlands, stream and pond banks, and damp thickets.

CHARACTERISTICS: This thorny plant rarely reaches a metre in height. Stems are red with many purple-red bristles and a few larger prickles. The pinnately compound, alternate leaves have seven to nine elliptical, toothed, shiny dark green leaflets. Fall foliage turns orange and red.

In July and August, shining rose produces highly fragrant, five-petalled, 4- to 6-centimetre-diameter, dark pink flowers, singly or in small clusters. Stiff glandular hairs cover the flower stalk. In fall, it produces globular, bristly red hips. The calyx remnants give the hips a "crown" (or bump, if the calyx drops off). The fruit often persists through winter and can be used to make jelly.

Prickly rose (*R. acicularis*) is a rare species found in Nova Scotia and New Brunswick. It also has bristly, prickly stems, but leaf undersides are slightly sticky and appear powdery. Its hips are tapered and smooth.

Top: Dark green leaves are highly glossy; flowers have five pink petals. **Middle:** Shining rose stems are densely covered in bristles and prickles. **Bottom:** The globular hips are also covered in bristles.

Rose family / Rosaceae

Swamp rose
Rosa palustris

VITAL STATISTICS
Maximum height: 2.5 metres
Flowering season: July

HABITAT: Swamp rose, an Atlantic Coastal Plain species, grows in wet thickets, marshes, and swamps, and along stream and lake margins. Rare in southern Nova Scotia, it is extremely rare in southern New Brunswick and absent from Prince Edward Island.

CHARACTERISTICS: Swamp rose, a suckering deciduous shrub, has many stout prickles at the base of its canes. Paired prickles—stout, broad-based, and curving downward—also grow at each leaf base. Stems are smooth and green or purple-tinted.

Alternate pinnate leaves have five to nine, dull green, finely toothed, elliptical leaflets. Above the midpoint of each leaflet are 12 to 25 teeth—the similar Carolina rose (*R. carolina*) has only 5 to 15. Leaflets are finely hairy along the mid-rib. Fall colour is a mix of red and orange.

Fragrant, pink, five-petalled flowers (4 to 5.5 centimetres across) are produced singly or in small clusters. They develop into globular to oval-shaped red hips that can persist through winter. Smooth or covered in stiff glandular hairs, hips can be used to make jelly.

Top: Dull green leaves are finely toothed. **Middle:** The upper prickles are paired and curve downward. **Bottom:** These rosehips are covered in stiff glandular hairs.

Rose family / Rosaceae
Shrub rose species
Rosa species

Introduced Species

VITAL STATISTICS
Maximum height: 2.5 metres
Flowering season: July to August

HABITAT: Several non-native ornamental roses can be found in untended urban areas and roadsides throughout the Maritimes. They include briar rose (*R. rubiginosa*), cinnamon rose (*R. cinnamomea*), dog rose (*R. canina*), French rose (*R. gallica*), glaucous rose (*R. glauca*), multiflora rose (*R. multiflora*), and rugosa rose (*R. rugosa*).

CHARACTERISTICS: "Wild" shrub roses produce upright to arching canes 2 metres or more in height—they are generally much taller than native Maritime roses. Canes have many broad-based prickles (except rugosa rose, which has thinner, straighter prickles).

The alternate leaves are pinnately compound with five to nine toothed leaflets. The leaf surface is smooth in all except rugosa rose, which has wrinkly and veiny leaves. Glaucous rose has distinctly reddish purple foliage.

Top: Multiflora rose produces an open spray of relatively small white flowers. **Middle:** Distinctively, the leaves of glaucous rose are purple-grey. **Bottom:** Briar rose produces clusters of pale pink flowers.

Flowers can be produced singly but more commonly are in loose clusters. Multiflora rose produces an open spray of many flowers. Flower diameter ranges from 2 to 3 centimetres (multiflora) to 9 centimetres (rugosa). Generally, blossoms have five petals in shades of pink or white. Some rugosa roses and the cinnamon rose have double flowers. All are highly fragrant. July is the main blooming season, but a few blossoms may appear later in the summer.

In autumn, all species produce orange to red, berry-like hips, from 5 millimetres (multiflora) to 3 centimetres (rugosa) in diameter. Hips generally retain the old calyx, giving them a "crown" (or a bump, if it drops off), and can persist into early winter. Hips from some species of shrub rose can be used to make jellies or rosehip tea.

Top: Rugosa rose leaves are veiny; their hips are the largest of the Maritimes' naturalized rose species. **Middle:** Cinnamon rose often has double flowers. **Bottom:** Multiflora rosehips are the smallest of any naturalized Maritimes rose species.

Rose family / Rosaceae
Virginia rose
Rosa virginiana
Pasture rose

Native Species

VITAL STATISTICS
Maximum height: 2 metres
Flowering season: July

HABITAT: Virginia rose is the most common rose in the Maritimes. It grows in a range of habitats, including forest clearings, rocky slopes, barrens, pastures, and roadsides.

CHARACTERISTICS: A somewhat suckering shrub, Virginia rose can reach 2 metres in height. Stem bases are prickly; the upper portions are smooth but for a pair of downward-curving prickles at the base of each leaf. New stems are green or purple-tinted.

The compound leaves are alternate, relatively shiny, and have five to eleven elliptical, hairless leaflets, toothed only on the outer three-quarters of the leaf edge. Fall foliage turns red and purple.

Five-petalled flowers are 5 to 7 centimetres in diameter and range from pale to dark pink. Highly fragrant, they appear singly or in small clusters in July and August.

The fruit—a red hip—has a few bristles. The calyx remnants form a "crown," which can fall off, leaving only a bump. Hips can persist into the winter and be used to make jelly.

Top: Pink flowers have five petals. **Middle:** Smooth upper stems have a pair of downward-curving prickles at each leaf base; note how the leaves shine. **Bottom:** The crowns of these ripe hips have fallen off, leaving only a bump.

Rose family / Rosaceae

American mountain-ash
Sorbus americana

Dogberry

VITAL STATISTICS
Maximum height: 10 metres
Flowering season: Late June to mid-July

HABITAT: American mountain-ash grows in a variety of habitats throughout the Maritimes, including on rocky slopes, in woodlands, on barrens, along roadsides, and on old burned sites.

CHARACTERISTICS: This shrub-like, small deciduous tree grows from 6 to 10 metres tall. Winter buds are alternate, sticky, and shiny wine red to black. Twigs and bark are smooth and mottled grey with elongate, slightly raised lenticels.

The alternate leaves are 15 to 25 centimetres long and compound. Each of the 11 to 17 lance-shaped, finely toothed leaflets gradually narrows to a pointed tip and is four to five times as long as it is wide. The upper leaf surface is somewhat shiny; the underside is pale green. Fall colour is a mix of yellow, orange, and red.

Flat-topped clusters of tiny, white, five-petalled flowers are produced in late June and July, followed by relatively shiny, orange-red, berry-like pomes (September and October). The calyx remnants leave a star-like scar.

Native and naturalized mountain-ash fruit is edible but acidic; all species provide food for fruit-eating birds.

Top: Lance-shaped leaflets are somewhat shiny on the upper surface. **Middle:** Flowers are produced in dense, flat-topped clusters. **Bottom:** Relatively shiny fruit is also in dense clusters; note star-like tips left by calyx remnants.

Rose family / Rosaceae
European mountain-ash
Sorbus aucuparia
Rowan, rowan tree

Introduced Species

VITAL STATISTICS
Maximum height: 12 metres
Flowering season: June

HABITAT: This species, native throughout Europe, is a popular landscape tree in the Maritimes. Its ability to self-seed (aided by fruit-eating, seed-dispersing birds) has spread European mountain-ash to roadsides, pathways, scrubland, and even forested areas in and near larger communities.

CHARACTERISTICS: A small deciduous tree, European mountain-ash is only rarely shrub-like (multi-trunked). Relatively large, brown to black winter buds have, distinctively, conspicuous grey to white hairs.

The alternate compound leaves have oval-shaped leaflets with toothed edges. When leaves emerge, the underside is covered in fine white hairs. As they mature, the upper surface becomes matte green and the underside white with fine pubescence. Leaflets are mostly dull-tipped. Foliage has no distinctive fall colour.

June flowers resemble those of the two native Maritimes mountain-ash species—they are flat-topped clusters of minute, creamy white blossoms. They produce dull orange-red, edible (though acidic), berry-like pomes in September. The calyx remnants give the fruit a star-like scar. The fruit is an important food source for fruit-eating birds.

Top: Newly emerging leaves are covered in pale brown hairs. **Middle:** Flowers are produced in a dense, flat-topped cluster. **Bottom:** Clustered fruit has a dull finish: note the star-like tips created by calyx remnants.

Rose family / Rosaceae
Showy mountain-ash
Sorbus decora
Northern mountain-ash, dogberry

HABITAT: Throughout the Maritimes, showy mountain-ash grows in woodlands and on rocky slopes, barrens, and old burned sites. It is more common near seacoasts than inland.

CHARACTERISTICS: Showy mountain-ash is a small shrub-like tree of 3 to 6 metres. Winter buds are alternate, distinctly sticky, and shiny wine red to black. Twigs and bark are smooth and grey with elongate, slightly raised lenticels.

The alternate, pinnately compound leaves are 15 to 25 centimetres long and have 11 to 17 lance-shaped, finely toothed leaflets. Each leaflet—two to three times longer than its width—abruptly narrows to a pointed tip. The upper leaf surface is dull blue- to grey-green; the underside is pale green and may have a few fine hairs in spring. Fall colour is a mix of yellow, orange, and red.

Flat-topped clusters of tiny, white, five-petalled flowers are produced from mid-June to mid-July, followed by orange-red, berry-like pomes in September. The calyx remnants create a star-like scar. Acidic but edible, the pomes are a food source for fruit-eating birds.

VITAL STATISTICS
Maximum height: 10 metres
Flowering season: Mid-June to mid-July

Top: Dull grey-green leaves have elliptical leaflets. **Middle:** Flowers are produced in dense, flat-topped clusters. **Bottom:** Fruit is also in dense clusters; note the blue-green tint of these leaves.

Rose family / Rosaceae
False spiraea
Sorbaria sorbifolia
Ural false spiraea

Introduced Species

VITAL STATISTICS
Maximum height: 2.5 metres
Flowering season: Late June through July

HABITAT: A native of Siberia, false spiraea is commonly grown as an ornamental throughout the Maritimes. Its suckering habit has allowed it to spread in a few areas to disturbed ground and roadsides.

CHARACTERISTICS: False spiraea is a deciduous suckering shrub that can reach 2.5 metres. Bark is smooth and light brown; twigs can be smooth or slightly pubescent. Winter buds are oval and reddish brown.

The alternate leaves are pinnately compound, 20 to 30 centimetres long, with 11 to 17 lance-shaped leaflets. False spiraea is among the earliest shrubs to leaf; new foliage is often tinted red. Leaves are sharply double-toothed with a smooth upper surface and smooth or fuzzy undersides. Fall foliage is yellow.

Plants produce upright or arching sprays of numerous tiny, five-petalled, white flowers. The spray can be 15 to 25 centimetres long. Flowers fade and develop into a dense cluster of star-shaped capsules that often remain attached through the winter.

Top: False spiraea can grow in large clumps. **Middle:** Leaflets are sharply toothed. **Bottom:** Each arching spray has many small flowers.

Cashew family / Anacardiaceae
Staghorn sumac
Rhus typhina
Velvet sumac

Native Species

VITAL STATISTICS
Maximum height: 6 metres
Flowering season: June and July

HABITAT: Throughout the Maritimes, staghorn sumac grows along dry forest edges, rocky slopes, and old pastures.

CHARACTERISTICS: Staghorn sumac is a broad suckering and forking shrub with multiple stems. New stems are stout, brown, and covered in a velvet-like coating of fine hairs reminiscent of deer antlers. Old trunks are scaly and grey-brown. Winter buds are small and pointed.

The alternate leaves are pinnately compound with up to 31 lance-shaped leaflets. Toothed leaflets can be 5 to 12 centimetres long. The leaf stalk is covered in hairs. The entire leaf can reach up to 60 centimetres in length, making staghorn sumac the largest-leaved native shrub in the Maritimes. In autumn, leaves turn orange and red.

Plants are dioecious. Flowers are minute and yellow-green, tightly packed into dense, upright clusters of up to 20 centimetres in length. Female flowers develop into a dense, upright cluster of fuzzy red drupes that often persist through winter.

Poison sumac (*Toxicodendron vernix*) is restricted to the Tefler Lake area in Queens County, Nova Scotia. It resembles staghorn sumac but has smooth twigs and shiny, hairless, smooth-edged, pinnate leaves (seven to thirteen leaflets per leaf). **All parts of the plant are toxic and can cause severe dermatitis.**

Top: Large compound leaves have many toothed leaflets; note the ripe red fruit. **Middle:** Flowers form tight upright clusters. **Bottom:** Stems have a velvet-like coating of fine hair.

Mixed Forest

Hardwood Forest

Disturbed

199

Rose family / Rosaceae
Sorbaronia hybrids
X *Sorbaronia* hybrids

Black mountain-ash

Native Species

VITAL STATISTICS
Maximum height: 5 metres
Flowering season: Mid-June to mid-July

HABITAT: Plants called sorbaronia include a collection of natural hybrids of chokeberry (*Aronia* species) and mountain-ash (*Sorbus* species). Though rare, they appear in New Brunswick, where the two parents are found.

CHARACTERISTICS: These large multi-stemmed shrubs grow 3 to 5 metres tall. Reddish brown new twigs soon turn grey. Grey bark has a few raised lenticels. Narrow, pointed winter buds have shiny black scales and may be fringed with tawny hairs.

Leaves are pinnately compound. Oval leaflets are toothed mostly on the outer edges. On some specimens, a few (or all) leaflets are fused. Leaves are dark green and glossy on the upper surface; the underside is pale and lightly pubescent. Fall foliage is a mix of orange, red, and burgundy.

As on mountain-ash, flowers grow in flat-topped clusters—but blossoms are fewer and larger. Stamens are pink (as on the chokeberry parent). Flowers bloom from mid-June to mid-July; loose clusters of wine red, berry-like pomes follow (September and October). Calyx remnants leave a star-like scar on the fruit.

Top: Some sorbaronia have bizarrely shaped leaves with partially fused leaflets.
Middle: Flowers resemble mountain-ash blossoms but can be larger. Note the pink stamens, commonly seen on chokeberry.
Bottom: The fruit is similar to that of mountain-ash but larger, less profuse, and wine red.

Native Species

Rose family / Rosaceae

Shrubby cinquefoil

Dasiphora fruticosa
(formerly *Potentilla fruticosa*)

Bush cinquefoil, golden hardhack

HABITAT: Shrubby cinquefoil prefers open, damp, gravelly, rocky areas, especially on limestone substrates. It occurs in New Brunswick and Nova Scotia but is not native to Prince Edward Island.

CHARACTERISTICS: This dense deciduous shrub can grow in different forms, from prostrate to upright and rounded. Only rarely does shrubby cinquefoil exceed a metre in height. Older stems are reddish brown with exfoliating bark; finely pubescent young twigs are purple-red to purplish green.

Leaves are alternate and pinnately compound with five to seven, narrow, elliptical to lanceolate leaflets. Leaf edges are smooth and both surfaces are covered in fine hairs. Foliage has no distinctive fall colour.

Shrubby cinquefoil produces yellow, 2-centimetre-wide, five-petalled flowers at branch tips. Flowers are either single or in small clusters and have a long blooming season: from late June through August.

VITAL STATISTICS
Maximum height: 1 metre
Flowering season: Late June to August

Top: Shrubby cinquefoil commonly takes the form of a rounded low shrub. **Middle:** Leaves are pinnately compound with five lance-shaped leaflets. **Bottom:** Five-petalled yellow flowers are produced in small clusters.

Pea family / Fabaceae
Black locust
Robinia pseudoacacia
Common locust, yellow locust

Introduced Species

VITAL STATISTICS
Maximum height: 20 metres
Flowering season: June and July

HABITAT: This native of the southeastern United States has been planted as an ornamental throughout the Maritimes. It is now occasionally found as a naturalized species along roadsides near towns and cities.

CHARACTERISTICS: A large shrub or medium-sized tree, black locust is narrow with upright, often crooked, branches. It may sucker from the root to form larger clumps. Bark is grey to light brown with a ropy texture. Reddish brown stems are somewhat stout, zigzagged, and hairless. They often have a pair of spines at each leaf base. Tiny winter buds are located between the spines.

The alternate leaves are pinnately compound with 7 to 19 hairless, oval, smooth-edged leaflets of 2.5 centimetres. The entire leaf can be up to 30 centimetres long. Fall colour is insignificant to yellow.

The fragrant flowers are white and shaped like pea-blossoms. Produced in a hanging chain up to 12 centimetres long, they later develop brown pea-pods 5 to 10 centimetres in length.

Top: Pinnate leaves have smooth-edged leaflets. **Bottom:** White pea-like flowers are produced in a hanging chain.

Introduced Species

Pea family / Fabaceae
Clammy locust
Robinia viscosa

HABITAT: Clammy locust is native to the southeastern United States but has been planted as an ornamental throughout the Maritimes. It is now occasionally found as a naturalized species along roadsides near towns and cities.

CHARACTERISTICS: A large shrub or small tree, clammy locust can sucker from the root to form larger clumps. Bark is grey to light brown with a ropy texture. New stems are covered in reddish purple, glandular hairs. Winter buds are tiny and nondescript.

The alternate leaves are pinnately compound with 13 to 25 hairless, oval, smooth-edged leaflets that measure 2.5 centimetres long—and the whole leaf can reach up to 30 centimetres. Fall colour is yellow.

Flowers are pink, pea-blossom-shaped, and produced in dense hanging clusters. The flowers have no fragrance. They develop sticky brown pea-pods 5 to 10 centimetres long.

VITAL STATISTICS
Maximum height: 13 metres
Flowering season: June and July

Top: The compound leaves have smooth-edged oval leaflets. **Bottom:** Pink, fragrance-free, pea-like flowers are produced in a hanging chain.

Disturbed

WOODY SPECIES WITH AT-RISK STATUS

Several native woody plant species found in the Maritimes—tree and shrub—are currently at risk in the region. They are all listed in the following chart with their province-by-province status.

Generally, if a plant is designated as "at risk" in a province, it is because its range is severely restricted or because it grows only in a specific type of (localized) habitat. Designations can and do vary from one province to another.

Some designated plants are not given a full listing in this guide; some are only mentioned in the description of a similar species. The choice to minimize discussion of rare or endangered plants was made because they are infrequently encountered. In addition, limiting the scope helps make the book a more manageable size for carrying into the field. An asterisk (*) in the table denotes a species that is not mentioned in this book.

The at-risk designations shown in the chart follow *Wild Species 2010: The General Status of Species in Canada* by the Canadian Endangered Species Conservation Council (CESCC), 2012. Note that a species' status can change over time.

The CESCC uses three main categories of endangerment:
1. Species for which a formal, detailed risk assessment has been completed, through a Committee on the Status of Endangered Wildlife in Canada (COSEWIC) status assessment or a provincial or territorial equivalent, and which are deemed to be **at risk of extirpation or extinction**; such species have either Endangered or Threatened status (COSEWIC).
2. Species that **may be at risk of extirpation or extinction** and are therefore candidates for a detailed risk assessment by COSEWIC or a provincial or territorial equivalent.
3. Sensitive species, which are *not* believed to be at risk of immediate extirpation or extinction but **may require special attention or protection** to prevent them from becoming at risk.

Identifying a rare or endangered species can be an exciting event in the field. You are reminded never to pick or harm any uncommon or designated plant you encounter.

SPECIES	NB	NS	PEI
alpine bilberry / *Vaccinium uliginosum*	2	3	2
American witch-hazel / *Hamamelis virginiana*			2
* autumn willow / *Salix serissima*	2		
balsam poplar / *Populus balsamifera*			3
* bayberry willow / *Salix myricoides*	3		
* bearberry willow / *Salix uva-ursi*		2	
black ash / *Fraxinus nigra*		3	2
black willow / *Salix nigra*	3		
bog birch / *Betula pumila*		3	3
bog rosemary / *Andromeda polifolia*			2
* bog willow / *Salix pedicellaris*		3	
broom crowberry / *Corema conradii*	2		3
burr oak / *Quercus macrocarpa*	2		
butternut / *Juglans cinerea*	1		
Carolina rose / *Rosa carolina*			3
coastal sweet pepperbush / *Clethra alnifolia*		3	
common bearberry / *Arctostaphylos uva-ursi*			3
common buttonbush / *Cephalanthus occidentalis*	3	3	
dwarf bilberry / *Vaccinium caespitosum*		3	
dwarf white birch / *Betula minor*	3	3	
eastern baccharis tree / *Baccharis halimifolia*		2	
eastern hop-hornbeam / *Ostrya virginiana*			2
eastern leatherwood / *Dirca palustris*	2	2	
eastern white cedar / *Thuja occidentalis*		1	3
* entire-leaved mountain avens / *Dryas integrifolia*	2		
fan-leaved hawthorn / *Crataegus flabellata*		3	
Fernald's serviceberry / *Amelanchier fernaldii*	2		
fleshy hawthorn / *Crataegus succulenta*	3		
glandular birch / *Betula glandulosa*	2	2	
* grey-leaved willow / *Salix glauca*		2	
* hairy willow / *Salix vestita*		2	
highbush blueberry / *Vaccinium corymbosum*	3		
hobblebush / *Viburnum lantanoides*			2

SPECIES	NB	NS	PEI
jack pine / *Pinus banksiana*			3
Jones' hawthorn / *Crataegus jonesiae*	2		
Lapland diapensia / *Diapensia lapponica*		2	
Lapland rosebay / *Rhododendron lapponicum*		2	
* low blueberry willow / *Salix myrtillifolia*	2		
maple-leaved viburnum / *Viburnum acerifolium*	2		
meadow willow / *Salix petiolaris*			2
Nantucket serviceberry /*Amelanchier nantucketensis*		2	
* net-veined willow / *Salix reticulata*		2	
Newfoundland dwarf birch / *Betula michauxii*	2	3	
northern blueberry / *Vaccinium boreale*	2	2	
oval-leaved blueberry / *Vaccinium ovalifolium*		2	
partridgeberry / *Mitchella repens*			2
pinebarren golden heather / *Hudsonia ericoides*		3	2
pink crowberry / *Empetrum eamesii*		3	3
poison ivy / *Toxicodendron radicans*	3		
poison sumac / *Toxicodendron vernix*		2	
prickly rose / *Rosa acicularis*	2		
purple clematis / *Clematis occidentalis*		2	
Québec hawthorn / *Crataegus submollis*	3		
red ash / *Fraxinus pennsylvanica*		2	
rough hawthorn / *Crataegus scabrida*	3		
round-leaved dogwood / *Cornus rugosa*			2
sage willow / *Salix candida*	3	2	2
shrubby cinquefoil / *Dasiphora fruticosa*			2
silky dogwood / *Cornus amomum*	3		
silky willow / *Salix sericea*		2	
smooth alder / *Alnus serrulata*	3	3	
soapberry / *Shepherdia canadensis*	3	3	
squashberry / *Viburnum edule*		3	
staghorn sumac / *Rhus typhina*			2
swamp fly honeysuckle / *Lonicera oblongifolia*	3		
swamp loosestrife / *Decodon verticillatus*	2	3	2
Swedish bunchberry / *Cornus suecica*		3	
Virginia clematis / *Clematis virginiana*			3
white elm / *Ulmus americana*			3
woolly heather / *Hudsonia tomentosa*		2	

GLOSSARY

aerial roots: above-ground roots that help nourish and support a plant

allelopathy: a natural phenomenon in which one plant species produces chemicals that inhibit the growth of another species

anther: the tip of the stamen; anthers produce pollen

aril: a fleshy, brightly coloured seed covering

axil: the angle created by (and between) two leaves

basal sheath: a paper-like covering at the base of some pine-needle clusters

bill: the dried remnants of the pistil

bloom: a waxy, whitened surface coating

bract: a leaf (often modified) located immediately under a flower

branchlet: a smaller side branch that grows out of a larger branch

bristle: a stiff hair

burr: a seed or fruit with short, stiff bristles or hooks

calcareous: soil that contains calcium carbonate (limestone), often chalky

calyx: the outermost covering of a flower, which often protects the flower in the bud stage

catkin: a modified flower spike that is often scaly and usually unisexual (i.e., either male or female)

colonial: plants that form colonies (groups) through underground stems (rhizomes)

cordate: heart-shaped

corolla: flower petals

cutting: a portion of a plant snipped from a larger plant and put into soil or water to grow roots (also called a "slip")

deltoid: triangular in outline

dieback: the gradual dying of a plant shoot that usually starts at the tip, mainly caused by disease or environmental factors such as cold winds

dioecious: unisexual plants in which male and female flowers are on separate plants

disjunct: a plant population that is far removed from the main distribution of its species

drupe: a fleshy fruit with a stony seed at its centre (e.g., a peach)

drupelet: a small drupe

elongate(d): long or lengthened

endemic: plant populations that are confined to a single and relatively small geographic area

ericaceous: belonging to the heath family (Ericaceae)

escape: a non-native species that has become naturalized

felted: densely covered in fine hairs

filament: the stalk of the stamen, to which the anther is attached

fire-adapted species: plants that usually release their seeds only after they have been exposed to temperatures above 60°C (which occurs during most forest fires)

glandular: having glands that excrete a substance that makes stems or leaves sticky

globular: rounded

herbaceous: plants with stems that die back to the ground in winter

hermaphroditic: a flower that has both male and female parts

lanceolate: lance-shaped

leader: the primary or tallest stem or trunk on a single plant

leaf scars: the mark left behind on a stem after a leaf falls off

lenticel: corky, somewhat soft spots on young bark

linear: long and narrow with parallel edges

mid-rib: the central or main rib of a leaf, which runs from stem to tip

monoecious: species in which male and female flowers grow on the same plant

net veins: distinct veins on a leaf that form a net-like pattern

nodding: an upright stem or structure that droops at the tip

nutlet: a small nut

oblanceolate: lance-shaped with the widest part of the leaf at the tip (farthest from the stem)

oblong: two to three times longer than broad, with parallel sides

obovate: inverted egg-shaped: narrowest at the base, widest at the terminal end

orbicular: circular

ornamental: species that are planted to beautify gardens

ovate: egg-shaped

palmate: a lobed leaf with a hand-like silhouette

panicle: a loose cluster of flowers

pendant: hanging downward from a stem

persistent: continuing for a long time, such as fruit or leaves that remain on a plant well into winter

petiole: the stalk of a leaf

pioneer species: the first species to grow in disturbed sites (e.g., scraped, logged, or burned); usually shade-intolerant plants

pistil: the entire female portion of a flower, composed of the ovary (where seeds are produced), style (stalk), and stigma (pollen-receptive tip)

plumose: feather-like

pome: a fleshy fruit with several seeds at its centre (e.g., an apple)

prickle: a sharp, slender outgrowth from bark that is thinner than a thorn and not anchored as deeply in the branch

prostrate: growing flat along the ground

pubescent: covered in short, downy hairs (not as dense as "felted")

raceme: a cluster of flowers growing at the end of an elongate flower stalk

recurved: curving downward

reflexed: curled back toward the stem

reniform: kidney-shaped

reticulated: covered with distinct veins that interconnect in a net-like pattern (see also net veins)

revolute: rolled under (usually referring to the leaf edge)

rhizome: a prostrate or underground stem

rhombic: square-shaped

rugose: wrinkled

samara: a winged fruit

scurfy: bark or leaves that are covered in scale- or bran-like particles

seed head: a dense cluster of seeds

shatter: breaking apart while still attached to a tree (in reference to cones)

shrub: a plant that is typically shorter than 5 metres and has several stems smaller than 10 centimetres in diameter; branches occur near or at ground level

sinus: the cleft between two adjacent lobes on a leaf

slip: a portion of a plant snipped from a larger plant and put into soil or water to grow roots (also called a "cutting")

stamen: the male portion of a flower, which is composed of a filament (stalk) and anther (tip)

stigma: the pollen-receptive tip of the pistil (the female part of a flower)

stipule: a small leaf-like appendage at the base of a regular leaf

style: the narrow, elongate portion of a pistil (the female part of a flower)

sub-opposite: almost opposite

sub-shrub: a small shrub that appears almost herbaceous

substrate: a plant's growing medium—the soil

suckering: producing vegetative shoots from underground roots and rhizomes

taproot: a plant's main or primary root

tepal: the name for a "petal" on flowers (such as tulips) in which petals (corolla) and sepals (calyx) look identical

thorn: a sharp woody outgrowth from a stem that is anchored more deeply—and is often thicker—than a prickle

tree: a plant that can reach a minimum mature height of 5 metres and attain a minimum trunk diameter of 10 centimetres; branches are supported clear of the ground

umbel: a group of flowers that arises from a single point on the flower stalk, often resulting in flat-topped flower clusters

undulate(d): with a wavy edge

villous: having long silky hairs

MARITIMES WOODY PLANTS BY FAMILY

The following pages list all the woody plants in the Maritimes according to their taxonomic family relationship.
- Species found in all three Maritime provinces have no province cited after their name; species found in only one or two Maritimes provinces have the relevant location(s) listed.
- Species not mentioned in this book have been printed in grey type.
- Introduced species have an "(i)" after their name, as well as the relevant provincial initials if they are not introduced in all three Maritime provinces.

Taxaceae   **Yew family**
   Taxus canadensis   Canada yew

Pinaceae   **Pine family**
   Abies balsamea   balsam fir
   Larix decidua (i) NS   European larch (i) NS
   Larix laricina   tamarack
   Picea abies (i) NS   Norway spruce (i) NS
   Picea glauca   white spruce
   Picea mariana   black spruce
   Picea rubens   red spruce
   Pinus banksiana   jack pine
   Pinus resinosa   red pine
   Pinus strobus   eastern white pine
   Pinus sylvestris (i)   Scotch pine (i)
   Tsuga canadensis   eastern hemlock

Cupressaceae   **Cypress family**
   Juniperus communis   common juniper
   Juniperus horizontalis   creeping juniper
   Thuja occidentalis   eastern white cedar

Smilacaceae
    Smilax rotundifolia NS

Salicaceae
    Populus alba (i)
    Populus balsamifera
    Populus grandidentata
    Populus nigra (i) NS, PEI
    Populus tremuloides
    Populus X canadensis (i) NS
    Populus X canescens (i) NB
    Populus X jackii (i)
    Salix alba (i)
    Salix bebbiana
    Salix candida
    Salix caprea (i) NS
    Salix cinerea (i) NS
    Salix discolor
    Salix eriocephala
    Salix glauca NS
    Salix humilis
    Salix interior NB
    Salix lucida
    Salix myricoides NB
    Salix mrytillifolia NB
    Salix nigra NB
    Salix pedicellaris NB, NS
    Salix pellita NB, NS
    Salix pentandra (i)
    Salix petiolaris
    Salix purpurea (i)
    Salix pyrifolia
    Salix reticulata NS
    Salix sericea NB, NS
    Salix serissima NB
    Salix uva-ursi NS
    Salix vesitita NS
    Salix viminalis (i)
    Salix X fragilis (i)

Myricaceae
    Comptonia peregrina
    Morella pensylvanica
    Myrica gale

Greenbrier family
    common greenbrier NS

Willow family
    white poplar (i)
    balsam poplar
    large-toothed aspen
    black poplar (i) NS, PEI
    trembling aspen
    Canada poplar (i) NS
    grey poplar (i) NB
    Jack's hybrid poplar (i)
    white willow (i)
    Bebb's willow
    sage willow
    goat willow (i) NS
    European grey willow (i) NS
    pussy willow
    cottony willow
    grey-leaved willow NS
    prairie willow
    sandbar willow NB
    shining willow
    bayberry willow NB
    low blueberry willow NB
    black willow NB
    bog willow NB, NS
    satiny willow NB, NS
    laurel willow (i)
    meadow willow
    purple willow (i)
    balsam willow
    net-veined willow NS
    silky willow NB, NS
    autumn willow NB
    bearberry willow NS
    hairy willow NS
    basket willow (i)
    crack willow (i)

Wax-myrtle family
    sweet-fern
    northern bayberry
    sweet gale

Juglandaceae — **Walnut family**
    Juglans cinerea NB; (i) NS, PEI — butternut NB; (i) NS, PEI

Betulaceae — **Birch family**
    Alnus glutinosa (i) NS — European black alder (i) NS
    Alnus incana subsp. *rugosa* — speckled alder
    Alnus serrulata — smooth alder
    Alnus viridis subsp. *crispa* — American green alder
    Betula alleghaniensis — yellow birch
    Betula cordifolia — heart-leaved birch
    Betula glandulosa NB, NS — glandular birch NB, NS
    Betula michauxii NB, NS — Newfoundland dwarf birch NB, NS
    Betula minor NB, NS — dwarf white birch NB, NS
    Betula papyrifera — paper birch
    Betula pendula (i) — weeping birch (i)
    Betula populifolia — grey birch
    Betula pubescens (i) NS — downy birch (i) NS
    Betula pumila — bog birch
    Betula X *caerulea-grandis* — blue birch
    Betula X *sandbergii* NB — Sandberg's birch NB
    Corylus cornuta — beaked hazelnut
    Ostrya virginiana — eastern hop-hornbeam

Fagaceae — **Beech family**
    Fagus grandifolia — American beech
    Quercus macrocarpa NB — burr oak NB
    Quercus robur (i) — English oak (i)
    Quercus rubra — northern red oak

Ulmaceae — **Elm family**
    Ulmus americana — white elm
    Ulmus glabra (i) NB, NS — wych elm (i) NB, NS
    Ulmus procera (i) NB, NS — English elm (i) NB, NS
    Ulmus pumila (i) NB — Siberian elm (i) NB

Ranunculaceae — **Buttercup family**
    Clematis occidentalis NB, NS — purple clematis NB, NS
    Clematis virginiana — Virginia clematis

Berberidaceae — **Barberry family**
    Berberis thunbergii (i) — Japanese barberry (i)
    Berberis vulgaris (i) — common barberry (i)

Philadelphaceae — **Mock orange family**
    Philadelphus coronarius (i) NB — sweet mock orange (i) NB

Grossulariaceae **Currant family**
    Ribes americanum NB; (i) NS   wild black currant NB; (i) NS
    Ribes cynosbati NB   eastern prickly gooseberry NB
    Ribes glandulosum   skunk currant
    Ribes hirtellum   swamp gooseberry
    Ribes lacustre   bristly black currant
    Ribes nigrum (i)   European black currant (i)
    Ribes rubrum (i)   European red currant (i)
    Ribes triste   swamp red currant

Hamamelidaceae   **Witch-hazel family**
    Hamamelis virginiana   American witch-hazel

Rosaceae   **Rose family**
    Amelanchier arborea NB, NS   downy serviceberry NB, NS
    Amelanchier bartramiana   Bartram's serviceberry
    Amelanchier canadensis   shadblow serviceberry
    Amelanchier fernaldii   Fernald's serviceberry
    Amelanchier gaspensis NB   Gaspé serviceberry NB
    Amelanchier interior   inland serviceberry
    Amelanchier intermedia   purple serviceberry
    Amelanchier laevis   smooth serviceberry
    Amelanchier nantucketensis NS   Nantucket serviceberry NS
    Amelanchier sanguinea NB   round-leaved serviceberry NB
    Amelanchier spicata   dwarf serviceberry
    Aronia arbutifolia   red chokeberry
    Aronia melanocarpa   black chokeberry
    Aronia X *prunifolia*   purple chokeberry
    Crataegus brainerdii NB, NS   Brainerd's hawthorn NB, NS
    Crataegus crus-galli (i) NS   cock-spur hawthorn (i) NS
    Crataegus chrysocarpa   fireberry hawthorn
    Crataegus flabellata NB, NS   fan-leaved hawthorn NB, NS
    Crataegus intricata NS   Copenhagen hawthorn NS
    Crataegus jonesiae   Jones' hawthorn
    Crataegus macrosperma NB, NS   big-fruit hawthorn NB, NS
    Crataegus mollis NS   downy hawthorn NS
    Crataegus monogyna (i)   English hawthorn (i)
    Crataegus punctata NB, NS   dotted hawthorn NB, NS
    Crataegus scabrida NB, NS   rough hawthorn NB, NS
    Crataegus submollis NB, NS   Quebec hawthorn NB, NS
    Crataegus succulenta   fleshy hawthorn
    Dasiphora fruticosa NB, NS   shrubby cinquefoil NB, NS
    Dryas integrifolia NB   entire-leaved mountain avens NB
    Malus baccata (i) NB, NS   Siberian crabapple (i) NB, NS
    Malus pumila (i)   common apple (i)

Physocarpus opulifolius NB, NS	eastern ninebark NB, NS
Prunus americana NB	American plum NB
Prunus avium (i) NB, NS	sweet cherry (i) NB, NS
Prunus cerasus (i) NB, NS	sour cherry (i) NB, NS
Prunus domestica (i) NB, NS	European plum (i) NB, NS
Prunus nigra	Canada plum
Prunus pensylvanica	pin cherry
Prunus pumila NB	sand cherry NB
Prunus serotina NB, NS	black cherry NB, NS
Prunus spinosa (i) NS	blackthorn (i) NS
Prunus virginiana	chokecherry
Pyrus communis (i) NS	common pear (i) NS
Rosa acicularis NB	prickly rose NB
Rosa blanda	smooth rose
Rosa canina (i)	dog rose (i)
Rosa carolina	Carolina rose
Rosa cinnamomea (i)	cinnamon rose (i)
Rosa gallica (i)	French rose (i)
Rosa glauca (i)	glaucous rose (i)
Rosa multiflora (i)	multiflora rose (i)
Rosa nitida	shining rose
Rosa palustris NB, NS	swamp rose NB, NS
Rosa rubiginosa (i)	briar rose (i)
Rosa rugosa (i)	rugosa rose (i)
Rosa virginiana	Virginia rose
Rubus allegheniensis	Alleghaney blackberry
Rubus canadensis	Canada blackberry
Rubus chamaemorus	cloudberry
Rubus flagellaris NS, PEI	northern dewberry NS, PEI
Rubus hispidus	bristly dewberry
Rubus idaeus	wild red raspberry
Rubus occidentalis NB	black raspberry NB
Rubus odoratus (i) NB, NS	purple-flowering raspberry (i) NB, NS
Rubus pensilvanicus	Pennsylvania blackberry
Rubus pubescens	dewberry
Rubus setosus	bristly blackberry
Sorbaria sorbifolia (i)	false spiraea (i)
Sorbus americana	American mountain-ash
Sorbus aucuparia	European mountain-ash
Sorbus decora	showy mountain-ash
Spiraea latifolia	broad-leaved meadowsweet
Spiraea tomentosa	steeplebush
X *Sorbaronia arsenei*	Arsen's sorbaronia
X *Sorbaronia* hybrids NB	sorbaronia hybrids NB

Fabaceae   **Pea family**
    Caragana arborescens (i) NB   Siberian pea shrub (i) NB
    Cytisus scoparius (i) NS, PEI   Scotch broom (i) NS, PEI
    Genista tinctoria (i) NS   dyer's greenwood (i) NS
    Robinia hispida (i) NS   bristly locust (i) NS
    Robinia pseudoacacia (i) NB, NS   black locust (i) NB, NS
    Robinia viscosa (i)   clammy locust (i)

Anacardiaceae   **Cashew family**
    Rhus typhina   staghorn sumac
    Toxicodendron radicans   poison ivy
    Toxicodendron vernix NS   poison sumac NS

Aquifoliaceae   **Holly family**
    Ilex glabra NS   inkberry NS
    Ilex mucronata   mountain holly
    Ilex verticillata   common winterberry

Celastraceae   **Staff-tree family**
    Celastrus orbiculatus (i) NB, NS   oriental bittersweet (i) NB, NS
    Euonymus europaeus (i) NB   European euonymus (i) NB

Aceraceae   **Maple family**
    Acer negundo (i)   Manitoba maple (i)
    Acer pensylvanicum   striped maple
    Acer platanoides (i)   Norway maple (i)
    Acer pseudoplatanus (i)   sycamore maple (i)
    Acer rubrum   red maple
    Acer saccharinum NB   silver maple NB
    Acer saccharum   sugar maple
    Acer spicatum   mountain maple

Hippocastanaceae   **Buckeye family**
    Aesculus hippocastanum (i) NB   horse chestnut (i) NB

Rhamnaceae   **Buckthorn family**
    Frangula alnus (i)   glossy buckthorn (i)
    Rhamnus alnifolia   alder-leaved buckthorn
    Rhamnus cathartica (i)   European buckthorn (i)

Vitaceae   **Grape family**
    Parthenocissus inserta NB, NS   thicket creeper NB, NS
    Parthenocissus quinquefolia   Virginia creeper
    Vitis labrusca (i) NB, NS   northern fox grape (i) NB, NS
    Vitis riparia NB; (i) NS   riverbank grape NB; (i) NS

Malvaceae	**Mallow family**
    Tilia americana NB	 basswood NB
    Tilia cordata (i) NB, NS	 little-leaved linden(i) NB, NS
    Tilia heterophylla (i) NB	 white basswood (i) NB
    Tilia platyphyllos (i) NB	 large-leaved linden (i) NB
    Tilia X vulgaris (i)	 European linden (i)

Cistaceae	**Rockrose family**
    Hudsonia ericoides NS, PEI	 pinebarren golden heather NS, PEI
    Hudsonia tomentosa	 woolly heather

Thymelaeaceae	**Mezereum family**
    Daphne mezereum (i)	 February daphne (i)
    Dirca palustris NB, NS	 eastern leatherwood NB, NS

Elaeagnaceae	**Oleaster family**
    Elaeagnus angustifolia (i) NB	 Russian olive (i) NB
    Shepherdia canadensis NB, NS	 soapberry NB, NS

Lythraceae	**Loosestrife family**
    Decodon verticillatus NB, NS	 swamp loosestrife NB, NS

Cornaceae	**Dogwood family**
    Cornus alternifolia	 alternate-leaved dogwood
    Cornus amomum NB	 silky dogwood NB
    Cornus canadensis	 bunchberry
    Cornus rugosa NB, NS	 round-leaved dogwood NB, NS
    Cornus stolonifera	 red-osier dogwood
    Cornus suecica NB, NS	 Swedish bunchberry NB, NS

Clethraceae	**White alder family**
    Clethra alnifolia NS	 coastal sweet pepperbush NS

Ericaceae	**Heath family**
    Andromeda polifolia var. *latifolia*	 bog rosemary
    Arctostaphylos uva-ursi	 common bearberry
    Calluna vulgaris (i) NB, NS	 Scottish heather (i) NB, NS
    Chamaedaphne calyculata	 leatherleaf
    Chimaphila umbellata	 common pipsissewa
    Corema conradii NS, PEI	 broom crowberry NS, PEI
    Empetrum atropurpureum NS	 purple crowberry NS
    Empetrum eamesii NS	 pink crowberry NS
    Empetrum nigrum	 black crowberry
    Epigaea repens	 trailing arbutus
    Gaultheria hispidula	 creeping snowberry

Gaultheria procumbens	eastern teaberry
Gaylussacia baccata	black huckleberry
Gaylussacia bigeloviana	dwarf huckleberry
Kalmia angustifolia	sheep laurel
Kalmia polifolia	pale bog laurel
Rhododendron canadense	rhodora
Rhododendron groenlandicum	common Labrador tea
Rhododendron lapponicum NS	Lapland rosebay NS
Vaccinium angustifolium	early lowbush blueberry
Vaccinium boreale NB, NS	northern blueberry NB, NS
Vaccinium caespitosum NB, NS	dwarf bilberry NB, NS
Vaccinium corymbosum NB, NS	highbush blueberry NB, NS
Vaccinium macrocarpon	large cranberry
Vaccinium mrytilloides	velvet-leaved blueberry
Vaccinium ovalifolium NS	oval-leaved blueberry NS
Vaccinium oxycoccus	small cranberry
Vaccinium uliginosum	alpine bilberry
Vaccinium vitis-idaea	mountain cranberry

Diapensiaceae — **Diapensia family**

Diapensia lapponica NS — Lapland diapensia NS

Oleaceae — **Olive family**

Fraxinus americana	white ash
Fraxinus excelsior (i) NB, NS	European ash (i) NB, NS
Fraxinus nigra	black ash
Fraxinus pennsylvanica NB, NS; (i) PEI	red ash NB, NS; (i) PEI
Syringa vulgaris (i)	common lilac (i)

Solanaceae — **Nightshade family**

Solanum dulcamara (i) — bittersweet nightshade (i)

Rubiaceae — **Madder family**

Cephalanthus occidentalis NS	common buttonbush NS
Mitchella repens	partridgeberry

Diervillaceae — **Bush-honeysuckle family**

Diervilla lonicera — northern bush-honeysuckle

Linnaeaceae — **Twinflower family**

Linnaea borealis — twinflower

Caprifoliaceae — **Honeysuckle family**

Lonicera canadensis	Canada fly honeysuckle
Lonicera caprifolium (i) NS	Italian honeysuckle (i) NS
Lonicera morrowii (i) NB	Morrow's honeysuckle (i) NB

Lonicera oblongifolia NB	swamp fly honeysuckle NB
Lonicera periclymenum (i) NS	European honeysuckle (i) NS
Lonicera tatarica (i) NB, NS	Tartarian honeysuckle (i) NB, NS
Lonicera villosa	mountain fly honeysuckle
Lonicera xylosteum (i) NB	dwarf honeysuckle (i) NB
Symphoricarpos albus (i)	common snowberry (i)

Adoxaceae — Muskroot family

Sambucus canadensis	common elderberry
Sambucus racemosa subsp. *pubens*	red elderberry
Viburnum acerifolium NB	maple-leaved viburnum NB
Viburnum edule NB, NS	squashberry NB, NS
Viburnum lantana (i) NB	wayfaring viburnum (i) NB
Viburnum lantanoides	hobblebush
Viburnum lentago NB	nannyberry NB
Viburnum nudum var. *cassinoides*	northern wild raisin
Viburnum opulus subsp. *opulus* (i) NB, NS	cranberry viburnum (i) NB, NS
Viburnum opulus subsp. *trilobum*	highbush cranberry
Viburnum recognitum NB; (i) NS	smooth arrowwood NB; (i) NS

Asteraceae — Aster family

Baccharis halimifolia NS	eastern baccharis NS
Erechtites hieraciifolia	eastern burnweed
Iva frutescens subsp. *oraria* NS	big-leaved marsh-elder NS

INDEX / PLANTS BY LATIN NAME

- Species in black type are included in this book with a full-page description.
- Species in grey type are mentioned in the description of another species.
- Former (but still familiar) Latin names are in grey type and indented.

Abies balsamea 21
Acer negundo 172
Acer pensylvanicum 63
Acer platanoides 67
Acer pseudoplatanus 68
Acer rubrum 69
Acer saccharinum 70
Acer saccharum 71
Acer spicatum 64
   Alnus crispa 120
Alnus incana subsp. *rugosa* 118
   Alnus rugosa 118
Alnus serrulata 119
Alnus viridis subsp. *crispa* 120
Amelanchier bartramiana 90
Amelanchier species: shrub 91
   A. fernaldii
   A. gaspensis
   A. nantucketensis
   A. sanguinea
   A. spicata
Amelanchier species: tree 92
   A. arborea
   A. canadensis
   A. interior
   A. intermedia
   A. laevis
Andromeda glaucophylla 84

Andromeda polifolia var. *latifolia* 84
Arctostaphylos uva-ursi 147
Aronia arbutifolia 94
   Aronia floribunda 94
Aronia melanocarpa 93
Aronia X *prunifolia* 94

Baccharis halimifolia 142
Berberis thunbergii 144
Berberis vulgaris 130
Betula alleghaniensis 121
Betula cordifolia 122
Betula glandulosa 126
   Betula lutea 121
Betula michauxii 126
Betula minor 126
Betula papyrifera 123
Betula pendula 124
Betula populifolia 125
Betula pubescens 124
Betula pumila 126
Betula X *caerulea-grandis* 122

Calluna vulgaris 41
Caragana arborescens 182
Celastrus orbiculatus 139
Cephalanthus occidentalis 48
Chamaedaphne calyculata 107

Chimaphila umbellata 167
Clematis occidentalis 170
Clematis virginiana 171
Clethra alnifolia 100
Comptonia peregrine 78
Corema conradii 35
Cornus alternifolia 106
Cornus amomum 59
Cornus canadensis 57
Cornus rugosa 58
Cornus stolonifera 59
Cornus suecica 57
Corylus cornuta 127
Crataegus monogyna 134
Crataegus species 132
    C. brainerdii
    C. chrysocarpa
    C. crus-galli
    C. flabellata
    C. intricata
    C. jonesiae
    C. macrosperma
    C. mollis
    C. punctata
    C. scabrida
    C. submollis
    C. succulenta
Cytisus scoparius 182

Daphne mezereum 83
Dasiphora fruticosa 201
Decodon verticillatus 169
Diapensia lapponica 43
Diervilla lonicera 44
Dirca palustris 146

Empetrum atropurpureum 36
Empetrum eamesii 36
Empetrum hermaphroditica 37
Empetrum nigrum 37
Epigaea repens 148

Fagus grandifolia 89
Frangula alnus 145

Fraxinus americana 173
Fraxinus excelsior 174
Fraxinus nigra 175
Fraxinus pennsylvanica 176

Gaultheria hispidula 149
Gaultheria procumbens 101
Gaylussacia baccata 108
Gaylussacia bigeloviana 109
    Gaylussacia dumosa 109

Hamamelis virginiana 131
Hudsonia ericoides 34
Hudsonia tomentosa 40
Humulus lupulus 88

Ilex glabra 98
Ilex mucronata 105
Ilex verticillata 99
Iva frutescens subsp. *oraria* 46

Juglans cinerea 186
Juniperus communis 33
Juniperus horizontalis 38

Kalmia angustifolia 168
Kalmia polifolia 42

Larix decidua 22
Larix laricina 23
   Ledum groenlandicum 111
Linnaea borealis 54
Lonicera canadensis 49
Lonicera caprifolium 50
Lonicera morrowii 51
Lonicera oblongifolia 49
Lonicera periclymenum 50
Lonicera tatarica 51
Lonicera villosa 52
Lonicera xylosteum 51

   Malus domestica 95
Malus pumila 95
Mitchella repens 61

Morella pensylvanica   104
Myrica gale   87
   Myrica pensylvanica   104

   Nemopanthus mucronata   105

Ostrya virginiana   88

Parthenocissus quinquefolia   183
Parthenocissus inserta   183
Physocarpus opulifolius   157
Picea abies   24
Picea glauca   25
Picea mariana   26
Picea rubens   27
Pinus banksiana   28
Pinus resinosa   29
Pinus strobus   30
Pinus sylvestris   31
Populus alba   158
Populus balsamifera   114
Populus grandidentata   115
Populus tremuloides   116
Populus X canescens   158
Populus X jackii   114
  Potentilla fruticosa   201
Prunus avium   96
Prunus cerasus   96
Prunus nigra   135
Prunus pensylvanica   79
Prunus pumila   80
Prunus serotina   97
Prunus virginiana   136
Pyrus communis   95

Quercus macrocarpa   154
Quercus robur   155
Quercus rubra   153

Rhamnus alnifolia   140
Rhamnus cathartica   53
  Rhamnus frangula   145
Rhododendron canadense   110
Rhododendron groenlandicum   111
Rhododendron lapponicum   110

Rhus radicans 181
Rhus typhina   199
Ribes americanum   159
Ribes cynosbati   161
Ribes glandulosum   160
Ribes hirtellum   161
Ribes lacustre   162
Ribes nigrum   159
Ribes rubrum   163
Ribes triste   163
Robinia pseudoacacia   202
Robinia viscosa   203
Rosa acicularis   190
Rosa blanda   188
Rosa canina   192
Rosa carolina   189
Rosa cinnamomea   192
Rosa gallica   192
Rosa glauca   192
Rosa multiflora   192
Rosa nitida   190
Rosa palustris   191
Rosa rubiginosa   192
Rosa rugosa   192
Rosa virginiana   194
Rubus chamaemorus   164
Rubus flagellaris   180
Rubus hispidus   180
Rubus idaeus   187
Rubus odoratus   165
  Rubus plicatifolius   180
Rubus pubescens   179
  Rubus recurvicaulis   180
Rubus species   184
    R. allegheniensis
    R. canadensis
    R. pensilvanicus
    R. setosus

Salix alba   74
Salix bebbiana   85
Salix candida   81
Salix discolor   86
Salix eriocephala   72
Salix humilis   86

223

Salix interior   76
Salix lucida   73
Salix nigra   74
Salix pentandra   75
Salix petiolaris   76
Salix purpurea   77
Salix pyrifolia   117
Salix sericeae   72
Salix viminalis   82
Salix X *fragilis*   74
Sambucus canadensis   177
   Sambucus pubens   178
Sambucus racemosa var. *pubens*   178
Shepherdia canadensis   47
Smilax rotundifolia   143
Solanum dulcamara   156
Sorbaria sorbifolia   198
Sorbus americana   195
Sorbus aucuparia   196
Sorbus decora   197
Spiraea latifolia   137
Spiraea tomentosa   138
Symphoricarpos albus   62
Syringa vulgaris   60

Taxus canadensis   20
Thuja occidentalis   39
Tilia americana   141
Tilia cordata   141
Tilia platyphyllos   141
Toxicodendron radicans   181
Toxicodendron vernix   199
Tsuga canadensis   32

Ulmus americana   128
Ulmus glabra   129
Ulmus procera   129
Ulmus pumila   128

Vaccinium angustifolium   102
Vaccinium boreale   102
Vaccinium caespitosum   103
Vaccinium corymbosum   102
Vaccinium macrocarpon   112
Vaccinium myrtilloides   113
Vaccinium ovalifolium   151
Vaccinium oxycoccus   150
Vaccinium uliginosum   151
Vaccinium vitis-idaea   152
Viburnum acerifolium   55
   Viburnum alnifolium   56
   Viburnum cassinoides   45
   Viburnum dentatum   55
Viburnum edule   65
Viburnum lantana   56
Viburnum lantanoides   56
Viburnum lentago   45
Viburnum nudum var. *cassinoides*   45
Viburnum opulus subsp. *trilobum*   66
Viburnum opulus subsp. *opulus*   66
Viburnum recognitum   55
   Viburnum trilobum   66
Vitis labrusca   166
Vitis riparia   166

X *Sorbaronia* hybrids   200

INDEX / PLANTS BY COMMON NAME

- Species in black type are included in this book with a full-page description.
- Species in grey type are mentioned in the description of another species.

alder
    American green alder 120
    smooth alder 119
    speckled alder 118
alder-leaved buckthorn 140
Alleghaney blackberry 184
alpine bilberry 151
alternate-leaved dogwood 106
American beech 89
American green alder 120
American hop 88
American mountain-ash 195
American witch-hazel 131
apple (common) 95
arrowwood (smooth) 55
ash
    black ash 175
    European ash 174
    red ash 176
    white ash 173
aspen
    large-toothed aspen 115
    trembling aspen 116

baccharis (eastern) 142
balsam fir 21
balsam poplar 114
balsam willow 117

barberry
    common barberry 130
    Japanese barberry 144
Bartram's serviceberry 90
basket willow 82
basswood 141 *(see also linden)*
bayberry (northern) 104
beaked hazelnut 127
bearberry (common) 147
Bebb's willow 85
beech (American) 89
big-fruit hawthorn 132
big-leaved marsh-elder 46
bilberry
    alpine bilberry 151
    dwarf bilberry 103
birch
    blue birch 122
    bog birch 126
    downy birch 124
    dwarf white birch 126
    glandular birch 126
    grey birch 125
    heart-leaved birch 122
    Newfoundland dwarf birch 126
    paper birch 123
    weeping birch 124
    yellow birch 121

bittersweet (oriental)   139
bittersweet nightshade   156
black ash   175
black cherry   97
black chokeberry   93
black crowberry   37
black currant
    bristly black currant   162
    wild black currant   159
black huckleberry   108
black locust   202
black spruce   26
black willow   74
blackberry species
    Alleghaney blackberry   184
    bristly blackberry   184
    Canada blackberry   184
    Pennsylvania blackberry   184
blueberry
    highbush blueberry   102
    early lowbush blueberry   102
    northern blueberry   102
    oval-leaved blueberry   151
    velvet-leaved blueberry   113
blue birch   122
bog birch   126
bog rosemary   84
Brainerd's hawthorn   132
briar rose   192
bristly black currant   162
bristly blackberry   184
bristly dewberry   180
broad-leaved meadowsweet   137
broom crowberry   35
broom (Scotch)   182
buckthorn
    alder-leaved buckthorn   140
    European buckthorn   53
    glossy buckthorn   145
bunchberry
    bunchberry   57
    Swedish bunchberry   57
burr oak   154
bush-honeysuckle (northern)   44
butternut   186

buttonbush (common)   48

Canada blackberry   184
Canada fly honeysuckle   49
Canada plum   135
Canada yew   20
Carolina rose   189
cedar (eastern white)   39
cherry
    black cherry   97
    chokecherry   136
    pin cherry   79
    sand cherry   80
    sour cherry   96
    sweet cherry   96
chokeberry
    black chokeberry   93
    purple chokeberry   94
    red chokeberry   94
chokecherry   136
cinnamon rose   192
cinquefoil (shrubby)   201
clammy locust   203
clematis
    purple clematis   170
    Virginia clematis   171
cloudberry   164
coastal sweet pepperbush   100
cockspur hawthorn   132
common apple   95
common barberry   130
common bearberry   147
common buttonbush   48
common elderberry   177
common greenbrier   143
common juniper   33
common Labrador tea   111
common lilac   60
common pear   95
common pipsissewa   167
common snowberry   62
common winterberry   99
Copenhagen hawthorn   132
cottony willow   72
crack willow   74

cranberry
- cranberry viburnum 66
- highbush cranberry 66
- large cranberry 112
- mountain cranberry 152
- small cranberry 150

creeper
- thicket creeper 183
- Virginia creeper 183

creeping juniper 38
creeping snowberry 149

crowberry
- black crowberry 37
- broom crowberry 35
- pink crowberry 36
- purple crowberry 36

currant
- bristly black currant 162
- Eurasian black currant 159
- European red currant 163
- skunk currant 160
- swamp red currant 163
- wild black currant 159

daphne (February) 83
dewberry
- bristly dewberry 180
- dewberry 179
- northern dewberry 180

diapensia (Lapland) 43
dog rose 192
dogwood
- alternate-leaved dogwood 106
- red-osier dogwood 59
- round-leaved dogwood 58
- silky dogwood 59

dotted hawthorn 132
downy birch 124
downy hawthorn 132
downy serviceberry 92
dwarf bilberry 103
dwarf honeysuckle 51
dwarf huckleberry 109
dwarf serviceberry 91
dwarf white birch 126

eastern baccharis tree 142
early lowbush blueberry 102
eastern hemlock 32
eastern hop-hornbeam 88
eastern leatherwood 146
eastern ninebark 157
eastern prickly gooseberry 161
eastern teaberry 101
eastern white cedar 39
eastern white pine 30

elderberry
- common elderberry 177
- red elderberry 178

elm
- English elm 129
- Siberian elm 128
- white elm 128
- wych elm 129

English hawthorn 134
English oak 155
Eurasian black currant 159
European ash 174
European buckthorn 53
European honeysuckle 50
European larch 22
European mountain-ash 196
European red currant 163

false spiraea 198
fan-leaved hawthorn 132
February daphne 83
Fernald's serviceberry 91
fir (balsam) 21
fireberry hawthorn 132
fleshy hawthorn 132
fox grape (northern) 166
French rose 192

Gaspé serviceberry 91
glandular birch 126
glaucous rose 192
glossy buckthorn 145
gooseberry
- eastern prickly gooseberry 161
- swamp gooseberry 161

227

grape
- northern fox grape   166
- riverbank grape   166

greenbrier (common)   143
grey birch   125
grey poplar   158

hawthorn
- English hawthorn   134
- hawthorn species
  - big-fruit hawthorn   132
  - Brainerd's hawthorn   132
  - cockspur hawthorn   132
  - Copenhagen hawthorn   132
  - dotted hawthorn   132
  - downy hawthorn   132
  - fan-leaved hawthorn   132
  - fireberry hawthorn   132
  - fleshy hawthorn   132
  - Jones' hawthorn   132
  - Quebec hawthorn   132
  - rough hawthorn   132

hazelnut (beaked)   127
heart-leaved birch   122
heather
- pinebarren golden heather   34
- Scottish heather   41
- woolly heather   40

hemlock (eastern)   32
highbush blueberry   102
highbush cranberry   66
hobblebush   56
honeysuckle
- Canada fly honeysuckle   49
- dwarf honeysuckle   51
- European honeysuckle   50
- Italian honeysuckle 50
- Morrow's honeysuckle   51
- mountain fly honeysuckle   52
- northern bush-honeysuckle   44
- swamp fly honeysuckle   49
- Tartarian honeysuckle   51

hop (American)   88
hop-hornbeam (eastern)   88

huckleberry
- black huckleberry   108
- dwarf huckleberry   109

inkberry   98
inland serviceberry   92
Italian honeysuckle   50

jack pine   28
Jack's hybrid poplar   114
Japanese barberry   144
Jones' hawthorn   132
juniper
- common juniper   33
- creeping juniper   38

Labrador tea (common)   111
Lapland diapensia   43
Lapland rosebay   110
larch (European)   22
large cranberry   112
large-leaved linden   141
large-toothed aspen   115
laurel
- pale bog laurel   42
- sheep laurel   168

laurel willow   75
leatherleaf   107
leatherwood (eastern)   146
lilac (common)   60
linden
- large-leaved linden   141
- little-leaved linden   141
- (*see also basswood*)

locust
- black locust   202
- clammy locust   203

loosestrife (swamp)   169

maple
- Manitoba maple   172
- mountain maple   64
- Norway maple   67
- red maple   69

silver maple   70
striped maple   63
sugar maple   71
sycamore maple   68
maple-leaved viburnum   55
marsh-elder (big-leaved)   46
meadow willow   76
meadowsweet (broad-leaved)   137
Morrow's honeysuckle   51
mountain cranberry   152
mountain fly honeysuckle   52
mountain holly   105
mountain maple   64
mountain-ash
    American mountain-ash   195
    European mountain-ash   196
    showy mountain-ash   197
multiflora rose   192

nannyberry   45
Nantucket serviceberry   91
Newfoundland dwarf birch   126
nightshade (bittersweet)   156
ninebark (eastern)   157
northern bayberry   104
northern blueberry   102
northern bush-honeysuckle   44
northern dewberry   180
northern fox grape   166
northern red oak   153
northern wild raisin   45
Norway maple   67
Norway spruce   24

oak
    burr oak   154
    English oak   155
    northern red oak   153
oriental bittersweet   139
oval-leaved blueberry   151

pale bog laurel   42
paper birch   123
partridgeberry   61

pear (common)   95
peashrub (Siberian)   182
Pennsylvania blackberry   184
pepperbush (coastal sweet)   100
pin cherry   79
pine
    eastern white pine   30
    jack pine   28
    red pine   29
    Scotch pine   31
pinebarren golden heather   34
pink crowberry   36
pipsissewa (common)   167
plum (Canada)   135
poison ivy   181
poison sumac   199
poplar
    balsam poplar   114
    grey poplar   158
    Jack's hybrid poplar   114
    white poplar   158
prairie willow   86
prickly rose   190
purple chokeberry   94
purple clematis   170
purple crowberry   36
purple serviceberry   92
purple willow   77
purple-flowering raspberry   165
pussy willow   86

Quebec hawthorn   132

raspberry
    purple-flowering raspberry   165
    wild red raspberry   187
red ash   176
red chokeberry   94
red currant
    European red currant   163
    swamp red currant   163
red elderberry   178
red maple   69
red oak (northern)   153

red pine   29
red spruce   27
red-osier dogwood   59
rhodora   110
riverbank grape   166
rose
    Carolina rose   189
    prickly rose   190
    shining rose   190
    smooth rose   188
    swamp rose   191
    Virginia rose   194
    (*see also shrub rose species*)
rough hawthorn   132
round-leaved dogwood   58
round-leaved serviceberry   91
rugosa rose   192

sage willow   81
sand cherry   80
sandbar willow   76
Scotch broom   182
Scotch pine   31
Scottish heather   41
serviceberry
    Bartram's serviceberry   90
    serviceberry shrub species
        dwarf serviceberry   91
        Fernald's serviceberry   91
        Gaspé serviceberry   91
        Nantucket serviceberry   91
        round-leaved serviceberry   91
    serviceberry tree species
        downy serviceberry   92
        inland serviceberry   92
        purple serviceberry   92
        shadblow serviceberry   92
        smooth serviceberry   92
sheep laurel   168
shining rose   190
shining willow   73
showy mountain-ash   197
shrub rose species
    briar rose   192
    cinnamon rose   192

    dog rose   192
    French rose   192
    glaucous rose   192
    multiflora rose   192
    rugosa rose   192
    (*see also rose*)
shrubby cinquefoil   201
Siberian elm   128
Siberian peashrub   182
silky dogwood   59
silky willow   72
silver maple   70
skunk currant   160
small cranberry   150
smooth alder   119
smooth arrowwood   55
smooth rose   188
smooth serviceberry   92
snowberry
    common snowberry   62
    creeping snowberry   149
soapberry   47
sorbaronia hybrids   200
sour cherry   96
speckled alder   118
spiraea (false)   198
spruce
    black spruce   26
    Norway spruce   24
    red spruce   27
    white spruce   25
squashberry   65
staghorn sumac   199
steeplebush   138
striped maple   63
sugar maple   71
sumac
    poison sumac   199
    staghorn sumac   199
swamp fly honeysuckle   49
swamp gooseberry   161
swamp loosestrife   169
swamp red currant   163
swamp rose   191
Swedish bunchberry   57

sweet cherry   96
sweet gale   87
sweet-fern   78
sycamore maple   68

tamarack   23
Tartarian honeysuckle   51
teaberry (eastern)   101
thicket creeper   183
trailing arbutus   148
trembling aspen   116
twinflower   54

velvet-leaved blueberry   113
viburnum
    maple-leaved viburnum   55
    wayfaring viburnum   56
Virginia clematis   171
Virginia creeper   183
Virginia rose   194

wayfaring viburnum   56
weeping birch   124
white ash   173
white elm   128
white poplar   158
white spruce   25
white willow   74

wild black currant   159
wild raisin (northern)   45
wild red raspberry   187
willow
    balsam willow   117
    basket willow   82
    Bebb's willow   85
    black willow   74
    cottony willow   72
    crack willow   74
    laurel willow   75
    meadow willow   76
    prairie willow   86
    purple willow   77
    pussy willow   86
    sage willow   81
    sandbar willow   76
    shining willow   73
    silky willow   72
    white willow   74
winterberry (common)   99
witch-hazel (American)   131
woolly heather   40
wych elm   129

yellow birch   121
yew (Canada)   20

PHOTO CREDITS

All plant photographs by Todd Boland except those by the following photographers, whom we acknowledge with appreciation:

PER AASEN: wild black currant (p. 159: bottom photo)

ANNA ARMITAGE: big-leaved marsh-elder (p. 46: top photo)

MARK BIRKLE: sugar maple (p. 71: middle photo)

MADONNA BISHOP: creeping snowberry (p. 149: middle photo)

WILLIAM BROWN: alternate-leaved dogwood (p. 106: bottom photo)

WILL COOK: silky willow (p. 72: top photo)

ALAN CRESSLER: clammy locust (p. 203: bottom photo)

LAYLA DISHMAN: eastern hop-hornbeam (p. 88: top and middle photos)

PAUL DUPONT: butternut (p. 186: bottom photo)

JIM GOLTZ: common greenbrier (p. 143: top and middle photos), red spruce (p. 27: bottom photo)

JOHN HAGSTROM: American witch-hazel (p. 131: top photo), black willow (p. 74: top photo), common buttonbush (p. 48: bottom photo), eastern leatherwood (p. 146: top and bottom photos), eastern white cedar (p. 39: bottom photo), little-leaved linden (p. 141: bottom photo), purple-flowering raspberry (p. 165: top photo), red spruce (p. 27: middle photo), sandbar willow (p. 76: bottom photo), smooth arrowwood (p. 55: top and bottom photos), sugar maple (p. 71: top and bottom photos), swamp loosestrife (p. 169: top photo), sweet-fern (p. 78: top photo), white elm (p. 128: middle photo), white willow (p. 74: bottom photo)

AUDREY HOFF: common greenbrier (p. 143: bottom photo)

JASON HOLLINGER: striped maple (p. 63: top photo)

NELSON HORSLEY: fireberry hawthorn (p. 132: middle photo)

MICHAEL HOUGH: bristly dewberry (p. 180: middle photo)

THOMAS JACKSON: dwarf bilberry (p. 103: middle photo)

ELIZABETH KILMARX: Alleghaney blackberry (p. 184: middle photo)

LOUIS M. LANDRY: cottony willow (p. 72: top photo), sand cherry (p. 80: top and bottom photos), smooth rose (p. 188: top and middle photos)

MATT LAVIN: dwarf serviceberry (p. 91: middle photo), red ash (p. 176: top and middle photos), Tartarian honeysuckle (p. 51: top photo), white poplar (p. 158: top photo)

DAVID LEIBMAN: black ash (p. 175: bottom photo)

JOHN LOOMIS: black huckleberry (p. 108: top and bottom photo)

ULI LORIMER: American witch-hazel (p. 131: middle photo), bristly dewberry (p. 180: top photo), broom crowberry (p. 35: top, middle and bottom photos), swamp loosestrife (p. 169: bottom photo), sweet-fern (p. 78: bottom photo), woolly heather (p. 40: bottom photo)

ALAIN MAIRE: eastern hop-hornbeam (p. 88: bottom photo), eastern ninebark (p. 157: middle photo), glossy buckthorn (p. 145: bottom photo), hobblebush (p. 56: top and bottom photos), purple-flowering raspberry (p. 165: middle photo), steeplebush (p. 138: middle photo), yellow birch (p. 121: bottom photo)

MALCOLM MANNERS: swamp rose (p. 191: middle photo)

JOHN MAUNDER: heart-leaved birch (p. 122: bottom photo)

SUSAN MEADES: Canada plum (p. 135: top photo), round-leaved dogwood (p. 58: bottom photo), sand cherry (p. 80: middle photo), shining willow (p. 73: bottom photo)

WILLIAM MEADES: Canada plum (p. 135: middle photo)

PHILLIP MERRITT: American beech (p. 89: middle and bottom photos), big-leaved marsh-elder (p. 46: bottom photo), swamp rose (p. 191: top photo)

MILLETTE PHOTOGRAPHY: bristly dewberry (p. 180: bottom photo), clammy locust (p. 203: top photo)

ROBBIN MORAN: swamp fly honeysuckle (p. 49: bottom photo)

CLEA MORAY: balsam willow (p. 117: top photo), Canada fly honeysuckle (p. 49: middle photo), shining willow (p. 73: top photo)

JASON M. MORRIS: common pipsissewa (p. 167: top and middle photos)

KEIR MORSE: smooth rose (p. 188: bottom photo), meadow willow (p. 76: top photo)

RUTH PARTHENUIK: purple clematis (p. 170: bottom photo)

JOHN POYSTON: alternate-leaved dogwood (p. 106: middle photo)

COREY RAIMOND: round-leaved dogwood (p. 58: middle photo), woolly heather (p. 40: top and middle photos)

KATIE SAVALCHAK: sweet-fern (p. 78: middle photos)

JENNIFER SCHLICK: swamp rose (p. 191: bottom photos)

KATJA SCHULTZ: eastern baccharis (p. 142: bottom photos)

ROBERT STRUSIEVICZ: common pipsissewa (p. 167: bottom photos)

JOSH SULMAN: Carolina rose (p. 189: bottom photo)

SUPERIOR NATIONAL FOREST: Canada fly honeysuckle (p. 49: top photos), dwarf bilberry (p. 103: top and bottom photos), round-leaved dogwood (p. 58: top photo)

TIM WALSH: fireberry hawthorn (p. 132: top photo)

CHARLES WOHLERS: bristly blackberry (p. 184: bottom photo)

ABOUT THE AUTHOR

Todd Boland is the author of *Trees & Shrubs of Newfoundland and Labrador* and *Wildflowers of Fogo Island and Change Islands*, and the Research Horticulturist at the Memorial University of Newfoundland Botanical Garden.

Todd has written about and lectured on various aspects of horticulture and native plants internationally. He is a founding member of the Newfoundland and Labrador Wildflower Society (1990), and an active website volunteer with the North American Rock Garden Society.

Born and raised in St. John's, Newfoundland and Labrador, Todd graduated from Memorial University of Newfoundland with an M.Sc. in Biology and a specialization in Plant Ecology. Alpine plants are his longstanding outdoor gardening passion; indoors he maintains an ever-increasing orchid collection. Photography and bird watching occupy any non-gardening downtime.